Concise German Review Grammar

I 1   1835

Jack Moeller
Oakland University

Helmut Liedloff
Southern Illinois University

Helen Lepke
Clarion University

with
Constanze Kirmse
Goethe Institute
Munich

Houghton Mifflin Company   **Boston**

Dallas   Geneva, Illinois   Palo Alto   Princeton, New Jersey

Acknowledgments

Page 3: Courtesy Dr. Poelman & Co. GmbH., Herdecke; p. 8: Courtesy Guhl Kosmetik AG, Münchenstein, Schweiz; p. 11: Courtesy Hamburg Information; p. 12: © J. Douglas Guy; p. 20: Courtesy Robert Krause GmbH. & Co. KG, Espelkamp; p. 35: Courtesy VARTA Batterie AG, Hannover; p. 36: Courtesy Eberhard Karls Universität Tübingen; p. 40: Courtesy Der Sportler, Freiburg; p. 42: Courtesy Commodore Büromaschinen GmbH., Frankfurt; p. 45: Foto Helmut Newton, © Villeroy & Boch, Mettlach; p. 47: Courtesy Mövenpick, Stuttgart; p. 55: Courtesy Der Landgraf Gasthaus, Osnabrück; p. 57: Courtesy Der Salatgarten, Freiburg; p. 59: Courtesy Jeans und Sportswear, Tübingen; p. 69: Courtesy Mobil, Germany; p. 71: Courtesy Grotrian-Steinweg Pianofortefabrikanten, Braunschweig; p. 77: Courtesy Machiavelli Scuola, Florence, Italy; p. 80: Courtesy Schlossmühle Zellerndorf; p. 88 (left): Courtesy Austrian Tourist Office; (right): Courtesy Schweizer Verkehrsbüro, Frankfurt/Main; p. 91: Courtesy Staatl. Indisches Verkehrsbüro, Frankfurt; p. 95: Courtesy Gesellschaft Hochtaunusstraße, Bad Homburg v.d. Höhe; p. 100: Courtesy Tourist Information, Würzburg; p. 109: Courtesy Hamburg Information/Reichelt; p. 111: Courtesy Stähle Party Service, Freiburg; p. 114: Courtesy Sport Kiefer, Freiburg im Breisgau; p. 117: Courtesy Holland Hotel, Baden Baden; p. 123: Courtesy Heihoff Internationale Damenmoden, Hamburg; p. 125: Courtesy Mandel, Osnabrück; p. 129: Courtesy Braun, Inc.; p. 141: Courtesy Bridgestone Corp., Brussels, Belgium; p. 146: Courtesy Landesbausparkasse, Hannover. Portions of this book from Jack Moeller, Helmut Liedloff, Helen Lepke *Kaleidoskop: Kultur, Literatur und Grammatik*, Second Edition. Copyright © 1987 Houghton Mifflin Company. Used with permission.

Printed in the U.S.A.

Library of Congress Catalog Card Number: 89-82368

ISBN: 0-395-54686-9

ABCDEFGHIJ-H-96543210

Contents

Introduction

Concise German Review Grammar provides a complete review of the grammar topics normally covered in beginning courses and introduces new elements as appropriate for intermediate-level courses.

The text is organized to provide review and easy access to information for student reference as well as extensive opportunities for practice of the structures in context. Clear, concise explanations help students increase their mastery of German grammar. These explanations are in English so that there will be no opportunity for students to misunderstand the concepts.

The exercises that follow the grammatical explanations are built around a theme or an everyday situation—thus helping students use form to express meaning. The use of fill-in and question-answer formats, as well as translation exercises, permits the production of whole conversations that are in "genuine" language. Models are provided throughout so that students clearly understand how to do each exercise and know what type of response is needed. The culminating activity in each *Kapitel* consists of one or more composition topics that implicitly or explicitly require students to use the grammatical features reviewed in the chapter.

So that students can concentrate on the grammar point being reviewed without the distraction of unfamiliar words, the vocabulary in the exercises is limited to a basic list of 1,200 high-frequency words. Occasionally, words not on this list will be used to avoid artificiality; in such cases, they are glossed. By continually using these basic words, students will gain mastery of high-frequency vocabulary—an additional advantage of this unique feature.

The reference section of the text contains four separate elements: (1) a grammar summary with tables and charts and a list of strong verbs and irregular weak verbs with their principal parts; (2) a German-English vocabulary of all words used in the text; (3) an English-German vocabulary of the words needed to do the translation exercises; and (4) an index of grammatical features that enables students and instructors to look up a particular grammar point easily.

Students may begin by reviewing the grammatical presentations paying particular attention to anything that is new to them or that they may have forgotten. They should then do the exercises focusing on the points that cause them difficulty. If questions arise while doing the exercises on their own, students should be encouraged to consult the reference grammar in the Appendix to look up such grammatical features as case endings, verb forms, or verbs and prepositions with special meanings.

Additional exercises for each *Kapitel* are available on six audiocassettes. These recorded exercises are based on situations and provide opportunities for oral work. Since these exercises are different from those in the text, they provide additional practice in new formats. The recorded material may form the basis for work in the language lab, or students may purchase the cassettes to listen to on their own and at a time that fits into their schedules. To order, instructors and students should request Audiocassettes, Part 2 *Kaleidoskop* (code number: 3-38006).

The instructor may use *Concise German Review Grammar* in a course with a reader or readers or in conversation or composition courses. The clarity, conciseness, and easy accessibility of material make the text a useful core or adjunct to any intermediate-level course or beyond.

No matter how the book is used, it provides a clear format for grammar review coupled with a variety of activities in situational formats to allow for student production of real language.

BUNDESREPUBLIK DEUTSCHLAND/DEUTSCHE DEMOKRATISCHE REPUBLIK

Concise German Review Grammar

Kapitel 1

- Infinitives
- Present tense of verbs
- Imperatives
- Verbs with separable prefixes
- Modal auxiliaries

1. Infinitive stems and endings

Infinitive	Stem + ending	English equivalent
arbeiten	**arbeit** + **en**	*to work*
sammeln	**sammel** + **n**	*to collect*

The infinitive is the basic form of a verb, the form listed in dictionaries and vocabularies. A German infinitive consists of a stem plus the ending **-en** or **-n**.

2. Basic present-tense endings

	fragen	arbeiten	heißen	sammeln
ich	frage	arbeite	heiße	samm(e)le
du	fragst	arbeitest	heißt	sammelst
er es sie	fragt	arbeitet	heißt	sammelt
wir	fragen	arbeiten	heißen	sammeln
ihr	fragt	arbeitet	heißt	sammelt
sie	fragen	arbeiten	heißen	sammeln
Sie	fragen	arbeiten	heißen	sammeln

Most German verbs form the present tense from the stem of the infinitive. Most verbs add the following endings to the stem: **-e, -st, -t, -en.**

1. If the verb stem ends in **-d** or **-t**, or if it ends in **-m** or **-n** preceded by another consonant (except **-l** or **-r**), the endings **-st** and **-t** expand to **-est** and **-et: arbeiten>arbeitest, arbeitet; atmen> atmest, atmet.**
2. If the verb stem ends in **-s, -ss, -ß, -tz,** or **-z,** the **-st** ending contracts to **-t: heißen>du heißt; sitzen>du sitzt.**
3. In many verbs with the stem ending in **-el,** the **-e** of the 1st person singular (**ich**-form) drops out: **sammeln>ich sammle.**

3. Present tense of stem-changing verbs

	tragen (a>ä)	laufen (au>äu)	nehmen (e>i)	lesen (e>ie)
ich	trage	laufe	nehme	lese
du	**trägst**	**läufst**	**nimmst**	**liest**
er/es/sie	**trägt**	**läuft**	**nimmt**	**liest**

Many verbs with the stem vowels **a** or **au** take umlaut in the 2nd person (**du**-form) and 3rd person (**er/es/sie**-form): **a>ä; au>äu.** Many verbs with the stem vowel **e** also exhibit a vowel change in the 2nd and 3rd person singular: **e>i** or **e>ie.** The verbs with stem-vowel change are all strong verbs. For a list of the vowel-change verbs used in this text see pages 163-166. Some basic stem-changing verbs are:

a>ä		au>äu	e>i		e>ie
backen	raten	laufen	brechen	sterben	befehlen
fahren	schlafen		essen	treffen	geschehen
fallen	schlagen		geben	treten	lesen
fangen	tragen		helfen	vergessen	sehen
halten	wachsen		nehmen	werden	stehlen
lassen	waschen		sprechen	werfen	

4. Present tense of *haben, sein,* and *werden*

	haben	sein	werden
ich	habe	bin	werde
du	hast	bist	wirst
er/es/sie	hat	ist	wird
wir	haben	sind	werden
ihr	habt	seid	werdet
sie	haben	sind	werden
Sie	haben	sind	werden

The verbs **haben, sein,** and **werden** are irregular in the present tense.

5. Use of the present tense

Ute **arbeitet** schwer. = $\begin{cases} \textit{Ute works hard.} \\ \textit{Ute is working hard.} \\ \textit{Ute does work a lot.} \end{cases}$

Arbeitet Gerhard auch schwer? = $\begin{cases} \textit{Is Gerhard also working hard?} \\ \textit{Does Gerhard also work hard?} \end{cases}$

1. German verbs have one present-tense form to express what English expresses with two or three different forms of the verb.

Jürgen **wohnt** schon lange in München.	*Jürgen has been living in Munich for a long time.*
Uschi **arbeitet** seit September bei dieser Firma.	*Uschi has been working for this company since September.*

2. The present tense in German can be used to express an action begun in the past that continues into the present.

Ilse **macht** in einer Woche Examen.	*Ilse is taking her (final) exam in one week.*
Kommen Sie heute abend?	*Are you coming tonight?*

3. German, like English, can use the present tense to express an action intended or planned for the future.

6. Imperative forms

	fragen	warten	tragen	laufen	nehmen	lesen
Familiar singular:	frag(e)!	wart(e)!	trag(e)!	lauf(e)!	nimm!	lies!
Familiar plural:	fragt!	wartet!	tragt!	lauft!	nehmt!	lest!
Formal:	fragen Sie!	warten Sie!	tragen Sie!	laufen Sie!	nehmen Sie!	lesen Sie!

Imperatives are verb forms used to express commands such as orders, instructions, suggestions, and wishes. Each German verb has three imperative forms, corresponding to the three forms of address: the familiar singular imperative (**du**-form), the familiar plural imperative (**ihr**-form), and the formal imperative (**Sie**-form), which is the same for both singular and plural.

1. The familiar singular imperative is used when addressing someone to whom you would say **du**. The imperative is formed from the infinitive verb stem. An **-e** may be added to the imperative form, but it is usually omitted in conversation: **frag(e)!** If the verb stem ends in **-d, -t,** or **-ig,** or in **-m** or **-n** (except when preceded by **-l** or **-r**), an **-e** is added in written German: **rede! warte! entschuldige! atme! öffne!**

   Verbs with stems that change from **e>i** or **e>ie** retain the stem-vowel change but do not add **-e: nehmen>nimm! lesen>lies!** Verbs with stems that change from **a>ä** do not take umlaut in the familiar singular imperative: **tragen>trag(e)! laufen>lauf(e)!**

   The pronoun **du** is occasionally used for emphasis or clarification: **Warum muß ich immer Kaffee holen? Geh du mal!**

2. The familiar plural imperative is used when addressing people to whom you would say **ihr.** It is identical to the present-tense **ihr**-form of the verb. The pronoun **ihr** is occasionally used for emphasis or clarification: **Es ist noch Kuchen da. — Eßt ihr doch!**

3. The formal imperative is used when addressing one or more persons to whom you would say **Sie.** It is identical to the present-

tense **Sie**-form of the verb. The pronoun **Sie** is always used in the imperative and follows the verb: **Warten Sie bitte einen Augenblick!**

Wir-imperative

Dieter: Was machen wir heute abend?

What'll we do tonight?

Jürgen: **Gehen wir** mal ins Kino!

Let's go to the movies!

English imperatives beginning with *let's* can be expressed in German with the 1st person plural present-tense form of the verb followed by the pronoun **wir**.

7. Separable-prefix verbs

mitkommen	**Kommst** du heute **mit?**	*Are you coming along today?*
aufpassen	**Paß auf!**	*Watch out!*
anrufen	Ich **rufe** um sieben **an.**	*I'll call at seven.*

A separable-prefix verb consists of a basic verb plus a prefix that is separated from the verb under certain conditions. In the infinitive, a separable prefix is attached to the base form of the verb. In the present tense, the imperative, and the simple past tense (see *Kapitel 2*), a separable prefix is separated from the base form of the verb and stands at the end of the main clause.

Separable prefixes are usually prepositions or adverbs. Some of the most common separable prefixes are listed below:

ab	bei	her	nach	weg
an	ein	hin	nieder	zu
auf	entlang	los	vor	zurück
aus	fort	mit	vorbei	zusammen

Zwei Mädchen setzen sich durch

Warum Désirée und Tanja in New York so erfolgreich sind

8. Present tense of modal auxiliaries

	dürfen	können	mögen	müssen	sollen	wollen
ich	darf	kann	mag	muß	soll	will
du	darfst	kannst	magst	mußt	sollst	willst
er						
es	darf	kann	mag	muß	soll	will
sie						
wir	dürfen	können	mögen	müssen	sollen	wollen
ihr	dürft	könnt	mögt	müßt	sollt	wollt
sie	dürfen	können	mögen	müssen	sollen	wollen
Sie	dürfen	können	mögen	müssen	sollen	wollen

German modal auxiliaries have no verb endings in the 1st and 3rd person singular. All modals except **sollen** and **wollen** exhibit stem-vowel changes in the singular forms of the present tense.

9. Use of modal auxiliaries

Ich **kann** bis acht Uhr **bleiben.**	*I can stay until eight o'clock.*
Wir **wollen** die Musik **hören.**	*We want to hear the music.*
Peter **muß** jetzt **gehen.**	*Peter has to leave now.*

Modal auxiliaries in both German and English convey an attitude about an action, rather than expressing that action itself. For this reason, modals are generally used with dependent infinitives that express that action.

Ich **muß** um fünf nach Hause
    (gehen).

I have to go home at five.

Barbara **kann** gut Deutsch
    (sprechen).

Barbara knows German well.

The dependent infinitive is often omitted in a sentence containing a
modal when the meaning of the infinitive is clear from the context.

10. Meaning of the modal auxiliaries

dürfen	*permission*	Sie **darf** heute mitkommen.	*She's allowed to come along today.*
können	*ability*	Sie **kann** heute mitkommen.	*She can (is able to) come along today.*
mögen	*liking, personal preference*	**Magst** du Jazz?	*Do you like jazz?*
müssen	*compulsion*	Sie **muß** heute mitkommen.	*She has to (must) come along today.*
sollen	*obligation*	Sie **soll** heute mitkommen.	*She is supposed to (is to) come along today.*
wollen	*wanting, intention, wishing*	Sie **will** heute mitkommen.	*She wants (intends) to come along today.*

Mögen usually expresses a fondness or a dislike for someone or
something. With this meaning it appears most frequently in the
interrogative and in the negative without a dependent infinitive:

Magst du Dieter? —Nein, ich **mag** ihn nicht.

11. The *möchte*-forms

ich **möchte**	*wir* **möchten**
du **möchtest**	*ihr* **möchtet**
er/es/sie **möchte**	*sie* **möchten**
Sie **möchten**	

The modal **mögen** is most frequently used as **möchte**. The möchte-
forms are subjunctive forms of **mögen** and are equivalent to English
would like (see *Kapitel 8*).

Ober: **Möchten** Sie jetzt
    bestellen?

Would you like to order now?

Jens: Ja, ich **möchte** eine
    Tasse Kaffee, bitte.

*Yes, I'd like a cup of coffee,
    please.*

12. Negative of *müssen* and *dürfen*

Compulsion

Positive:	Ich **muß** heute arbeiten.	I must *work today.*
		I have to *work today.*
Negative:	Ich **muß** heute **nicht** arbeiten.	I don't have to *work today.*

Permission

Positive:	Ich **darf** wieder arbeiten.	I may *work again.*
		I'm allowed to *work again.*
Negative:	Ich **darf** noch **nicht** arbeiten.	I mustn't *work yet.*
		I'm not allowed to *work yet.*

English *must* and *have to* have the same meanings in positive sentences. They have different meanings in negative sentences and hence different German equivalents.

Ich **muß** heute **nicht** arbeiten.	*I don't have to work today (but I will).*
Ich **brauche** heute **nicht zu** arbeiten.	*I don't have to work today (and I won't).*

Übungen

A. Verben.   Restate with the cued subject.

▶ ich lese (du)   *du liest*

1. ich sehe (er)
2. wir essen (du)
3. er hilft (ich)
4. sie sprechen (sie sg.)
5. er nimmt (ihr)
6. ich backe (sie sg.)
7. wir fahren (du)
8. er läßt (ich)
9. sie schlafen (er)
10. ich trage (sie sg.)
11. sie fängt an (ihr)
12. ich rate (er)

B. Stefanies Tag.   Alex and Stefanie are talking about Stefanie's typical day. Complete their conversation with the appropriate forms of the verbs in parentheses.

Stefanie: Ich *stehe* schon um 7 *auf* . (aufstehen)
Alex: Und dann *trinkst* du Kaffee? (trinken)

Stefanie: Ja, und ich _esse_ drei Brötchen zum Frühstück. Das _gibt_ mir Energie für den ganzen Morgen. (essen/geben)

Alex: _Fahrst_ du mit dem Fahrrad in die Uni? (fahren)

Stefanie: Ja, meistens. Oft mit meinem Freund Gerd. Er _wartet_ immer vor Hertie. Wir _gehen_ sofort in die Bibliothek. (warten/gehen)

Alex: In der Bibliothek _sah_ ich euch manchmal. Ihr _lest_ viel dort. Ihr _sitzt_ immer am Fenster. (sehen/lesen/sitzen).

Stefanie: Stimmt. Gerd _____ viel. Am Nachmittag _spricht_ er mit dem Professor für Englisch. (arbeiten/sprechen)

Alex: Und was _____ dann? (geschehen)

Stefanie: Dann _trinken_ wir zusammen Kaffee und ich _komme_ nach Hause und _bin_ kaputt. (trinken/kommen/sein).

C. Peter in Hamburg. You have received a letter from your friend Peter. Tell about his experience in Hamburg by translating the following information.

1. Peter has been living in Hamburg for four weeks.
2. He's going to stay there for six months.
3. He already knows a lot of people.
4. He has a new girlfriend.
5. He has known her for a couple of weeks.
6. They're spending a lot of time together.
7. Next weekend they're going to visit her parents.

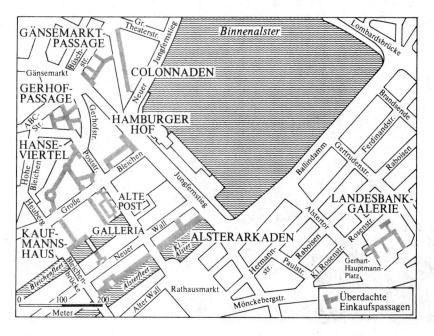

D. Kleine Konversationen. Complete the following sentences with the expressions given in parentheses.

1. Aua! _____! Du _____! (aufpassen / mir wehtun)
   — Oh, Entschuldigung!
2. _____? (du / mit mir / spazierengehen)
   — Hm, ich glaube, ich _____. (lieber / radfahren)
3. Was _____? (du / vorhaben / heute abend)
   — Nichts, ich _____ (vielleicht / fernsehen)
4. _____? (du / gern / skilaufen)
   — Oh ja, sehr gern.
5. _____? (du / anziehen / dein neues Kleid)
   Es _____. (aussehen / so hübsch)
   — Das ist ein schönes Blau, nicht?
6. Ich _____. (dich / anrufen / später)
   — Gut, ich bin zu Hause.

E. Reiseführer. You are helping a German tourist in Bonn by giving directions from the Beethovenhalle to the Hauptbahnhof.

▶ am Fluß entlanggehen   *Gehen Sie am Fluß entlang!*

1. an der Brücke nach rechts abbiegen
2. geradeaus bis zur Haltestelle laufen
3. dort auf die Straßenbahn warten
4. die 21 nehmen
5. vorher die Fahrkarte am Automaten kaufen
6. am Bahnhof aussteigen

Entschuldigen Sie, wie kommt man am besten von hier aus zum Hauptbahnhof?

F. Noch einmal.   Just as you finish telling the tourist how to get to the **Hauptbahnhof**, a young person asks for the same directions. Give them to her/him.

▶ am Fluß entlanggehen   *Geh am Fluß entlang!*

G. Machen wir es! Construct sentences using the **wir**-imperative with the cues provided.

▶ gehen / jetzt   *Gehen wir jetzt!*

1. fahren / mit dem Bus
2. besuchen / Peter und Eva / heute abend
3. anrufen / sie doch
4. spazierengehen / später
5. bleiben / lieber zu Hause
6. machen / unsere Arbeit / erstmal

H. Modalverben.   Restate with the cued modal.

▶ Ich gehe jetzt. (müssen)   *Ich muß jetzt gehen.*

1. Ich verstehe es nicht. (können)
2. Hilfst du mir? (können)
3. Arbeitest du bei uns? (wollen)
4. Ich höre heute abend Musik. (wollen)
5. Es regnet morgen. (sollen)
6. Wir arbeiten mehr. (sollen)
7. Gehst du schon? (müssen)
8. Er liest viel. (müssen)
9. Ich esse keinen Zucker. (dürfen)
10. Lars trinkt keinen Kaffee. (dürfen)
11. Bleibt ihr hier? (möchten)
12. Wir gehen wandern. (möchten)

I. Vorbereitungen.   Yvonne and Andreas are preparing for a party. Give their conversation by using the cues.

Andreas: sollen / einkaufen / im Supermarkt?
Yvonne: Ja, bitte, gute Idee. du / können / kaufen / die Getränke° / auch?   drinks
Andreas: ich / müssen / gehen / aber / vorher / zur Bank
Yvonne: was / Uwe / sollen / machen?
Andreas: er / können / decken / den Tisch / und / vorbereiten / die Salatsauce
Yvonne: wir / dürfen / ausgeben / nicht zuviel Geld
Andreas: aber / du / wollen / haben / doch alles schön

J. Wim braucht ein Auto.   Wim needs to go to the airport and asks Veronika for her car. Complete their conversation with the modal that fits best. (dürfen, können, mögen, möchten, müssen, sollen, wollen).

Wim: Brauchst du dein Auto heute nachmittag?

Veronika: Warum? _willst_ du es haben?

Wim: Weißt du, ich _muß_ um vier am Flughafen sein. Ich _muß_ _surprise_
meinen Freund Gerd abholen. Ich _möchte_ ihn damit überraschen. Und da _darf_ ich nicht zu spät kommen. Ich _kann_
nämlich erst um halb vier wegfahren. _____ ich dich um dein
Auto bitten?

Veronika: Aber sicher. Oder _soll_ ich dich zum Flughafen
bringen?

Wim: Ach, ich _kann_ gut allein fahren. Du _mußt_ sicher arbeiten. In einer halben Stunde _muß_ ich es gut schaffen. Aber
wenn du gern _willst_?

Veronika: Ja, fahren wir zusammen! Ich _mag_ die Atmosphäre am
Flughafen. Da _kann_ man immer von der weiten Welt träumen.
_____ wir uns dann um halb vier hier treffen?

Wim: Ja, das _können_ wir machen.

K. Kurze Gespräche. Complete the mini-dialogues with the
appropriate forms of *mögen* or *möchte*.

1. Wie findest du Harald? _magst_ du ihn?
   —Nein, ich _mag_ ihn nicht besonders. Er ist so unfreundlich.
2. Fräulein, wir _möchten_ zwei Tassen Tee und ein Stück Apfel-
   kuchen, bitte.
   —_Möchten_ Sie auch Sahne?
   —Nein, danke, ich _möchte_ keine Sahne.
   —Aber ich _möchte_ bitte gern eine Portion.
3. _möchtest_ du eine Tasse Kaffee?
   —Nein, danke, ich _möchte_ keinen Kaffee. Ich trinke lieber Tee.
4. Karin ist immer so nett. Ich _mag_ sie wirklich gern.

L. Nach der Vorlesung. Nadine and Daniel are having a little talk
after the lecture. Express the following conversation in German.

Nadine: Would you like to (go to) drink a cup of coffee?

Daniel: I'd like to° but I can't. I have to go to a seminar°. History, you   schon / ins Seminar
know.

Nadine: Oh, is Professor Lange good?

Daniel: Yes. He's excellent. I like him. We have to work hard, but we
can also learn a lot.

Nadine: Do you have to write many papers°?   die Seminararbeit, pl.
    Seminararbeiten / man /
Daniel: We are supposed to write two. But if you° want, you° may also   man / ein Referat halten
give an oral report°.

M. Kurze Aufsätze

1. Make plans for the weekend; describe how you like to spend your free time. Use verbs in the present tense.
2. An exchange student is going to live with you for a month; describe your day for her or him. Use present tense and modals.

Kapitel 2

- Simple past tense
- Present perfect tense
- Past participles
- Past perfect tense

1. Simple past tense

Letzte Woche **arbeitete** Inge nur vormittags. Nachmittags **spielte** sie Tennis oder **besuchte** Freunde. Abends **blieb** sie zu Hause und **sah fern.**

Last week Inge worked *mornings only. In the afternoon she* played *tennis* or visited *friends. Evenings she* stayed *home and* watched *TV.*

The simple past tense, often called the narrative past, is used to narrate a series of connected events that took place in the past. It is used more frequently in formal writing such as literature and expository prose than in conversation.

Ein strahlendes Prinzenpaar des MKC besuchte gestern die „Presse-Basis"

Närrische Untertanen stürmten Gemächer in der „Prinz-Reiner-Straße"

spelling change — laut wechsel

2. Weak verbs in the simple past

Infinitive	Stem	Tense marker	Simple past
warnen	warn-	-te	warnte
arbeiten	arbeit-	-ete	arbeitete
öffnen	öffn-	-ete	öffnete

to warn

A regular weak verb is a verb whose infinitive stem remains unchanged in the past tense forms. In the simple past a weak verb adds the past tense marker -te to the infinitive stem. The past tense marker -te becomes -ete when the verb stem ends in -d or -t, or in -m or -n preceded by another consonant (except -l or -r).

ich spielte	_wir_ spielten
_du_ spieltest	_ihr_ spieltet
er/es/sie spielte	_sie_ spielten
Sie spielten	

All forms except the first- and third-person singular form add endings to the -te tense marker.

Karin **machte** die Tür **auf.**	_Karin opened the door._
Der Tourist **packte** den Koffer **aus.**	_The tourist unpacked his suitcase._

In the simple past, as in the present, the separable prefix is separated from the base form of the verb and is in final position.

3. Irregular weak verbs in the simple past

Infinitive	Simple past	Examples
brennen	brannte	Das Holz **brannte** nicht.
kennen	kannte	Sie **kannte** die Stadt gut.
nennen	nannte	Sie **nannte** das Kind nach dem Vater.
rennen	rannte	Er **rannte** jede Woche zum Arzt.
denken	dachte	Du **dachtest** an uns.
bringen	brachte	Ich **brachte** ihr Blumen.
wissen	wußte	Wir **wußten** die Antwort nicht.
haben	hatte	Ihr **hattet** nicht viel Zeit.

A few weak verbs are irregular in that they have a stem-vowel change and occasionally a consonant change in the simple past. Common irregular weak verbs are **brennen, kennen, nennen, rennen, denken, bringen, wissen,** and **haben.**

4. Modals in the simple past

Infinitive	Simple past	Examples
dürfen	durfte	Ich **durfte** ihr helfen.
können	konnte	Du **konntest** nicht mitkommen.
mögen	mochte	Er **mochte** unsere Suppe nicht.
müssen	mußte	Wir **mußten** Inge helfen.
sollen	sollte	Ihr **solltet** es gestern machen.
wollen	wollte	Sie **wollten** früher fahren.

The modals **dürfen, können, mögen,** and **müssen** lose the umlaut in the simple past tense. In addition, **mögen** exhibits a consonant change.

5. Strong verbs in the simple past

Infinitive	Simple past stem
sprechen	sprach
schreiben	schrieb
fahren	fuhr
ziehen	zog
gehen	ging

A strong verb is a verb that has a stem-vowel change in the simple past: **sprechen>sprach.** A few verbs also have a consonant change: **ziehen>zog.** (See pp. 163-166 for a list of strong verbs in the simple past.) The tense marker -**te** is not added to the strong verbs in the simple past.

ich sprach	*wir* sprachen
du sprachst	*ihr* spracht
er/es/sie sprach	*sie* sprachen
Sie sprachen	

In the simple past the first and third person singular have no endings.

6. The present perfect tense

Ist Inge schon **gegangen?**	*Has Inge gone already?*
Ja, sie **hat** mir auf Wiedersehen **gesagt.**	*Yes, she said good-by to me.*
Weißt du, wann sie **gegangen ist?**	*Do you know when she left?*

The present perfect tense consists of the present tense of the auxiliary **haben** or **sein** plus the past participle of the verb. In compound tenses such as the present perfect tense, it is the auxiliary **haben** or **sein** that takes person and number endings, while the past participle remains unchanged. The past participle is in last position, except in a dependent clause (see *Kapitel 3*).

7. The present perfect versus simple past

Was **habt** ihr gestern **gemacht**?	*What did you do yesterday?*
Wir **sind** zu Hause **geblieben**.	*We stayed home.*

The present perfect tense is often called the conversational past because it is used most frequently in conversation to refer to events in past time.

Benno **war** gestern sehr müde. Er **schlief** bis zehn, **frühstückte** und **ging** dann wieder ins Bett.	*Benno was very tired yesterday. He slept until ten, ate breakfast, and then went back to bed.*

The simple past (narrative past) tense is used to narrate connected events in past time.

einbeziehen (klick) → (klack) **einbezogen**

RINGBUCHTECHNIK **KRAUSE**

8. Past participles of regular weak verbs

Infinitive	Past participle	Present perfect tense
spielen	ge + spiel + t	Jörg hat Tennis **gespielt.**
arbeiten	ge + arbeit + et	Ilse hat lange **gearbeitet.**
öffnen	ge + öffn + et	Ich **habe** das Fenster **geöffnet.**

The past participle of a weak verb is formed by adding -**t** to the unchanged stem. If the verb stem ends in -**d** or -**t**, or if it ends in -**m** or -**n** preceded by another consonant (except -**l** or -**r**), the ending -**t** expands to -**et**. The past participle of most weak verbs has the prefix **ge-**.

9. Past participles of irregular weak verbs

Infinitive	Past participle	Present perfect tense
brennen	ge + brann + t	Das Holz **hat** nicht **gebrannt.**
kennen	ge + kann + t	Sie **hat** die Familie gut **gekannt.**
nennen	ge + nann + t	Sie **haben** das Kind nach dem Vater **genannt.**
rennen	ge + rann + t	Er **ist** jede Woche zum Arzt **gerannt.**
bringen	ge + brach + t	Ich **habe** dir Blumen **gebracht.**
denken	ge + dach + t	**Hast** du an uns **gedacht?**
wissen	ge + wuß + t	Wir **haben** es nicht **gewußt.**
haben	ge + hab + t	Ihr **habt** nicht viel Zeit **gehabt.**

The past participle of an irregular weak verb has the **ge-** prefix and the ending **-t.** Note the changes in the stem vowel and in some of the consonants.

10. Past participles of strong verbs

Infinitive	Past participle	Present perfect tense
sprechen	ge + sproch + en	**Hast** du mit Inge **gesprochen?**
schreiben	ge + schrieb + en	Ich **habe** das **geschrieben.**
fahren	ge + fahr + en	Jan **ist** allein **gefahren.**
ziehen	ge + zog + en	Sie **haben** das Boot an Land **gezogen.**
gehen	ge + gang + en	Wann **bist** du nach Hause **gegangen?**

The past participle of a strong verb is formed by adding **-en** to the participle stem. Most strong verbs also add the **ge-** prefix in the past participle. Many strong verbs have a change in the stem vowel of the past participle, and some verbs also have a change in the consonants.

11. Past participles of separable-prefix verbs

Infinitive	Past participle	Present perfect tense
abholen	ab + ge + holt	**Hast** du Ute **abgeholt?**
mitnehmen	mit + ge + nommen	Erik **hat** den Schlüssel **mitgenommen.**

The **ge-** prefix of the past participle comes between the separable prefix and the stem of the participle. Both weak and strong verbs can have separable prefixes.

12. Past participle without ge- prefix

Present tense	Present perfect tense
Inge bezahlt das Essen.	Inge **hat** das Essen **bezahlt.**
Ich verstehe die Frage nicht.	Ich **habe** die Frage nicht **verstanden.**

Some prefixes are never separated from the verb stem. Common inseparable prefixes are **be-, emp-, ent-, er-, ge-, ver-,** and **zer-.** Inseparable prefix verbs do not add the **ge-** prefix. Both weak and strong verbs can have inseparable prefixes.

Present tense	Present perfect tense
Wann passiert das?	Wann **ist** das **passiert?**
Benno studiert in Bonn.	Benno **hat** in Bonn **studiert.**

Verbs ending in **-ieren** do not add the **ge-**prefix to form the past participle.

Musik und Bildkunst sinnvoll kombiniert

13. Use of the auxiliary *haben*

Ich **habe** den Brief selber **geschrieben.**

I wrote the letter myself.

Hast du **ferngesehen?**

Did you watch TV?

The auxiliary **haben** is used to form the present perfect tense of most verbs.

14. Use of the auxiliary *sein*

Ingrid **ist** gerade **weggegangen.**

Ingrid has just left.

Benno **ist** auf dem Sofa **eingeschlafen.**

Benno fell asleep on the sofa.

Some verbs use **sein** instead of **haben** as an auxiliary in the present perfect tense. Verbs that require **sein** must meet two conditions. They must:

1. be intransitive verbs (i.e. verbs without a direct object) and
2. indicate a change in location (**weggehen**) or condition (**einschlafen**).

Wie lange **bist** du dort **geblieben**?

How long did you stay there?

Wo **bist** du die ganze Zeit **gewesen**?

Where were you all this time?

The verbs **bleiben** and **sein** also require the auxiliary **sein,** even though they do not indicate a change of location or condition.

Wie **war** das Wetter?

How was the weather?

Wir **waren** gestern nicht zu Hause.

We weren't home yesterday.

The simple past of **sein** is used more commonly than the present perfect tense of **sein** (**ist gewesen**).

15. The past perfect tense

Ich **hatte** schon zwei Tage **gewartet.**

I had waited already for two days.

Sie **war** am Montag **angekommen.**

She had arrived on Monday.

The past perfect tense consists of the simple past of **haben** or **sein** plus the past participle of the main verb. Verbs that use **haben** in the present perfect tense use **haben** in the past perfect; those that use **sein** in the present perfect use **sein** in the past perfect.

Ich wollte am Mittwoch ins Kino gehen.	*I wanted to go to the movies on Wednesday.*
Leider **hatte** mein Freund den Film am Montag schon **gesehen.**	*Unfortunately my friend had already seen the film on Monday.*
Wir sind zu spät angekommen. Die Vorstellung **hatte** schon **angefangen**.	*We arrived too late. The performance had already begun.*

The past perfect tense is used to report an event or action that took place before another event or action in the past.

Übungen

A. Ein Film.   Robert describes a scene from the movie he saw last night. Complete his account by using the simple past tense of the cued verbs.

1. Die Männer _____ sich an den Tisch und _____ Karten. (setzen / spielen)
2. Erik _____ die Spielregeln°. (erklären)   the rules of the game
3. Da _____ er Julia. (bemerken)
4. Sie _____ die Gläser auf den Tisch und _____ nichts. (stellen / sagen)
5. Niels _____ eine verrückte Geschichte, und die Männer _____. (erzählen / lachen)
6. Dann _____ er seine Karten, und alle _____ ein ziemlich dummes Gesicht. (zeigen / machen)

B. Was will er denn?   Tell about your attempts to help a friend. Use the simple past tense of the modal auxiliary.

▶ Mein Freund kann seine Arbeit nicht allein machen.
   Mein Freund konnte seine Arbeit nicht allein machen.

1. Ich soll ihm helfen.
2. Ich will es also versuchen.
3. Gut. Ich muß ihm alles genau erklären.
4. Und er kann es nicht verstehen.
5. Er muß die Arbeit bis Freitag fertig haben.
6. Bald mag er mich nicht mehr sehen.
7. Eigentlich will er gar keine Hilfe.
8. Schließlich darf ich gar nichts mehr sagen.

C. Verben.   Give the simple past of the following verbs. Use the sie-singular form as in the model.

▶ beginnen   *sie begann*

1. nennen, denken, bringen, wissen, haben
2. essen, geben, helfen, bitten, finden, sitzen, kommen, tun
3. fliegen, schließen, umziehen
4. gefallen, halten, schlafen, laufen, bleiben, scheinen, rufen
5. fahren, tragen, waschen, wissen
6. leiden, schneiden, gehen

D. Ein komischer Mensch.   In the park you meet a strange person. Tell a friend about it. Use the simple past tense.

1. Heute fahre ich mit dem Rad durch den Park.
2. Da sehe ich einen Mann.
3. Er sitzt auf einer Bank.
4. Er trägt lustige Kleider.
5. Sein Hut ist viel zu klein.
6. Die Hosen sind zu eng.
7. Das Hemd paßt nicht.
8. Er hat ganz große Schuhe an.
9. Er liest eine alte, schmutzige Zeitung.
10. Ich will ihn ansprechen, aber ich bekomme keine Antwort.
11. Vielleicht versteht er kein Deutsch.
12. Später steht er auf und geht weg.

E. Ein schöner Abend.   Gerd tells you about his impromptu date with Annette. Use the simple past tense.

1. In the evening I wanted to invite Annette to dinner.
2. But I didn't call her up.
3. I simply picked her up.
4. She opened the door and looked at me curiously.
5. I told her my plan.
6. She didn't think about it very long.
7. She shut her books.
8. She put on her coat, and we left.

F. Verben.   Give the present perfect of the following verbs. Use the forms as in the models.

▶ essen   *ich habe gegessen*
▶ fahren   *ich bin gefahren*

1. spielen, zeigen, machen, kaufen
2. kennen, denken, wissen, haben, bringen, rennen

3. sehen, geben, lesen
4. helfen, nehmen, schließen
5. schlafen, tragen
6. schneiden, leiden, reiten
7. rufen, finden
8. schreiben, bleiben
9. fliegen, kommen, gehen
10. abholen, einkaufen, einladen, vorschlagen, aufstehen, anfangen
11. bekommen, beginnen, erfahren, gewinnen, verbieten, verlieren

G. Mini-Gespräche. Restate the following conversational exchanges in the present perfect.

▶ Was machst du am Wochenende?
Was hast du am Wochenende gemacht?

▶ Ich lese und gehe spazieren.
Ich habe gelesen und bin spazierengegangen.

1. — Lädst du Erik zu deinem Fest ein?
   — Ja, ich rufe ihn an.
2. — Wie lange bleibst du in der Schweiz?
   — Ich fahre gar nicht hin.
3. — Wieviel kostet das Bild?
   — Zuviel. Ich kaufe es nicht.
4. — Spielst du heute morgen Tennis?
   — Ja, ich fange um 10 an.
5. — Warum fliegst du nach Berlin?
   — Ich gebe dort ein Konzert.
6. — Warum lachst du?
   — Oh, ich denke gerade an einen guten Witz.

H. Rate mal, was mir passiert ist!   Ingrid tells her roommate what happened to her during the afternoon. Complete her account with the cued verbs. Use the tense indicated.

1. Stell dir vor, was mir heute nachmittag _____. (passieren; pres. perf.)
2. Ich _____ die Mozartstraße entlang, und da _____ plötzlich ein Auto ganz langsam neben mir her. (gehen, fahren; simple past)
3. Na, was will der denn, _____ ich mich. (fragen; simple past)
4. Weißt du, wer es _____? (sein; simple past)
5. Michael! Wir _____ zusammen in Hamburg _____. (studieren; pres. perf.)

6. Er _____ _____ und wir _____ beide herzlich _____. (aussteigen, lachen; pres. perf.)
7. Wir _____ uns natürlich sehr! (freuen; simple past)
8. Wir _____ uns seit zwei Jahren nicht mehr _____. (sehen; pres. perf.)
9. Im Café Mozart _____ wir eine Tasse Kaffee _____ und lange _____. (trinken, erzählen; pres. perf.)

I. Von Hamburg nach Berlin.   Jan thought Rita spent her vacation in Hamburg and he has just learned was in Berlin. Give the German equivalents.

1. Jan: How did you get from Hamburg to Berlin?
   Rita: I flew.
2. Jan: When did you buy the ticket?
   Rita: I didn't buy it (at all). My mother sent it.
3. Jan: How nice! How long did you stay there?
   Rita: I came back yesterday.
4. Jan: Did you visit friends?
   Rita: Oh yes, and I went to the museum frequently.

J. Probleme.   Tell about the problems you had last night when you were going to the theater. Use the past perfect tense of the cued verbs.

▶ Wir sind zu spät ins Theater gekommen.
  Das Stück / anfangen / schon
  Das Stück hatte schon angefangen.

1. Wir wollten mit der Straßenbahn fahren. Aber / sie / wegfahren / gerade
2. Wir gingen in eine Telefonzelle°, um ein Taxi anzurufen. Aber / da / man / stehlen / Telefonbuch   telephone booth
3. Nach 20 Minuten kam die nächste Bahn. Inzwischen / es / beginnen / zu regnen
4. Genau um 8 waren wir im Theater. Doch wo waren die Eintrittskarten°? / Ich / vergessen / sie / zu Hause   admission tickets
5. Ich mußte neue Karten kaufen. Für die alten / ich / ausgeben / viel Geld

K. Ein Brief.   Inge's friend has moved to another city and has written her a letter in a type of shorthand. Put the words into complete sentences using the tense indicated.

1. Liebe Inge! ich / ankommen / vor zwei Wochen (pres. perf.)
2. die Reise / gehen / gut (simple past)
3. ich / finden / ein schönes Zimmer (pres. perf.)
4. ich / müssen / suchen / gar nicht lange (simple past)
5. leider / ich / können / nicht besuchen / meine Freunde (simple past)
6. ich / verlieren / ihre Adresse (past perf.)
7. aber / ich / kennenlernen / schon / viele neue Leute (pres. perf.)
8. an der Uni / ich / treffen / zwei nette Mädchen (simple past)
9. wir / reden / lange (simple past)
10. sie / einladen / mich / zu einem Fest (pres. perf.)
11. du / hören / schon etwas von Karola / ? (pres. perf.)
    Herzliche Grüße, Heike.

L. Kurze Aufsätze

1. Tell your friend about a problem you had and how you solved it. You may use one of the following examples or create one of your own. You lost your German book before an exam; you ate in a restaurant and forgot your money.
2. Keep a diary for a week. Be sure to use verbs in the simple past.

Kapitel 3

- Verb position in statements, questions, and clauses
- Conjunctions
- Word order: time, manner, place
- Position of *nicht*

1. Position of the finite verb in statements

	1	2	3	4
Normal:	Wir	**trinken**	um vier	Kaffee.
Inverted:	Um vier	**trinken**	wir	Kaffee.
	Kaffee	**trinken**	wir	um vier.

In a German statement, or independent clause, the finite verb (the verb form that agrees with the subject) is always in second position.

In so-called "normal" word order, the subject is in first position. In so-called "inverted" word order, an element other than the subject is in first position, and the subject follows the verb. For stylistic variety or to emphasize a particular element, a German statement can begin with an adverb, prepositional phrase (**um vier**) or object (**Kaffee**).

"Männer und Frauen sind gleichberechtigt" (Art. 3 Abs. 2 GG)
Der Bundesminister für Jugend Familie und Gesundheit

BONN 2
30.12.83
5300

DEUTSCHE BUNDESPOST
0120
F 19   4692

2. Position of the finite verb in questions

a. Specific questions

Warum **findet** Ute den Film
  langweilig?

*Why does Ute find the film
  boring?*

Wann **hat** sie ihn gesehen?

When did she see it?

A specific question asks for a particular piece of information and begins with an interrogative such as **wie**, **wieviel**, **warum**, **wann**, or **wer**. The interrogative is followed by the finite verb, then the subject.

b. General questions

Hat Barbara einen festen
  Freund? — Ja.

*Does Barbara have a
  boyfriend? — Yes.*

Ist er gestern angekommen?
  — Nein.

*Did he arrive yesterday?
  — No.*

A general question can be answered with **ja** or **nein** and begins with the finite verb.

3. Independent clauses and coordinating conjunctions

Gabi hat ein neues Buch gekauft, **aber** sie liest es nicht, **denn** sie
  hat keine Zeit.

An independent, or main, clause can stand alone as a complete sentence. Two or more independent clauses may be connected by *coordinating* conjunctions. Coordinating conjunctions do not affect the order of subject and verb. Five common coordinating conjunctions are listed below.

aber	*but*
denn	*because (for)*
sondern	*but, on the contrary*
und	*and*
oder	*or*

Lore geht ins Café, **und** ihre Freundin lädt sie zu einem Kaffee ein.
Lore geht ins Café **und** trinkt einen Kaffee.
Lore geht ins Café **und** ihre Freundin auch.

In written German, coordinating conjunctions are generally preceded by a comma. However, **oder** and **und** are not preceded by a comma when the subject or verb in both clauses is the same and is not expressed.

4. The conjunctions *aber* and *sondern*

Inge geht ins Café, **aber** sie bestellt nichts.	*Inge goes into the café,* but *she doesn't order anything.*
Der Kuchen ist nicht teuer, **aber** Sabine kauft ihn trotzdem nicht.	*The cake is not expensive,* but *Sabine still doesn't buy it.*
Jürgen geht nicht ins Café, **sondern** in den Park.	*Jürgen doesn't go to the café,* but *to the park.*

Aber as a coordinating conjunction is equivalent to *but, however, nevertheless;* it may be used after either a positive or negative clause.

    Sondern is a coordinating conjunction that expresses a contrast or contradiction. It connects two ideas that are mutually exclusive. It is used only after a negative clause and is equivalent to *but, on the contrary, instead, rather.*

5. Two-part conjunctions

Entweder hilfst du mir,
Entweder du hilfst mir,   **oder** ich mache es nicht.
Either you help me or I won't do it.

Entweder ... oder is a two-part conjunction equivalent to English *either . . . or.* **Entweder** can be followed by normal or inverted word order.

Er kann **weder** dir **noch** mir helfen.	*He can help* neither *you* nor *me.*

Weder ... noch is the negative form of **entweder ... oder** and is equivalent to *neither . . . nor.*

Je später der Abend, desto freier die Leitung.

Post

6. Dependent clauses and subordinating conjunctions

main clause   dependent clause

Glaubst du, **daß Karin morgen kommt?**
Sie kommt bestimmt, **wenn sie Zeit hat.**

A dependent clause is a clause that cannot stand alone; it must be combined with a main clause to express a complete idea. A dependent clause is introduced by a subordinating conjunction (**daß, wenn**). In writing, a dependent clause is separated from the main clause by a comma.

Er möchte wissen, ob du heute Volleyball **spielst.**
                   ob du heute **mitspielst.**
                   ob du vielleicht Tennis **spielen willst.**
                   ob du gestern **gespielt hast.**

Unlike coordinating conjunctions, subordinating conjunctions affect word order.
    In dependent clauses:

a. The finite verb is in final position (**spielst**).
b. A separable prefix is attached to the base form of the verb which is in final position (**mitspielst**).
c. A modal auxiliary follows the infinitive and is in final position (**willst**).
d. In perfect tenses the auxiliary **haben** or **sein** follows the past participle and is in final position.

Da ich zuviel gegessen hatte, **habe** ich schlecht geschlafen.
Obwohl ich müde war, **mußte** ich früh aufstehen.

When a dependent clause begins a sentence, it is followed directly by the finite verb of the independent clause (**habe, mußte**).
    Common subordinating conjunctions are listed below:

als	*when*	**obgleich**	*although*
bevor	*before*	**obwohl**	*although*
da	*because, since* (causal)	**seit**	*since* (temporal)
damit	*so that*	**seitdem**	*since* (temporal)
daß	*that*	**sobald**	*as soon as*
ehe	*before*	**während**	*while; whereas*
nachdem	*after*	**weil**	*because*
ob	*if, whether*	**wenn**	*if, when*

7. Dependent clauses: indirect statements and questions

a. Conjunction introducing indirect statements: *daß*

Direct statement: Ich fahre morgen weg.
Indirect statement: Erika weiß, **daß** du morgen wegfährst.

Indirect statements are introduced by the subordinating conjunction **daß**.

b. Conjunction introducing indirect general questions: *ob*

General question: Habt ihr gewonnen?
Indirect question: Ich weiß nicht, **ob** wir gewonnen haben.

Indirect general questions are introduced by the subordinating conjunction **ob**.

c. Conjunction introducing indirect specific questions

Specific question: Warum erzählt Inge immer diese Geschichte?
Indirect question: Ich weiß nicht, **warum** sie immer diese
  Geschichte erzählt.

Indirect specific questions are introduced by the same question words, or interrogatives, that are used in direct specific questions, for example, **wann, warum, wie**.

8. Uses of *als, wenn,* and *wann*

Als wir letztes Jahr nach Kanada gereist sind, sind wir mit dem Auto gefahren.	When *we went to Canada last year we went by car.*
Als ich jung war, sind wir oft nach Kanada gefahren.	When *I was young we often went to Canada.*
Wenn wir nach Kanada reisten, fuhren wir immer mit dem Auto.	Whenever *we went to Canada, we always traveled by car.*
Ich weiß nicht, **wann** wir wieder nach Kanada reisen.	*I don't know* when *we're going to Canada again.*

Als, wenn, and **wann** are all equivalent to the English *when*, but they are not interchangeable. **Als** is used to introduce a clause concerned with a single event in the past or refers to a single block of time in the past (**als ich jung war**). **Wenn** is used to introduce a clause concerned with repeated events (*whenever*) or possibilities (*if*) in past time, or with single or repeated events in present or future time. **Wann** is used to introduce direct and indirect questions.

9. Word order: time, manner, and place

Wir fahren **heute mit dem Auto nach Spanien.**
Wir fahren **heute um acht Uhr mit dem Auto nach Spanien.**

When adverbs and adverbial prepositional phrases occur in a sentence, they occur in the following sequence: time (when?), manner (how?), place (where?). When a sentence contains two adverbial expressions of time, the general expression (**heute**) usually precedes the specific (**um acht Uhr**).

10. Position of *nicht*

Ich verstehe die Frage **nicht.**

When **nicht** negates a whole clause, it usually stands at the end of the clause.

Gerd ist **nicht** mein Freund.	*Gerd is not my friend.*
Er ist **nicht** nett.	*He's not nice.*
Ich arbeite **nicht** gern mit ihm zusammen.	*I don't like to work with him.*
Ich fahre **nicht** zu ihm.	*I'm not going to him.*
Du solltest **nicht** ihn bitten, sondern seine Schwester.	*You shouldn't ask him but his sister.*

Nicht precedes a number of sentence elements, e.g., a predicate noun (**Freund**), a predicate adjective (**nett**), an adverb (**gern**), or a prepositional phrase (**zu ihm**).

    Nicht may also precede any word that is given special negative emphasis (**ihn**).

Sie ist **nicht** hier.	*She's not here.*
Sie bleibt **nicht** gern allein.	*She doesn't like to be alone.*

Since **nicht** functions like an adverb of manner, it precedes adverbs of place (**hier**) and precedes other adverbs of manner (**gern**).

Wir gehen heute **nicht** in die Stadt.	*We're not going downtown today.*
Wir gehen **nicht** oft ins Kino.	*We don't go to the movies often.*

Nicht generally follows specific time expressions (**heute**) and precedes general time expressions (**oft**).

Übungen

A. Ein neues Auto.   Since Sabine has her own car, she visits her grandmother more often. Take the part of Sabine and tell about her visit.

▶ ich / haben / ein neues Auto   *Ich habe ein neues Auto.*

1. am Sonntag / ich / fahren / aufs Land
2. dort / ich / besuchen / meine Großmutter
3. sie / wohnen / in einem alten Bauernhaus
4. hinter dem Haus / ein großer, schöner Garten / liegen
5. in dem Garten / viele Apfelbäume / stehen
6. wir / gehen / oft / in den Garten
7. wir / setzen uns / in den Schatten
8. da / es / sein / schön kühl
9. meine Großmutter / erzählen / immer / verrückte Geschichten
10. wir / lachen / immer sehr viel

B. Freunde.   Give some information about Jutta and Frank. Combine each pair of sentences, using the coordinating conjunction indicated.

▸ Frank arbeitet bei Siemens. Jutta studiert. (und)
Frank arbeitet bei Siemens, und Jutta studiert.

1. Frank hat seine Arbeit nicht sehr gern. Jutta ist gern an der Uni. (aber)
2. Sie fahren jeden Tag mit der Straßenbahn. Sie haben kein Auto. (denn)
3. Frank ißt nicht im Restaurant. Er bringt sein Essen von zu Hause mit. Sie wollen sparen. (sondern / denn)
4. Im Sommer fahren sie nach Italien. Sie fliegen nach Amerika. (oder)
5. Dann muß er weiter bei Siemens arbeiten. Jutta studiert weiter. (und)

C. Peters Hauptfach.   Your friend Peter has changed majors. Tell about the change. Combine the sentences with *aber* or *sondern* as appropriate.

1. Peter studiert jetzt nicht mehr Mathematik, _____ er hat mit Geschichte angefangen.
2. Mit Geschichte verdient er vielleicht weniger Geld, _____ das Fach interessiert ihn mehr.
3. Das ist eine verrückte Idee, _____ er hat schon immer davon geträumt.
4. Seine Freunde verstehen ihn nicht, _____ das ist ihm egal.
5. Er hört nicht auf ihren Rat, _____ macht das, was er für gut hält.
6. Er muß jetzt viel Neues lernen, _____ das macht ihm auch großen Spaß.
7. Er arbeitet nicht nur viel, _____ auch gern.

D. Mit dem Fahrrad im Regen.   Tell about your experience bicycling in the rain. Combine each pair of sentences, using the conjunctions indicated.

1. Es regnete fürchterlich°. Ich fuhr von der Arbeit nach Hause.   terribly
   (als)
2. Ich fuhr mit dem Fahrrad. Das Wetter war so schlecht. (obwohl)
3. Ich fahre immer mit dem Fahrrad. Ich habe kein Auto. (weil)
4. Ich war schon ganz naß. Ich war zwei Straßen gefahren. (ehe)
5. Ich hoffe (es) sehr. Ich habe mich nicht erkältet. (daß)
6. Ich fahre nicht mehr mit dem Fahrrad. Es regnet wieder so.
   (wenn)
7. Ich kaufe mir ein Auto. Ich habe genug Geld. (sobald)

E. Restate the sentences in *Übung D*, beginning each sentence with the dependent clause.

F. Besuch von meiner Kusine.   Lore expects a visit from her cousin. Complete her account by supplying *als, wenn,* or *wann,* as appropriate.

1. _____ ich nach Hause kam, lag ein dicker Brief da.
2. Ich freue mich immer, _____ ich Post bekomme.
3. Ich war sehr überrascht, _____ ich ihn öffnete. Er war von meiner Kusine.
4. _____ sie kann, kommt sie mich besuchen.
5. Aber sie schreibt nicht, _____ sie kommen will.
6. Ich weiß gar nicht mehr, _____ ich das letzte Mal von ihr gehört habe.
7. Es wird ganz toll, _____ sie herkommt.
8. _____ sie mit dem Auto kommt, können wir schöne Ausflüge machen.
9. _____ sie mich das letzte Mal besucht hat, hatten wir viel Spaß miteinander.

G. Das Geld ist weg.   The other day your neighbor Mrs. Huber had a bad experience. Tell about it in German.

1. When Mrs. Huber came out of the store, she noticed° that she   merken
   had forgotten her money.
2. Although she went back immediately she couldn't find it.
3. She had taken along a lot of money, because she wanted to buy a jacket.
4. Now Mrs. Huber could buy nothing more but had to go home.
5. It annoyed her but she couldn't change it.

H. Wie war es in Italien?   Stefan is picking up his Italian friend Maria from the train station. She had spent a couple of weeks with her family in Italy. Report on their conversation by using indirect statements and questions. Use *daß* or *ob* when appropriate.

▶ Stefan fragt Maria: „Wie war es in Italien?"
  Stefan fragt Maria, wie es in Italien war.

1. Sie antwortet: „Es war herrlich."
2. Natürlich will er wissen: „Was hast du gemacht? Wo warst du? Wen hast du besucht?"
3. Er fragt auch: „War das Wetter schön?"
4. Sie sagt: „Es war sonnig und warm."
5. Er fragt sie: „Was gibt es sonst Neues?"
6. Sie erzählt: „Meine Eltern haben ein neues Haus. Es ist sehr groß und sehr schön."
7. Stefan fragt: „Bist du nach der langen Reise sehr müde?"
8. Maria antwortet: „Ich bin sehr müde und möchte am liebsten zwölf Stunden schlafen."

IM LAND, WO DIE ZITRONEN BLÜHEN, HATTE „MADE IN GERMANY" SCHON IMMER EINEN GUTEN NAMEN.

I. In Paris.   Mr. Bader often goes to Paris. Using the cued words, tell what he usually does when he first arrives there.

▶ Herr Bader fährt (nach Frankreich / oft).
  Herr Bader fährt oft nach Frankreich.

1. Er fährt (nach Paris / immer / mit dem Zug).
2. Der Zug fährt (vom Hauptbahnhof / um 8.30 Uhr) ab.
3. Herr Bader sitzt (in der Eisenbahn / gern).
4. Er kommt (in Paris / um vier Uhr / am Nachmittag) an.
5. Dort geht er (in ein Café / zuerst / jedesmal).
6. Er setzt sich (an einen Tisch / gleich) und trinkt (schnell / immer) einen Kaffee.
7. Er geht (an den Taxistand / dann).
8. Er fährt (in sein Hotel / meistens / mit dem Taxi).

J. Willst du sonst noch was wissen?   Rainer seems to be in a bad mood today. He answers all his friend's questions in the negative. Answer for Rainer.

▶ Gehst du heute in die Bibliothek?
Nein, ich gehe heute nicht in die Bibliothek.

1. Machst du dein Referat diese Woche fertig?
2. Hast du die Bücher für das Kafka-Seminar gelesen?
3. Arbeitest du für Professor Groß?
4. Findest du Professor Groß nett?
5. Gehst du mit mir eine Tasse Kaffee trinken?
6. Rufst du mich heute abend an?
7. Bist du heute schlecht gelaunt°?   in a bad mood

K. Die Amerikanerin.   Paul, who is rather shy, tells you about trying to meet a woman in a café in Cologne. Give his account in German. For sentences in past time use the tense indicated.

1. When I come home from work° in the evening I sometimes go to   von der Arbeit
   a café°.   ins Café
2. Yesterday I saw a woman in the café. (simple past).
3. I don't know whether she sits there every day, but I saw her
   there last week already°. (present perfect)   schon dort
4. When she ordered something, I realized° that she was [an] Amer-   bemerken
   ican. (simple past)
5. Her German was very good. (simple past)
6. Suddenly she looked at me and smiled°. (simple past)   lächeln
7. Before I could react°, the waiter came back to her table°. (simple   reagieren / schon an ihren Tisch
   past)
8. Although I am very shy° I spoke to her then. Great. (present   schüchtern
   perfect)

L. Kurze Aufsätze.   Describe how you do something. You may use one of the following processes or one of your own. Connect the steps of the process by using adverbs, such as **daher, dann, erst, später, zuerst,** and conjunctions, such as **aber, als, bevor, da, damit, daß, denn, nachdem, obgleich, sobald, während, weil, wenn.**

Kapitel 4

- Nominative and accusative cases
- Demonstrative pronouns
- Personal pronouns
- Interrogative pronouns
- *Dieser*-words
- *Ein*-words
- Accusative case prepositions
- Accusative of time, measure, and quantity

1. Definite article, nominative and accusative

	Masculine	Neuter	Feminine	Plural
Nominative:	der	das	die	die
Accusative:	den	das	die	die

...IN FREIBURG AM MARTINSTOR (VORM. SPORT KOTZ)...

...ALLES FÜR SPORT UND FREIZEIT...JUNG, AKTUELL, UND PREISWERT !

2. *Dieser*-words, nominative and accusative

	Masculine	Neuter	Feminine	Plural
Nominative:	dieser	dieses	diese	diese
Accusative:	diesen	dieses	diese	diese

3. Meanings and uses of *dieser*-words

dieser	this, these (*pl.*)
jeder	each, every (*used in singular only*)
jener	that, the one that
mancher	many a, several (*used mainly in the plural*)
solcher	such (*used mainly in the plural*)
welcher	which

Jener points to something known or previously mentioned:

Ich denke an **jene**, die nicht hier sein können.

Mancher and **solcher** are used mainly in the plural and replaced by a form of **manch ein** or **so ein** in the singular:

So einen Hut würde ich nicht tragen.

4. Demonstrative pronouns, nominative and accusative

	Masculine	Neuter	Feminine	Plural
Nominative:	**der** (*he, it*)	**das** (*it*)	**die** (*she, it*)	**die** (*they*)
Accusative:	**den** (*him, it*)	**das** (*it*)	**die** (*her, it*)	**die** (*them*)

Demonstrative pronouns are identical to the definite articles. A demonstrative pronoun often replaces a personal pronoun if the pronoun is to be emphasized. Demonstrative pronouns usually occur at or near the beginning of a sentence. The English equivalent is usually a personal pronoun.

Kaufst du **den** Mantel da?	*Are you going to buy that coat?*
Nein, **der** ist zu teuer.	*No, it is too expensive.*

5. Personal pronouns, nominative and accusative

Nominative:	ich *I*	du *you* (fam. sg.)	er *he, it*	es *it*	sie *she, it*
Accusative:	mich *me*	dich *you* (fam. sg.)	ihn *him, it*	es *it*	sie *her, it*

Nominative:	wir *we*	ihr *you* (fam. pl.)	sie *they*	Sie *you* (formal)
Accusative:	uns *us*	euch *you* (fam. pl.)	sie *them*	Sie *you* (formal)

The personal pronouns **er, es, sie** agree in gender and number with the noun to which they refer. Personal pronouns refer to both persons and things.

Kennst du **den Herrn** da? — Ja, **er** ist mein Onkel.
Der Wagen ist schon kaputt. — Wirklich? Die haben **ihn** doch letzte
 Woche gerade repariert.

6. The interrogative pronouns *wer* and *was*

Nominative:	wer (*who*)	was (*what*)
Accusative:	wen (*whom*)	was (*what*)

Wer ist die Frau da? — **Wen** meinst du? Die Frau im blauen Rock?
Was war das? — **Was** hast du eben gehört? — Ach, nur die Tür.

The accusative form of **wer** is **wen**. The accusative of **was** is identical to the nominative form.

7. The indefinite article *ein* and *kein*, nominative and accusative

	Masculine	Neuter	Feminine	Plural
Nominative:	ein	ein	eine	-----
Accusative:	einen	ein	eine	-----

The German indefinite article **ein** corresponds to the English *a, an*. It has no plural form.

The negative form of **ein** is **kein**. It is equivalent to English *not a, not any,* or *no*. **Kein** negates a noun that in the positive would be preceded by a form of **ein** or by no article at all.

Wo ist hier ein Telefon? — Es gibt hier **kein** Telefon.
Hast du jetzt Zeit? — Nein, ich habe im Moment **keine** Zeit.

8. Nouns indicating nationalities and professions

Kathrin ist **Deutsche**.	*Kathrin is (a) German.*
Sie ist **Studentin**.	*She's a student.*
Sie wird **Ingenieurin**.	*She's going to be an engineer.*

To state a person's nationality, profession, or membership in a group, German uses the noun directly after a form of the verbs **sein** or **werden**. The indefinite article **ein** is not used. English precedes such nouns with the indefinite article.

Florian ist **kein Ingenieur**.	*Florian is not an engineer.*

Kein is used to negate a sentence about someone's nationality, profession, or membership in a group.

Frau Dr. Braun ist **eine bekannte Deutsche**.	*Dr. Braun is a well-known German.*
Sie ist **eine gute Ärztin**.	*She's a good doctor.*

Ein is used with nouns designating professions, nationalities and membership in a group when the nouns are preceded by an adjective.

9. Possessive adjectives

Subject pronouns	Possessive adjectives	English equivalents
ich	mein	*my*
du	dein	*your (fam. sg.)*
er	sein	*his, its*
es	sein	*its*
sie	ihr	*her, its*
wir	unser	*our*
ihr	euer	*your (fam. pl.)*
sie	ihr	*their*
Sie	Ihr	*your (formal, sg. & pl.)*

Hast du **meinen** Kuli gesehen? — **Deinen** Kuli? Nein.

Possessive adjectives take the same endings as the indefinite article **ein**. They are therefore often called **ein**-words.

Ist Gerd **euer** Bruder und Ilse **eure** Schwester?
Nein, Kurt ist **unser** Bruder, und Martha ist **uns(e)re** Schwester.

Note that when **euer** has endings, the second -e is omitted (**euren**). In colloquial German, the -e in **unser** is also often omitted (**unsre**).

10. Masculine *N*-nouns in the accusative case

Nominative	Accusative
Ist das Herr Biermann?	Ich kenne keinen **Herrn** Biermann.
Wo ist hier ein Polizist?	Warum suchst du einen **Polizisten?**

A number of masculine nouns add -**n** or -**en** in the singular accusative. These nouns are often called masculine N-nouns or weak nouns. The accusative forms of common masculine nouns are: **den Bauern, den Gedanken, den Glauben, den Herrn, den Journalisten, den Jungen, den Juristen, den Kollegen, den Menschen, den Nachbarn, den Namen, den Neffen, den Patienten, den Polizisten, den Soldaten, den Studenten, den Touristen.**

11. Uses of the nominative case

Subject: **Meine Tochter** studiert Mathematik.

The subject designates a person, concept or thing to which the verb refers. It answers the question *who* or *what*. The subject of a sentence is in the nominative case.

Predicate nominative: Der junge Mann heißt **Jürgen**. Jürgen ist **ein netter junger Mann**. Er wird **Arzt**.

A predicate nominative designates a person, concept, or thing that is equated with the subject. A predicate nominative commonly follows verbs such as **heißen**, **sein**, and **werden**.

12. Uses of the accusative case

Direct object:	Kennst du **meinen Bruder?**
Object of prepositions:	Er arbeitet für **unseren Onkel.**
Time:	Wir bleiben nur **einen Tag** in Hamburg.
Measure:	Morgens laufen wir **einen Kilometer.**
Expression **es gibt:**	Gibt es hier **einen guten Arzt?**

Hallo Nachbarn, es gibt was zu sehen.

Villeroy & Boch

13. Direct object

Subject	Direct object
Wer ist **der Junge**?	Kennst du **den Jungen**?
Der rote Mantel ist schön.	Aber Julia kauft **den blauen Mantel**.
Wo ist **dein Freund**?	Ich habe **ihn** nicht gesehen.

The direct object receives the direct action of the verb and answers the questions *whom* (**wen**?) for persons and *what* (**was**?) for things and concepts. A noun or pronoun used as the direct object of a verb is in the accusative case.

14. Prepositions with the accusative case

Preposition	Meaning	Examples
bis	*until*	Ich bleibe **bis** nächsten Samstag.
	as far as	Ich fahre nur **bis** Nürnberg.
	by (time)	Kannst du **bis** morgen fertig sein?
durch	*through*	Sie fährt **durch** die Stadt.
entlang	*along*	Wir gehen den Fluß **entlang**.
für	*for*	**Für** wen kaufst du das?
gegen	*against*	Was hast du **gegen** ihn?
	about	Wir kommen **gegen** acht Uhr.
	(approximately)	
ohne	*without*	Er geht **ohne** seinen Freund.
um	*around*	Da kommt Inge **um** die Ecke.
	at (time)	Jörg fährt **um** zehn Uhr nach Hause.

The prepositions **bis**, **durch**, **entlang**, **für**, **gegen**, **ohne**, and **um** are used with the accusative case.

Usually **bis** is followed by other prepositions: Er geht **bis an** die Tür. Der Bus fährt nur **bis zum** Bahnhof.

Note that **entlang** follows the noun or pronoun in the accusative.

durch das → **durchs**	Sabine geht **durchs** Zimmer.
für das → **fürs**	Frau Lange kauft das **fürs** Geschäft.
um das → **ums**	Der Hund läuft **ums** Haus.

Some prepositions contract with the definite article **das**.

15. Time expressions with the accusative case

Definite point:	Sie kommen **nächsten Monat**.	*They're coming next month.*
Duration:	Sie bleiben **den ganzen Sommer**.	*They're staying the whole summer.*

Noun phrases expressing a definite point in time (answering the question **wann**?) or a duration of time (answering the question **wie lange**?) are in the accusative case. Examples for common expressions of time are given below.

Wann?	Wie lange?
nächsten Winter	den ganzen Tag
jedes Jahr	das ganze Jahr
diese Woche	die ganze Woche

16. Accusative of measure

Die Straße ist **einen Kilometer** lang.	*The street is one kilometer long.*
Die Äpfel wiegen **ein halbes Kilo.**	*The apples weigh one-half kilo.*
Das Kind ist erst **einen Monat** alt.	*The child is only one month old.*

Nouns expressing units of measurement, weight, or age are in the accusative case.

17. Units of measurement and quantity

Ich möchte **zwei Glas** Milch.   *I'd like two glasses of milk.*
Sie kauft **fünf Pfund** Kartoffeln.   *She's buying five pounds of potatoes.*

In German, masculine and neuter nouns expressing measure, weight, or number are in the singular.

Sie bestellt **zwei Tassen** Kaffee.   *She orders two cups of coffee.*
Sie kauft **zwei Flaschen** Cola.   *She's buying two bottles of coke.*

Feminine nouns ending in -**e** form plurals even when they express measure.

18. The expression *es gibt*

Es gibt hier keine guten Restaurants.   *There are no good restaurants here.*
Gibt es einen guten Grund dafür?   *Is there a good reason for that?*

The accusative case always follows the expression **es gibt** (*there is* or *there are*).

Übungen

A. Nominativ oder Akkusativ?   Identify each noun and pronoun in the nominative and accusative case and indicate its use in the sentence.

1. Petra hat einen neuen Freund.
2. Er ist Student.
3. Er studiert Sprachen an der Universität.
4. Er heißt Kai.
5. Kai ist ein sehr fleißiger Student.
6. Manchmal arbeitet Kai für seinen Professor.
7. Petra trifft den Freund am Nachmittag.
8. Gestern hat sie für ihn eine neue Platte gekauft.
9. Die Platte hat sie schon lange gesucht.
10. Sie lädt ihn zum Essen ein.

B. Mark braucht einen Koffer. Mark is going on a trip and is shopping for a new suitcase with his friend Susi. Complete their conversation by supplying the correct forms of the cued words.

1. Mark: _____ Koffer hier ist schön, nicht wahr? (jeder)
2. Susi: Nö. _____ Koffer gefallen mir, _____ nicht. Schau mal, wie gefällt dir _____ Tasche? (mancher, mancher, so ein)
3. Mark: Ach nein, _____ Art und _____ Farbe mag ich überhaupt nicht. (dieser, so ein)
4. Susi: Also, mußt du unbedingt° heute _____ Koffer kaufen, hm? (so ein)   absolutely
5. Mark: Ja, sei nicht ungeduldig°. Du weißt, wie ich _____ Sachen hasse. (solcher)   impatient
6. Susi: _____ Koffer nimmst du jetzt, _____ großen oder _____ kleinen? (welcher, dieser, jener)
7. Mark: Ich nehme _____ Tasche hier. Die mag ich. (dieser)
8. Susi: Also, _____ Leute haben schon einen merkwürdigen Geschmack°! (mancher)   taste

C. Kurze Gespräche. Complete the mini-dialogues by supplying the correct form of the demonstrative pronoun.

▶ —Der Pulli ist schön, nicht?
  —Meinst du? *Den* finde ich häßlich.

1. —Der neue Herzog-Film läuft im Thalia. _____ interessiert mich. Sollen wir uns _____ ansehen?
   —Nein, _____ kenne ich schon.
2. —Wo ist denn Monika?
   —_____ ist in Amerika.
   —_____ hab' ich doch gestern noch gesehen.
   —Nein. _____ ist vorgestern abgeflogen.
3. —Wem gehört das Auto da?
   —_____ gehört meinem Bruder.
   —Wann hat er _____ gekauft?
   —Gar nicht. _____ hat ihm mein Vater geschenkt.
4. —Wer sind die Leute da drüben?
   —_____ warten auf Professor Schwarz.
   —Was wollen _____?
   —_____ wollen mit ihm sprechen.
   —Wo ist denn _____?
   —_____ habe ich erst vor einer Stunde gesehen.

D. Alles über Oliver. Jutta is treating Sabine to a glass of wine. She hasn't seen Sabine for a while and asks a lot of questions about Sabine's friend Oliver. Take the role of Sabine and answer the questions with *ja* or *nein*. Use the personal pronoun in your answer.

▶ —Hat dir der Wein geschmeckt?
  —*Ja (Nein), er hat mir (nicht) geschmeckt.*

▶ —Kaufst du den Wein?
  —*Ja (Nein), ich kaufe ihn (nicht).*

1. Studiert Oliver in Marburg?
2. Kennst du seinen Bruder?
3. Hast du seine Eltern kennengelernt?
4. Ist seine Familie nett?
5. Hat er sein altes Auto verkauft?
6. Siehst du seine Freunde oft?
7. Laden die euch oft ein?
8. Mag dein Vater Oliver?
9. Liebst du Oliver?
10. Liebt er dich?
11. Willst du Oliver heiraten?

E. Eine internationale Familie. Give the German equivalent of the English sentences.

1. My sister is German. She is a teacher.
2. Her husband is English. He was a pharmacist. Now he works as a photographer.
3. Oh, I thought he's a doctor.
4. But your husband is American?
5. No, he's German.
6. And what does he do?
7. He's a professor.

F. Kurze Gespräche. Complete the mini-dialogues by using the correct form of the cued *ein*-word.

1. —_____ Herr will Sie sprechen. (ein)
   —Ich kenne _____ Herrn hier. Wie ist _____ Name? (kein, sein)
2. —Wo sind _____ Bücher? (mein)
   —Ich habe sie auf _____ Schreibtisch gelegt. (dein)
   —Ich sehe _____ Bücher. (kein)
3. —Ich möchte mir so gern _____ Paar neue Sommerschuhe kaufen, aber ich habe _____ Geld. (ein, kein)

—Warum? Hast du nicht mehr _____ Job? (dein)

—Doch, aber _____ Miete ist teurer geworden, und ich muß auch _____ Telefon bezahlen. (unser, unser)

4. —Wie ist _____ Professorin für Geschichte? (euer)

—Ich finde sie gut. _____ Kurs ist sehr interessant. _____ Noten sind auch besser geworden. Ich kenne _____ bessere Professorin. (unser, mein, kein)

G. Reisevorbereitungen. You are going on a trip with friends. Check to see whether everyone has packed his or her things.

▸ du / Kamm   *Hast du deinen Kamm eingepackt?*

1. Peter / Fotoapparat
2. Christa / Blusen
3. du / Seife
4. Gerd / Kassettenrecorder
5. Jürgen / Hemden

6. ihr / Zahnbürsten
7. du / Schuhe
8. Eva / Haartrockner
9. Gerd und Eva / Bücher

URLAUB

Tips für Ihre Ferienreise

H. Ein Märchen. You may know one version of this fairytale. Complete the story by filling in the blanks with appropriate forms of the definite and indefinite article, possessive adjectives, and pronouns.

Ein Mädchen will _____ Großmutter besuchen. _____ Mutter packt _____ Korb mit Essen (Eier, Kuchen, Wein, Butter, Wurst) für _____ und schickt _____ auf den Weg. Im Wald trifft das Mädchen _____ Wolf. Er fragt, wohin _____ geht. „Zu Oma", bekommt er zur Antwort.
Bei der Großmutter macht das Mädchen _____ Tür auf, geht ins Schlafzimmer und schaut _____ Großmutter an.
„Großmutter", sagt das Mädchen, „was für große Augen du hast."

„Damit ich _____ besser sehen kann.“

„Großmutter, was für große Ohren du hast.“

„Damit ich _____ besser hören kann.“

„Aber Großmutter, was für _____ großen Mund du hast.“

„Damit ich _____ besser fressen kann.“ _____ Wolf springt aus dem Bett und will das Mädchen fressen. Das Mädchen, es heißt übrigens Rotkäppchen, nimmt _____ Korb und wirft _____ dem Wolf an _____ Kopf. Der Wolf fällt um, und Rotkäppchen bringt _____ hinaus und macht _____ Tür zu.

„Hilfe, Hilfe“, hört Rotkäppchen.

„Oma, bist du's? Ich höre _____, aber ich sehe _____ nicht. Wo bist _____ denn?“

„Im Schrank.“

Rotkäppchen macht _____ Schrank auf. Sie küßt _____ Großmutter und gibt ihr _____ Korb. Die Großmutter freut sich auf das Essen, macht _____ Korb auf und schreit: „Aber Kindchen, was ist denn passiert? Die Eier sind alle kaputt. Das nächste Mal paß bitte besser auf!“

Die Moral: Einigen Menschen kann man nichts recht machen.

I. Viele Fragen.   Answer the questions in the negative using the cued words.

▶ Machst du es für deine Mutter? (mein Vater)
  Nein, für meinen Vater.

1. Seid ihr durch die Stadt gefahren? (die Felder und Wiesen)
2. Hast du Hans durch deine Arbeit kennengelernt? (ein Freund)
3. Machst du dir Sorgen um das Geld? (mein Job)
4. Mußt du das bis morgen fertig haben? (nächster Montag)
5. Bist du die Hauptstraße entlang gekommen? (der Fußweg)
6. Hast du etwas gegen Lisa? (mein Bruder)
7. Interessierst du dich für die Geschichte von Wien? (der Film über Wien)

J. Wie lange?   Say how long various activities lasted, using the nouns provided in expressions of time.

▶ Ausflug / Tag   *Der Ausflug hat einen Tag gedauert.*

1. Fest / Woche
2. Kurs / Sommer
3. Flug / Nachmittag
4. Gespräch / Stunde
5. Reise / Monat

K. Essen, trinken, einkaufen.   Answer the questions using the German equivalent of the English cues.

▶ Was trinkst du morgens? (two glasses of juice)
  Morgens trinke ich zwei Glas Saft.

1. Was ißt du morgens? (two pieces of bread)
2. Was trinkst du mittags? (three glasses of milk)
3. Was trinkst du nachmittags? (three cups of tea)
4. Was trinkt Gottfried auf seiner Fahrradtour? (two liters of water)
5. Was trinkst du mit deinen Gästen? (two bottles of wine)
6. Was kaufst du für das Abendessen? (500 grams of cheese)
7. Wieviel Kartoffeln kaufst du im Supermarkt? (five kilos)
8. Wieviel Orangen kaufst du auf dem Markt? (four pounds)

L. Was gibt es noch?   Herr Kurz is on the phone booking a room in a resort hotel for a week. He tries to find out about the amenities in the hotel and nearby.

▶ Blumenladen   *Gibt es da einen Blumenladen?*

1. Post
2. Garage im Hotel
3. Friseur
4. Apotheke
5. Kühlschrank im Zimmer
6. Arzt
7. Disco im Hotel
8. Lebensmittelgeschäft
9. Kino

M. Beim Umzug.   Brigitte is surprised that Astrid is moving after only one month in her apartment. She finds out why. Give the German equivalents.

1. Brigitte: Hey, where's your furniture?
2. Astrid: I'm moving.
3. Brigitte: Why? You only lived here one month!
4. Astrid: I know, but I've found an apartment with [a] garden. I can't live without [a] garden.
5. Brigitte: How did you find that apartment?
6. Astrid: Through a friend. I called him and he knew [of] something for me.
7. Brigitte: Not bad. Some people have to look for a long time°.   **lange**
8. Astrid: By° Sunday everything is supposed to be ready°. I'm having a party for our friends. Of course, you're invited, too.   **bis / fertig**
9. Brigitte: Great!

N. Kurze Aufsätze

1. You're showing your town to a friend who's visiting. Describe what you see so that your friend will find it interesting.
2. Discuss with a friend some gifts you have bought. Write out your conversation.

Kapitel 5

- Forms and uses of dative case
- Indirect object
- Order of dative and accusative objects
- Verbs with the dative case
- Prepositions with the dative case
- Adjectives with the dative case

1. Forms of the dative case

	Masculine	Neuter	Feminine	Plural
Definite article:	dem Mann	dem Kind	der Frau	den Freunden
Dieser-words:	diesem Mann	diesem Kind	dieser Frau	diesen Freunden
Indefinite article:	einem Mann	einem Kind	einer Frau	—
Negative **kein**:	keinem Mann	keinem Kind	keiner Frau	keinen Freunden
Possessive adjectives:	ihrem Mann	unserem Kind	seiner Frau	meinen Freunden

The chart above shows the dative forms of the definite article, **dieser**-words, the indefinite article, the negative **kein**, and the possessive adjectives.

2. Nouns in the dative plural

Nominative:	die Freunde	die Eltern	die Radios
Dative:	den Freunden	den Eltern	den Radios

Nouns in the dative plural add -**n** unless the plural form already ends in -**n** or -**s**.

3. Masculine N-nouns in the dative case

Nominative:	der Herr	der Student
Accusative:	den Herrn	den Studenten
Dative:	dem Herrn	dem Studenten

Masculine **N**-nouns add -**n** or -**en** in the dative as well as in the accusative case.

4. Personal pronouns in the dative case

	Singular					Plural			
Nominative:	ich	du	er	es	sie	wir	ihr	sie	Sie
Accusative:	mich	dich	ihn	es	sie	uns	euch	sie	Sie
Dative:	mir	dir	ihm	ihm	ihr	uns	euch	ihnen	Ihnen

The chart above shows the personal pronouns in the nominative, accusative, and dative case.

5. Demonstrative pronouns in the dative case

	Singular			Plural
Nominative:	der	das	die	die
Accusative:	den	das	die	die
Dative:	dem	dem	der	denen

The forms of the demonstrative pronouns are the same as the forms of the definite article except in the dative plural which is **denen**.

6. Dative of *wer*

Nominative:	**Wer** ist das?
Accusative:	**Wen** meinen Sie?
Dative:	Mit **wem** sprechen Sie?

The dative form of the interrogative pronoun **wer** is **wem**.

7. Uses of the dative case

Indirect object:	Sie schreibt **ihrer Mutter** einen Brief.
Object of prepositions:	Er wohnt bei **seinem Onkel.**
Object of certain verbs:	Ich danke **dir.**
Adjectives with the dative:	Das ist **mir** recht.

8. Indirect object

Sie gibt **ihrem Freund** ein Radio.

She's giving her friend *a radio.*
She's giving a radio to her friend.

The indirect object (**Freund**) is usually a person and answers the question *to whom* or *for whom* something is done. In German, the indirect object is in the dative case. This distinguishes it from the direct object (**Radio**) which is always in the accusative case.

SALAT GARTEN

**Das Salat- und Vollwertrestaurant
bietet Ihnen täglich frisch**

Schlecker-ecke
Müsli
Obstsalat
Apfelcreme

über
40 Sorten
Salate
leckere Dressings
Obst + Gemüse-Säfte

Gemüse-spezialitäten
+ Suppen
Nudel-Reis-gerichte

Kaffee
Tee
Vollkornkuchen
und
Torten

Vollkornpfann-kuchen, Hirse-Grünkern-Küchle
mit Gemüse oder
Kompott

Das erste alkoholfreie Lokal in Freiburg
Öffnungszeiten: Mo – Fr 10.45 – 20.00, Sa 1045 – 15.00, lg. Sa 10.45 – 20.00 Uhr
Restaurant DER SALATGARTEN
Löwenstraße 1 (Nähe Martinstor), 7800 Freiburg
Telefon 07 61 / 3 51 55

9. Word order of direct and indirect objects

	Indirect object	Direct object
Inge gibt	ihrem Bruder	ein **Radio**.
Inge gibt	ihm	ein **Radio**.

When the direct object is a noun it follows the indirect object.

	Direct object	Indirect object
Inge gibt	**es**	ihrem Bruder.
Inge gibt	**es**	ihm.

When the direct object is a personal pronoun, it precedes the indirect object.

10. Dative verbs

Ich **danke** Ihnen für Ihre Hilfe.	*I thank you for your help.*
Monika hat ihrer Freundin **verziehen**.	*Monika forgave her friend.*

Most German verbs take objects in the accusative, but a few verbs have objects in the dative. This dative object is usually a person. Such verbs are often called dative verbs. Some common dative verbs are **antworten, befehlen, begegnen, danken, dienen, fehlen, folgen, gefallen, gehorchen, gehören, gelingen, glauben, helfen, leid tun, passen, passieren, raten, schmecken, verzeihen, weh tun.**

For a more complete list see Appendix, p. 153.

Dative	Accusative
Er glaubt **ihm** nicht.	Er glaubt **es** nicht.
Ich kann **ihm** nicht verzeihen.	**So etwas** kann ich nicht verzeihen.

Some of the dative verbs can take impersonal objects in the accusative case: **befehlen, danken, glauben, raten, verzeihen.**

11. Prepositions with the dative case

Preposition	Meaning	Examples
aus	*out of*	Anja kommt gerade **aus** der Bibliothek.
	from	Helene kommt **aus** der Schweiz.
	made of	Der Teller ist **aus** Holz.
außer	*besides, except*	**Außer** deinem Bruder kommt niemand zum Abendessen.
	out of	Das Schiff ist **außer** Gefahr.
bei	*at the home of*	Jürgen wohnt immer noch **bei** seiner Mutter.
	near	Wo liegt der Ort? — **Bei** München.
	at	Inge arbeitet **bei** der Post.
	with	Hast du Geld **bei** dir?
gegenüber	*opposite, across from*	Schmidts wohnen uns **gegenüber**.
mit	*with*	Inge wohnt **mit** ihrer Schwester zusammen.
	by (vehicle)	Udo fährt heute **mit** dem Bus.
nach	*to* (cities, masc. and ntr. countries)	Fliegst du **nach** Österreich?
	after	**Nach** dem Frühstück spielen wir Tennis.
	according to	Meiner Meinung **nach** tust du immer zuviel.
seit	*since* (temporal)	**Seit** jenem Abend esse ich keinen Fisch mehr.
	for (temporal)	Der Student wartet **seit** einer Stunde im Büro.
von	*from*	Das Geschenk ist **von** meinen Eltern.
	by	Das Bild ist **von** Paul Klee.
	of, about	Die Touristen sprechen **von** ihrer Reise.
	of (relationship)	Jürgen ist ein Freund **von** mir.
zu	*to*	Wir gehen **zu** unseren Nachbarn.
		Ich gehe **zur** Bank.
	at	Bist du heute abend **zu** Hause?
	for	**Zum** Mittagessen gibt es heute Fisch.

The prepositions **aus, außer, bei, gegenüber, mit, nach, seit, von,** and **zu** are always followed by the dative case. Note that when **nach** means *according to,* it usually follows the noun. **Gegenüber** always follows a pronoun object. It may precede a noun object.

12. Contractions of dative prepositions

bei dem → beim	Ich sehe Helga immer **beim** Frühstück.
von dem → vom	Wir sprechen nicht **vom** Wetter.
zu dem → zum	Was gibt's **zum** Mittagessen?
zu der → zur	Ich muß schnell noch **zur** Post.

The prepositions **bei, von** and **zu** often contract with the definite article **dem,** and **zu** also contracts with the definite article **der.**

13. Adjectives with the dative case

Paul sieht seinem Bruder sehr
  ähnlich.

*Paul looks very much like his
  brother.*

Ich bin dir für den guten Rat
  sehr **dankbar.**

*I'm very grateful to you for the
  good advice.*

The dative case is used with many adjectives. Some common ones are:

ähnlich	böse	gleich	nahe	schuldig	wert
angenehm	dankbar	lieb	nützlich	teuer	willkommen
bekannt	fremd	möglich	recht		

Er ist seinem Vater ähnlich.

Übungen

A. Geben.   One can give all sorts of things—gifts, answers, even a kiss. Tell what the following people gave.

▶ Gerda / ihre Schwester Ulla / eine interessante Schallplatte
  *Gerda hat ihrer Schwester Ulla eine interessante Schallplatte
  gegeben.*

1. Karin / der Professor / ihr fertiges Referat
2. Paul / sein Bruder / der Kassettenrecorder
3. Dieter / der Lehrer / eine freche° Antwort   impudent
4. ich / die Schülerin / Privatunterricht°   private lessons
5. Susanne / ihre Mutter / viele schöne Blumen
6. der Bäcker / der Junge / die frischen Brötchen
7. Jürgen / seine Freundin / ein Kuß

B. Unsinn.   Gerd has lots of suggestions, all of which sound crazy to you. Use indirect object pronouns in your responses.

▶ Kauf deiner Großmutter ein Fahrrad!
 Unsinn, ich kauf' ihr doch kein Fahrrad!

▶ Schenk deinem Freund deine Bilder!
 Unsinn, ich schenk' ihm doch nicht meine Bilder.

1. Schenk deinen Eltern ein Klavier!
2. Schreib deiner Freundin eine Karte!
3. Kauf mir ein Telefon!
4. Kauf uns ein Auto!
5. Erzähl dem Professor einen Witz°!   joke
6. Gib dem Mechaniker deinen Führerschein!
7. Erklär deiner Chefin die Arbeit!
8. Gib mir die Schlüssel!
9. Wünsch dem Polizisten frohe Ostern!

C. Ja, das mache ich.   This time Gerd has better suggestions. Say you'll do them. Use a pronoun for the direct object in your answer.

▶ Schenkst du deinem Neffen diese Briefmarken?
 Ja, ich schenke sie meinem Neffen.

1. Kaufst du deiner Freundin diese Blumen?
2. Schreibst du deinen Eltern diese Karte?
3. Schenkst du deinem Freund dieses Radio?
4. Gibst du mir dein altes Fahrrad?
5. Erzählst du uns die Geschichte?
6. Beschreibst du uns deinen neuen Plan?
7. Schenkst du mir deinen alten Fernsehapparat?
8. Gibst du den Kindern den Kuchen?

D. Eine Reise nach Hamburg.   Angelika is telling about her friends, an American family, who visited Hamburg. Complete her account by using the cued words.

1. Hamburg hat _____ gut gefallen. (die Familie)
2. Die Leute in Hamburg waren so nett und haben _____ immer geholfen. (die Touristen)
3. Das deutsche Essen hat _____ recht gut geschmeckt. (die Amerikaner)
4. Viele tolle Sachen sind _____ dort passiert. (die Gäste)
5. Mitten in° Hamburg begegneten sie _____. (ein Kollege aus   in the middle of New York)

6. Das konnte ich _____ kaum glauben. (meine Freunde)
7. Auf der ganzen Reise folgten sie _____ aus einem Reisebuch. (ein Plan)
8. Es tat _____ sehr leid, daß sie nicht länger bleiben konnten. (ich)
9. Ich habe _____ geraten, länger zu bleiben. (sie)
10. Aber das hat _____ nicht gepaßt. (ihr Sohn Thomas)

E. Wie schmeckt's? Ingrid is baking a cake for her friend Max. Unfortunately it doesn't look as though it turned out well. Complete the account with appropriate personal pronouns.

▶ Ingrid: „Na, der ist _mir_ ja gar nicht gelungen!"

1. Ingrids Schwester hat _____ beim Kuchenbacken geholfen.
2. Sie fragt: „Ist _____ so etwas schon oft passiert?"
3. Ingrid antwortet _____ traurig: „Nein, noch nie."
4. Da stehen sie beide und schauen den Kuchen an. Das tut _____ jetzt sehr leid.
5. Max hatte sich so auf den Schokoladenkuchen gefreut. Der schmeckt _____ gerade am besten.
6. Später geben sie _____ den Kuchen: „Kannst du _____ verzeihen, Max?"
7. Max antwortet _____ und lacht: „Ach, natürlich! Ich danke _____ trotzdem."
8. „Der Kuchen gefällt _____ ganz gut und schmeckt _____ bestimmt ausgezeichnet!"

F. Auf deutsch bitte.

1. Yesterday I met a girl. She had a dog with her°.   mithaben
2. The dog followed her very slowly.
3. She commanded the dog, "Come."
4. But the dog didn't obey her.
5. I asked the girl, "Does the dog belong to you?"
6. She said, "Yes. He has been sick for a week. His leg hurts. I feel so sorry for him."
7. Too bad. I liked the dog.

G. Ein Paket aus der Schweiz. Ruth tells about the package she has received from her parents who are in Switzerland for a year. Complete the sentences with the German equivalents of the English cues.

1. Ich kam nach Hause, und da war ein Paket _für mich_. (for me)
2. Es war _____. (from my parents)
   von meinem Eltern

3. Es kam _aus der_____. (from Switzerland)
4. Meine Eltern wohnen _seit_ dort. (for a year)
5. Zu Weihnachten war ich _____. (with them) _bei ihnen_
6. Wir waren in einer kleinen Stadt im Hotel. Es war _dem_ _Rathaus_ gegenüber. (town hall)
7. _____ sehe ich sie nicht mehr. (until next summer) _Bis zum nächsten Sommer._
8. In dem Paket war eine neue Jacke. _____ habe ich doch schon _Aus diesem Stoff._ eine Hose! (made of this material) _Der Stoff_
9. Da paßt die Jacke sehr gut _____. (to the pants) _zu der Hose_
10. _____ war noch eine Menge Schweizer Schokolade drin. (besides the jacket) _Außerdem_
11. _____ kann ich nicht leben. Ich esse sie so gern! (without this chocolate) _Ohne diese Chokolad_

H. Eine frühere Freundin. Two art students, Karin and Doris, had been renting a studio from their friend Angie. Last week she made them move. They are pretty mad. Complete the account with the appropriate form of the cued words.

1. Doris und Karin sind _ihrer_____ sehr böse. (ihre Freundin Angie)
2. Denn es ist _____ nicht möglich, schnell etwas anderes nahe _____ zu finden. (die Studentinnen / die Universität) _den_   _den_
3. Doris: „So eine arrogante Person! Das sieht _ihr_ ähnlich!" (sie)
4. Sie sollte _uns_ dankbar sein! (wir)
5. Wir waren _ihr_ nie die Miete schuldig. (sie)
6. Karin: „Ja, wirklich, _mir_ ist das auch nicht recht." (ich)
7. _____ scheint ihre Freundin nicht viel wert zu sein. (manchen Leute)n
8. Aber _mir_ ist es jetzt auch gleich, was aus ihr wird. (ich)

I. Auf deutsch bitte! Kim's friend Benno has new plans that she finds a little weird. Say in German what she tells you about him.

1. Since the concert Benno wants to become a musician°.   **Musiker**
2. That's just like° him.   **ähnlich sehen**
3. In my opinion he should first° practice.   **erst einmal**
4. But he has already talked with his parents.
5. He says they like° this idea.   **gefallen**
6. Well°, I don't quite° believe him.   **na** / *not quite* = **nicht ganz**
7. For his birthday he got a piano.
8. His grandparents gave it to him.
9. Well, I'm curious.

J. Kurze Aufsätze

1. Tell about a trip you took or you'd like to take to another city or country with a friend.
2. In what ways are you similar to members of your family or in what ways are you different?
3. Describe five things you like and five you dislike.

Kapitel 6

- *Hin* and *her*
- Either-or prepositions
- Time expressions with the dative case
- *Da-* and *wo*-compounds
- The verbs *legen/liegen, setzen/sitzen, stellen/stehen, hängen*
- Forms and uses of genitive case
- Prepositions with genitive
- Expressions of indefinite time
- Dative as a genitive substitute

1. *Hin* and *her*

Wohin fährst du?	*Where are you going?*
Wo fährst du **hin?**	
Woher kommen Sie?	*Where do you come from?*
Wo kommen Sie **her?**	
Komm mal **herunter!**	*Come on down.*
Er ist gestern **hingefallen.**	*He fell down yesterday.*

The adverbs **hin** and **her** are used to show direction. **Hin** indicates motion in a direction away from the speaker, and **her** shows motion toward the speaker. **Hin** and **her** occupy last position in a sentence. They may also be combined with various parts of speech such as adverbs (**dorthin**), prepositions (**herunter**), and verbs (**hinfallen**).

2. Either-or prepositions

Ingrid arbeitet **in der Stadt.**	*Ingrid works in town.*
Alex fährt **in die Stadt.**	*Alex is going to town.*

German has nine prepositions that take either the dative or the accusative case. They may be called either-or, or two-way, prepositions. The dative case is used when the verb indicates position (place where) and answers the question **wo?** (*where?*). The accusative case is used when the verb indicates motion in a direction (change of location, destination) and answers the question **wohin?** (*where to?*).

Preposition	Meaning	Examples
an	*at (the side of)*	Ute steht **an der Tür.**
	to	Benno geht **an die Tür.**
	on (vertical surfaces)	Das Bild hängt **an der Wand.**
auf	*on top of* (horizontal surfaces)	Kurts Buch liegt **auf dem Tisch.**
		Sabine legt ihr Buch **auf den Tisch.**
	to	Ich gehe **auf die Post.**
hinter	*behind*	Inge arbeitet **hinter dem Haus.**
		Benno geht **hinter das Haus.**
in	*inside*	Paula arbeitet **in der Küche.**
	into	Jürgen geht **in die Küche.**
	to	Geht er **in die Schule?**
neben	*beside, next to*	**Neben dem Sofa** steht eine Lampe.
		Jan stellt eine zweite Lampe **neben das Sofa.**
über	*over, above*	**Über dem Tisch** hängt eine Lampe.
		Hugo hängt eine zweite Lampe **über den Tisch.**
	across	Ich gehe **über die Straße.**
unter	*under*	Kurts Schuhe stehen **unter dem Bett.**
		Er stellt auch Antons Schuhe **unter das Bett.**
vor	*in front of*	**Vor dem Sofa** steht ein Couchtisch.
		Ilse stellt einen zweiten **vor das Sofa.**
zwischen	*between*	**Zwischen den Büchern** liegt ein Stück Papier.
		Jens legt ein zweites Stück **zwischen die Bücher.**

3. Contractions of either-or prepositions

Accusative	Dative
an das → **ans**	an dem → **am**
in das → **ins**	in dem → **im**
auf das → **aufs**	

The prepositions **an** and **in** may contract with **das** and **dem**; **auf** may contract with **das**. Other either-or prepositions may also have contractions, but they are mostly colloquial, *e.g.* **hinterm, übers, vorm.**

4. Special meanings of either-or prepositions

Inge **schreibt an** ihren Freund Udo.	*Inge is writing to her friend Udo.*
Sie **denkt** oft **an** ihn.	*She often thinks of him.*
Udo **studiert an der Universität**.	*Udo is studying at the university.*
Inge **geht** jetzt **an die Arbeit**.	*Inge is starting her work now.*
Wann **bist** du **an der Reihe**?	*When is it your turn?*
Jürgen **antwortet** nicht **auf** meine Frage.	*Jürgen is not answering my question.*
Dieter **geht** nicht **auf die Universität**.	*Dieter doesn't go to college.*
Er wohnt **auf dem Land**.	*He lives in the country.*
Warten Sie **auf** den Bus?	*Are you waiting for the bus?*
Sie sagte es **auf deutsch**.	*She said it in German.*
Gehst du heute **ins Theater?**	*Are you going to the theater today?*
Morgen fahren wir **in die Schweiz**.	*Tomorrow we're going to Switzerland.*
Die Fahrkarte kostet **über 100 Mark**.	*The ticket costs over 100 marks.*
Lachst du **über** den Preis?	*Are you laughing about the price?*
Was ich jetzt sage, bleibt **unter uns**.	*What I'm about to say must remain between us.*
Die Jacke bekommst du nicht **unter 200 Mark**.	*You won't get the jacket for less than 200 marks.*
Das Kind **hat Angst vor** dem Hund.	*The child is afraid of the dog.*

In addition to their basic meanings, the either-or prepositions have special meanings when combined with specific verbs (**warten auf**) or in specific verb-noun combinations (**an der Reihe sein, an die Reihe kommen**). Since there is no way to predict the meaning and case, these expressions must be learned. When **über** means *about, concerning*, it is always followed by the accusative case.

5. Time expressions with the dative case

am Montag   on Monday
am Abend   in the evening

in einer Woche　　in a week
im Januar　　in January
vor einer Woche　　a week ago
vor dem Essen　　before dinner

When used in expressions of time, the prepositions **an, in,** and **vor** are followed by the dative case.

6. Da-compounds

Spricht er oft **von seiner Arbeit?**	Ja, er spricht oft **davon.**
Spricht er oft **von seinem Chef?**	Ja, er spricht oft **von ihm.**

A **da**-compound consists of the demonstrative adverb **da** plus a preposition and refers to things or ideas. A **da**-compound cannot refer to a person. **Da**- expands to **dar**- when combined with a preposition beginning with a vowel: **darüber, darauf.**

Woran Sie vor Ihrer Reise denken sollten:

Reiseunterlagen
☐ Personalausweis/Reisepaß (noch gültig?)
☐ Fahrkarten/Flugkarten
☐ Reservierungen und Informationen
☐ Führerschein/grüne Versicherungskarte
☐ Impfpaß
☐ Visum
☐ Krankenschein
☐ Unfall-, Reise- und Gepäckversicherung
☐ Reiseschecks, eurocheques und ec-Karte

☐ Benzingutscheine
☐ Wertgegenstände (Tresor der Sparkasse)

Für Autofahrer
☐ Ist das Auto fit?
☐ Notfallausrüstung in Ordnung?
☐ Autoapotheke vervollständigen
☐ D-Schild anbringen
☐ Reparaturwerkstätten-Verzeichnis des Reiselandes
☐ Reserveschlüssel!

Wohnung:
☐ Wasser, Gas und Strom abgestellt?
☐ Eisschrank abgetaut und offen?
☐ Fenster geschlossen?
☐ Postnachsendeantrag gestellt?
☐ Wohnungsschlüssel und Reiseadresse bei den Nachbarn?

Wir empfehlen Ihnen: Geben Sie uns rechtzeitig vor Ihrer Reise Dauerauftrags- oder Abbuchungsaufträge für anfallende Zahlungen.

Wir wünschen Ihnen gute Reise!

---

7. Wo-compounds

Wovon spricht sie?	Sie spricht **von ihrer Arbeit.**
Von wem spricht sie?	Sie spricht **von ihrem Chef.**

A **wo**-compound consists of the interrogative adverb **wo** plus a preposition and is used to ask questions referring to things or ideas. A **wo**-compound cannot refer to a person. **Wo**- expands to **wor**- when combined with a preposition beginning with a vowel: **worüber, worauf.**

8. The verbs *legen/liegen, setzen/sitzen, stellen/stehen, hängen*

Inge **legt** das Buch **auf den Tisch**.	Es **liegt** jetzt **auf dem Tisch**.
Marta **setzt** das Kind **auf den Stuhl**.	Es **sitzt** jetzt **auf dem Stuhl**.
Paul **stellt** die Lampe **in die Ecke**.	Sie **steht** jetzt **in der Ecke**.
Dieter **hängt** die Uhr **an die Wand**.	Sie **hängt** jetzt **an der Wand**.

To express movement to a position English uses the verb *to put*: Inge puts the book, Marta puts the child, Paul puts the lamp, etc. German uses several verbs: **legen, setzen, stellen, hängen**. With these verbs the case after the either-or preposition is accusative. To express the resulting position English uses the verb *to be*: The book is, the lamp is, the child is, etc. German uses the verbs **liegen, sitzen, stehen** and **hängen**. With these verbs the case after the either-or preposition is dative.

9. Forms of the genitive case

	Masculine	Neuter	Feminine	Plural
Definite article:	des Mannes	des Kindes	der Frau	der Freunde
Dieser-words:	dieses Mannes	dieses Kindes	dieser Frau	dieser Freunde
Indefinite article:	eines Mannes	eines Kindes	einer Frau	—
Kein:	keines Mannes	keines Kindes	keiner Frau	keiner Freunde
Ein-words:	ihres Mannes	unseres Kindes	seiner Frau	meiner Freunde

The chart above shows the genitive forms of the definite article, **dieser**-words, indefinite article, **kein**, and **ein**-words. The masculine and neuter forms end in -[e]s in the genitive, and feminine and plural forms in -[e]r.

10. Nouns in the genitive

Masculine / neuter	Feminine / plural
der Name des Mannes	der Name der Frau
ein Freund des Mädchens	ein Freund der Kinder

Masculine and neuter nouns of one syllable generally add -es in the genitive; masculine and neuter nouns of two or more syllables add -s. Feminine and plural nouns do not add a genitive ending.

11. Masculine N-nouns in the genitive

Nominative:	der Herr	der Student
Accusative:	den Herrn	den Studenten
Dative:	dem Herrn	dem Studenten
Genitive:	des Herrn	des Studenten

Masculine N-nouns that add -n or -en in the accusative and dative singular also add -n or -en in the genitive. A few masculine nouns add -ns: der Name>des Namens, der Gedanke>des Gedankens, der Glaube>des Glaubens. (See p. 155 for a list of common masculine N-nouns.)

12. Proper names in the genitive

Das ist **Ingrids** Buch.
Hans' Pullover gefällt mir.

The genitive of proper names is formed by adding -s. In writing, if the name already ends in an s-sound, no -s is added and an apostrophe is used.

13. The interrogative pronoun *wessen*

Wessen Buch ist das?   *Whose book is that?*
Wessen Jacke trägst du?   *Whose jacket are you wearing?*

Wessen is the genitive form of the interrogative **wer**; it is equivalent to *whose.*

14. Summary of uses of the genitive case

Possession and other relationships:	Das Haus **meines Freundes** ist 100 Jahre alt. Der Titel **des Buches** ist viel zu lang.
Object of prepositions:	**Trotz des Wetters** gehen wir schwimmen.
Indefinite time expressions:	**Eines Tages** ist etwas Komisches passiert.

The genitive case is used to show possession and other close relationships. It is also used for objects of certain prepositions and for expressions of indefinite time.

15. Possession and other close relationships

der Koffer **des Mädchens**	*the* girl's *suitcase*
die Farbe **des Koffers**	*the color* of the suitcase

English shows possession or other close relationships by adding 's to a noun or by using a phrase with *of*. English generally uses the 's-form only for persons. For things and ideas, English uses an *of*-construction. German uses the genitive case to show possession or other close relationships. The genitive is used for things and ideas as well as for persons. The genitive expression generally follows the noun it modifies.

Ingrids Koffer	*Ingrid's suitcase*
Marks Freund	*Mark's friend*

Proper names in the genitive generally precede the nouns they modify.

GROTRIAN
das königliche Instrument

Eine der großen Marken der Welt.

Grotrian Pianofortefabrikanten D-3300 Braunschweig

16. Genitive prepositions

Preposition	Meaning	Example
(an)statt	*instead of*	Kaufst du einen Stuhl **statt** eines Tisches?
trotz	*in spite of*	Kommst du **trotz** des Wetters?
während	*during*	**Während** des Essens sprach er kein Wort.
wegen	*on account of*	**Wegen** der vielen Arbeit blieb sie zu Hause.

The prepositions **(an)statt, trotz, während,** and **wegen** are the most commonly used prepositions that are always followed by the genitive case. **Statt** is the shortened form of **anstatt.** Some other genitive prepositions you should recognize are:

außerhalb	outside of	**unterhalb**	under
innerhalb	inside of	**diesseits**	on this side of
oberhalb	above	**jenseits**	on that side of

17. Expressions of indefinite time

Eines Tages (Abends, Nachts) hatte Jutta eine Idee.	*One day (evening, night) Jutta had an idea.*
Letzten Endes können wir nichts machen.	*After all, we can't do anything.*

Note that by analogy with **eines Tages** and **eines Abends** it is **eines Nachts** even though **Nacht** is feminine. Remember that definite time is expressed by the accusative (see p. 47): Sie bleibt **einen Tag.**

18. Special expressions

Ich fahre immer **erster Klasse.**	*I always go first class.*
Einmal **zweiter Klasse** München.	*A one-way ticket, second-class to Munich.*
Ich bin **ganz deiner Meinung.**	*I agree totally (I am of your opinion).*
Ich bin **anderer Meinung.**	*I am of another opinion.*

The genitive is also used in idiomatic expressions.

19. Dative as substitute for the genitive

a. Possession

die Freundin **von meinem Bruder** (meines Bruders)
zwei **von ihren Freunden** (ihrer Freunde)

In spoken German the genitive of possession is frequently replaced by **von** + *dative*.

die Ideen **von Studenten**
die Mutter **von vier Jungen**

Von + *dative* is regularly used if the noun of possession is not preceded by a word that shows genitive case (i.e. definite article, **dieser-**word, etc.).

ein Freund **von mir**
ein Freund **von Nicole**

Von + *dative* is also used in phrases similar to the English *of mine, of yours*, etc.

b. Prepositions

wegen **dem Wetter** (des Wetters)
trotz **dem Regen** (des Regens)
trotz **ihm**
wegen **dir**

In colloquial usage many people use the prepositions **statt**, **trotz**, **wegen**, and sometimes **während** with the dative.

Übungen

A. Wo sind meine Sachen? Mr. Stark, who is rather absent-minded, is ready to leave for work and asks his wife a lot of questions. Play her part and answer him, using the cues in parentheses.

▶ Wo sind meine Schuhe? (unter / Bett)   *Unter dem Bett.*

▶ Wohin hab' ich meine Handschuhe gesteckt? (in / Mantel)
   In den Mantel.

1. Wo hab' ich meine Brille? (auf / Nase)
2. Wo ist mein Hut? (in / Schrank)
3. Wo ist meine Tasche? (neben / Schreibtisch)

4. Wohin habe ich meine Schlüssel getan? (in / Tasche)
5. Wo hab' ich mein Auto geparkt? (hinter / Haus)
6. Wohin gehen wir heute Abend? (in / Kino)
7. Wo treffe ich dich? (vor / Kino)
8. Wohin gehen wir nach dem Film? (in / Gasthaus)
9. Wo ist das Gasthaus? (an / Marktplatz)

B. Ende gut, alles gut. Bernd's room is in chaos. Tell how he straightens it up. Make complete sentences using the cues given.

1. die Bücher / liegen / auf / der Boden
2. er / stellen / sie / in / das Regal°   bookcase
3. die Lampe / stehen / auf / der Fernseher
4. er / stellen / sie / auf / der Tisch
5. die Kleider / liegen / auf / das Bett
6. er / hängen / sie / in / der Schrank
7. seine neuen Poster / hängen / hinter / die Tür
8. er / hängen / sie / an / die Wand
9. seine Papers / liegen / unter / das Bett
10. er / legen / sie / auf / der Schreibtisch
11. seine kleine süße Katze / sitzen / auf / der Schrank
12. er / setzen / sie / auf / das Sofa
13. später / sitzen / er / dann auch / auf / das Sofa
14. er / legen / die Füße / auf / der Couchtisch / und betrachtet froh sein Werk

C. Noch einmal. Now tell the same story again, this time in the simple past tense.

D. Peters alte Freundin. Tell about Peter's former friend by completing the sentences with an appropriate preposition.

1. Peter hat Nicole _an_ der Universität Heidelberg kennengelernt.
2. Peter geht nicht mehr _auf_ die Universität.
3. Er wohnt jetzt _auf_ dem Land.
4. Nicole ist _in_ die Schweiz gegangen und studiert in Genf°   Geneva
   auf der Uni.
5. Peter denkt noch oft _an_ seine Freundin.
6. Er schreibt noch manchmal _an_ sie.
7. Nicole ist Französin, und Peter schreibt ihr _auf_ französisch.
8. Aber sie antwortet nicht mehr _auf_ seine Briefe.
9. Er wartet nicht mehr _auf_ sie.
10. Manchmal muß er schon _über_ seinen Liebeskummer° lachen.   lover's grief

E. Wie bitte? Susanne is talking to her grandfather about her boyfriend. Her grandfather is somewhat hard of hearing and never seems to get the end of the sentence. Take his part and ask Susanne to repeat what she said. Use a **wo**-compound or a preposition plus a pronoun, as appropriate.

▶ Ich interessiere mich nicht mehr für Heiner.
  Für wen interessierst du dich nicht mehr?

1. Heute mußte ich eine halbe Stunde auf ihn warten.
2. Ich glaube, er denkt nicht mehr an mich.
3. Er interessiert sich nicht für meine Arbeit.
4. Er denkt nur noch an China.
5. Er schreibt über chinesische Literatur.
6. Ich glaube, er hat auch Angst vor den Prüfungen am Semesterende.
7. Er interessiert sich überhaupt nicht mehr für Spaß, Musik und Tanzen.
8. Ich bin mit Heiner nicht mehr zufrieden.

F. Die Arbeit im Reisebüro. Evelyn is curious about Steffi's work in the travel agency. Take Steffi's part and confirm Evelyn's assumptions. Use a **da**-compound or a preposition plus a pronoun, as appropriate.

▶ Bist du mit deiner Stelle zufrieden? *Ja, ich bin damit zufrieden.*
  Bist du mit deiner Chefin auch zufrieden? *Ja, ich bin mit ihr auch zufrieden.*

1. Mußt du viel über fremde Länder wissen?
2. Arbeitest du jeden Tag mit dem Computer?
3. Arbeitest du gern mit deinen Kollegen? *mit ihnen*
4. Interessieren sich deine Kollegen für dein Privatleben?
5. Sprichst du oft über deine Freunde?
6. Erzählst du viel von deinem Privatleben?
7. Möchtest du viel von deinen Kollegen wissen? *von ihnen*
8. Arbeitest du gern für deine Chefin? *für sie*

G. Brigitte ist krank. Brigitte has been sick for two weeks and she is beginning to get cabin fever. Express the information about her in German.

1. Brigitte is standing at the window.
2. She is looking into the garden.
3. She has to stay in the house, because she is ill.
4. Most of the time she has to lie in bed.
5. Her friends come with flowers and put them beside her bed.
6. Brigitte is happy about this.
7. But she doesn't want to sit at home any more.
8. The doctor said in a week she can get up again.
9. Then she's going to the country.
10. She wants to hike in the mountains.

H. Aber nein! Answer the following questions in the negative, using the cues in parentheses.

▶ Ist das die Wohnung deiner Tochter? (mein Sohn)
   Nein, das ist die Wohnung meines Sohnes.

1. Ist das das Auto deines Vaters? (unser Nachbar)
2. Hast du das Haus deines Onkels gekauft? (meine Großeltern) er
3. Ist das die Telefonnummer deines Arztes? (das Krankenhaus)
4. Schreibst du über die Geschichte eurer Familie? (diese Stadt)
5. Ist das der Titel des Buches? (der Film)
6. Ist das ein Bild deiner Freundin? (ihre Schwester)
7. Ist das das Geschäft deiner Cousine? (ein Kollege) es,   en
8. Hast du die Adresse deines Professors? (seine Sekretärin)

I. Fragen über Gabi. You and a friend are in Gabi's apartment. Your friend asks all kinds of questions about Gabi. Reply, but remain non-committal.

▶ Sind das Gabis Bücher?   *Vielleicht. Ich weiß nicht, wessen Bücher das sind.*

1. Sind das Gabis Fotos auf dem Tisch?
2. Ist das die Telefonnummer ihres neuen Freundes?
3. Benutzt sie die Schreibmaschine ihrer Sekretärin?
4. Fährt sie mit dem Fahrrad ihres Freundes?
5. Liegt Gabis Bericht auf dem Schreibtisch?
6. Ist das die Stereoanlage ihrer Schwester?

J. Der dicke Fuß.   Thomas wants to know all about your swollen foot. Answer using the cues in parentheses.

▶ Wann warst du in Österreich? (während / die Ferien)
Während der Ferien.

1. Fahrt ihr im April wieder in die Berge? (ja, trotz / das Wetter)
2. Warum kannst du nicht so schnell gehen? (wegen / mein Fuß) *es , es*
3. Tut dein Fuß weh? (ja, trotz / die Wanderschuhe) *der*
4. Wann bist du gestürzt°? (während / unsere Alpenwanderung)   fall
5. Warum bist du gestürzt? (wegen / die Steine auf dem Weg)
6. Wann ist dein Fuß dick geworden? (während / diese Woche) *er*
7. Ist dein Bruder mit dir gewandert? (ja, statt / mein Vetter) *es , es*

K. Das Haus in Italien.   Tell about your stay in Italy. Complete the sentences using the German equivalent of the English cues.

1. Wo warst du _____? (during the vacation) *während der*
2. In Italien. Im Hause _____. (of my friends) *meiner Freunde*
3. Das Haus steht am Ufer _____, und man kann weit sehen. (of a *eines Flußes* river)
4. _____ hat es einen großen Hof. (instead of a garden) *Statt eines Gartens*
5. _____ ist es schön kühl dort (during the summer), *Während des Sommers* _____, der da steht. (because of a tree) *Wegen eines Baumes*
6. Die Fenster _____ sind klein (of the house), *des Hauses* damit es _____ schön kühl bleibt im Haus. (in spite of the sun)
7. Alle Häuser _____ sind so gebaut. (of this region)
8. Die Farbe _____ ist meistens gelb. (of the houses) *der Häuser*
9. Das sieht sehr schön aus zum Grün _____. Ich bin sehr gern dort. (of the trees) *der Bäume*

L. Anruf aus Amerika.   Gisela tells about a telephone call from her American friend. Complete the sentences using the German equivalent of the English cues.

1. _____ klingelte° mein Telefon. Es war mein Freund aus Amerika. (one night)   rang
2. Er vergißt _____, daß es hier sechs Stunden später ist. (every time)
3. Aber ich erinnere mich immer daran und rufe ihn nie _____ an. (in the morning)
4. Am Telefon erzählte ich ihm, daß ich _____ nach Amerika fliege. (next month)
5. _____ war ich schon einmal dort. (many years ago)
6. _____ beschloß ich einfach, eine große Reise zu machen. (one day)
7. _____ lernte ich viele Menschen kennen. (in a week)
8. _____ erlebte° ich etwas Neues. (every day)   experienced
9. Ich blieb insgesamt° _____. (two months)   all together

M. Regen am Wochenende.   Tell about your weekend in the rain. In German, naturally.

1. On the weekend a girl friend of mine came to see me°.   zu Besuch kommen
2. She always travels first-class.
3. I prefer to travel second-class.
4. In spite of the rain we went for many walks°.   viel spazierengehen
5. She put on° my sister's rain coat.   anziehen
6. Many people find rain boring but I am of a different opinion.
7. Because of the rain only a few people were outside.
8. In the evening two of my friends came and we cooked together.

N. Kurze Aufsätze

1. Describe your room as it is arranged now and then write how you could rearrange it.
2. Plan a trip; be sure to discuss where you will go, where you will shop, what it costs, and what you will do.
3. Write a short paragraph answering one of the following questions.

   a. Wovor hast du Angst?
   b. Woran denkst du oft?
   c. Worüber lachst du gern?

Kapitel 7

- Predicate adjectives
- Attributive adjectives
- Preceded adjectives
- Unpreceded adjectives
- Adjectives as nouns
- Ordinal numbers
- Participles as adjectives
- Comparison of adjectives and adverbs

1. Predicate adjectives

Mein Hut ist **neu.**
Fleisch ist **billig** geworden.
Das Brot bleibt **frisch.**

Predicate adjectives follow the verbs **sein, werden,** or **bleiben** and modify the subject of the sentence. They never add declensional endings.

2. Attributive adjectives

Mein **neuer** Hut ist schön, nicht?
Hast du das **billige** Fleisch gekauft?
Ich kaufe nur **frisches** Brot.

Attributive adjectives precede the nouns they modify. The declensional endings they have depend on whether the adjectives are preceded by a definite article, a **dieser**-word, an indefinite article, an **ein**-word, or no article. Adjective endings may be either strong (also called primary) or weak (also called secondary). Strong endings are the same as the endings of **dieser**-words. They show gender and case: **mein neuer Hut, frisches Brot.** Weak endings are either **-e** or **-en.** They do not show gender and case, which is indicated by the preceding article, **dieser**-word, or **ein**-word: **der neue Hut, diese schweren Aufgaben.**

Das ist ein **guter alter** Wein.
Wir haben ein **schönes neues** Auto.

Adjectives in a series have the same ending.

3. Adjectives preceded by the definite article or *dieser*-words

	Masculine	Neuter	Feminine	Plural
Nominative:	der **neue** Hut	das **neue** Hemd	die **neue** Hose	die **neuen** Schuhe
Accusative:	den **neuen** Hut	das **neue** Hemd	die **neue** Hose	die **neuen** Schuhe
Dative:	dem **neuen** Hut	dem **neuen** Hemd	der **neuen** Hose	den **neuen** Schuhen
Genitive:	des **neuen** Hutes	des **neuen** Hemdes	der **neuen** Hose	der **neuen** Schuhe

	M	N	F	Pl
Nominative:	e	e	e	en
Accusative:	en	e	e	en
Dative:	en	en	en	en
Genitive:	en	en	en	en

Adjectives preceded by a definite article or **dieser**-word have weak endings (**-e, -en**).

Der neue Feinschmeckertreff

Romantischer Schloßhof – Holzkohlengrill Kerzenlicht Lamm – Forellen Bodenständige Küche der Extraklasse – Hausgemachte Mehlspeisen

Schloßmühle

Zellerndorf

Rittermahl mit Tafelmusik jeden 2. Freitag im Monat, sechsgängiges Menü, Einheitspreis S 280,– **Kulinarium:** 22. August Prager Blech, Virtuoses Bläsersextett aus der Goldenen Stadt

Franz Gaunersdorfer
2051 Zellerndorf 1, Telefon (02952) 495

4. Adjectives preceded by the indefinite article or *ein*-words

	Masculine	Neuter	Feminine	Plural
Nominative:	ein **neuer** Hut	ein **neues** Hemd	eine **neue** Hose	meine **neuen** Schuhe
Accusative:	einen **neuen** Hut	ein **neues** Hemd	eine **neue** Hose	meine **neuen** Schuhe
Dative:	einem **neuen** Hut	einem **neuen** Hemd	einer **neuen** Hose	meinen **neuen** Schuhen
Genitive:	eines **neuen** Hutes	eines **neuen** Hemdes	einer **neuen** Hose	meiner **neuen** Schuhe

	M	N	F	Pl
Nominative:	**er**	**es**	**e**	en
Accusative:	en	**es**	**e**	en
Dative:	en	en	en	en
Genitive:	en	en	en	en

Adjectives preceded by an indefinite article or an **ein**-word have the weak endings (**-e**) or (**-en**) except in masculine nominative (**-er**) and neuter nominative and accusative (**-es**).

5. Adjectives not preceded by a definite article, *dieser*-word, indefinite article, or *ein*-word

	Masculine	Neuter	Feminine	Plural
Nominative:	**guter** Wein	**gutes** Brot	**gute** Wurst	**gute** Äpfel
Accusative:	**guten** Wein	**gutes** Brot	**gute** Wurst	**gute** Äpfel
Dative:	**gutem** Wein	**gutem** Brot	**guter** Wurst	**guten** Äpfeln
Genitive:	**guten** Weines	**guten** Brotes	**guter** Wurst	**guter** Äpfel

Adjectives not preceded by definite article, **dieser**-word, indefinite article, or **ein**-word have strong endings (the same as those of **dieser**-words), except the masculine and neuter genitive, which have the weak ending -en.

6. Adjectives preceded by indefinite adjectives

Einige neue Studenten kommen am Samstag.
Er kennt **viele schöne deutsche** Städte.

Both the indefinite adjectives **andere, einige, mehrere, viele,** and
wenige and the attributive adjectives following them have strong
endings.

Paul kennt nicht **alle deutschen** Städte.
Die Mütter **beider jungen** Menschen sind Verwandte.

An attributive adjective following the indefinite adjective **alle** or
beide has the weak ending **-en.**

7. Adjectives used as nouns

Das ist ein **Bekannter.** (Mann)	*That's a* friend. *(male)*
Das ist eine **Bekannte.** (Frau)	*That's a* friend. *(female)*
Das sind meine guten **Bekannten.** (Leute)	*Those are my* good friends. *(people)*

Many adjectives can be used as nouns in German. They retain the
adjective endings as though the noun were still there. In writing they
are capitalized.

Das Gute daran ist, daß es nicht so viel kostet.	The good thing *about it is that it doesn't cost so much.*
Wir haben **viel Schönes** gesehen.	*We saw* many beautiful things.
Alles Gute im Neuen Jahr.	Happy New Year.

Adjectives expressing abstractions *(the good, the beautiful)* are con-
sidered neuter nouns. They frequently follow words such as **etwas,
nichts,** and **viel (etwas Gutes).** Note that adjectives following **alles**
are weak **(alles Gute).**

8. Adjectives ending in -el or -er

Das ist eine **dunkle** Straße.	*That's a dark street.*
Das ist ein **teurer** Wagen.	*That's an expensive car.*
Das ist ein **hoher** Turm.	*That's a high tower.*

Adjectives ending in **-el** or **-er** omit the **e** when the adjective takes an
ending. **Hoch** becomes **hoh-** when it takes an ending.

9. Ordinal numbers

1.	erst-	**15.**	fünfzehnt-	**100.**	hundertst-
2.	zweit-	**16.**	sechzehnt-	**101.**	hunderterst-
3.	dritt-	**21.**	einundzwanzigst-	**105.**	hundertfünft-
6.	sechst-	**32.**	zweiunddreißigst-	**1000.**	tausendst-
7.	siebt-				
8.	acht-				

Ordinal numbers are used as adjectives. They are formed by adding -**t** to numbers 1–19 and -**st** to numbers beyond. Note the special forms **erst-, dritt-,** and **siebt-,** and the spelling of **acht-.**

Heute ist der **achtzehnte** Juni.
Hast du dir ein **zweites** Stück Kuchen genommen?

Ordinals take adjective endings. In writing, an ordinal is followed by a period: den **ersten Juni** > **den 1. Juni.** Dates in letter heads or news releases are in the accusative: **Hamburg, den 28. 7. 1990.**

Am 28. März 10.45 Uhr

10. Present participles as adjectives

Infinitive + d	Present participle	English
schlafen + d	**schlafend**	*sleeping*
lachen + d	**lachend**	*laughing*

Present participles are formed by adding -**d** to the infinitive.

die **schlafende** Katze   *the* sleeping *cat*
ein **lachendes** Kind   *a* laughing *child*

Present participles used as attributive adjectives take adjective endings. German does not use the present participle as a verb (compare English progressive forms): **sie lachte** *she was laughing.*

Ich hörte sie **lachen.**   *I heard her* laughing.

German uses an infinitive where English uses a participle.

11. Past participles as adjectives

Meine Eltern kauften einen **gebrauchten** Wagen.

My parents bought a used car.

Ich möchte ein weich **gekochtes** Ei.

I would like a soft boiled egg.

Past participles used as attributive adjectives take adjective endings.

12. Comparison of adjectives and adverbs

Base form:	**heiß**	*hot*	**schön**	*beautiful*
Comparative:	**heißer**	*hotter*	**schöner**	*more beautiful*
Superlative:	**heißest-**	*hottest*	**schönst-**	*most beautiful*

Adjectives and adverbs have three forms of degrees: base form (positive), comparative, and superlative. The comparative is formed by adding -er to the base form. The superlative is formed by adding -st to the base form. The ending -est is added to words ending in -d (**wildest-**), -t (**ältest-**), or a sibilant (**kürzest-**). The superlative of **groß** is **größt-**.

Base form:	alt	groß	jung
Comparative:	älter	größer	jünger
Superlative:	ältest-	größt-	jüngst-

Many one-syllable adjectives or adverbs with the stem vowel **a, o,** or **u** add an umlaut in the comparative and superlative. These adjectives and adverbs are noted in the end vocabulary as follows: **kalt (ä)**

Base form:	gern	gut	hoch	nah	viel
Comparative:	lieber	besser	höher	näher	mehr
Superlative:	liebst-	best-	höchst-	nächst-	meist-

Several adjectives and adverbs are irregular in the comparative and superlative.

13. Expressing comparisons

Sigrid ist nicht **so** groß **wie** Ursula.	*Sigrid is not as tall as Ursula.*
Es ist heute **so** kalt **wie** gestern.	*Today it's as cold as yesterday.*

The construction **so ... wie** is used to express the equality of one person or thing to another.

Ursula ist **größer als** Sigrid.	*Ursula is taller than Sigrid.*
Es ist heute **kälter als** gestern.	*Today it's colder than yesterday.*

The comparative form plus **als** is used to express a difference between two people or things.

Im Herbst ist es hier **am schönsten.**	*In the fall it's nicest here.*
Ich esse **am liebsten** Fisch.	*I like fish most of all.*

The pattern **am** + superlative + **-en** is used to express the superlative degree of predicate adjectives and adverbs.

Von den zehn Ländern in der Bundesrepublik ist Bremen **das kleinste** [Land].
Von meinen drei Brüdern ist Uwe **der größte** [Bruder].

A second superlative pattern in the predicate is one that shows gender and number. This construction is used when the noun is understood.

Base: Das ist kein **neues** Buch.
Comparative: Ich möchte ein **neueres** Buch lesen.
Superlative: Ist das dein **neuestes** Buch?

Attributive adjectives in the comparative and superlative take the same adjective endings as those in the base form.

Der kürzeste Weg nach Italien kann der preiswerteste sein.

Übungen

A. Ferien. Make the comments about vacation more descriptive by using the correct form of the cued adjectives before the italicized noun.

▶ Jeder *Lehrer* hat jetzt Ferien. (deutsch)
Jeder deutsche Lehrer hat jetzt Ferien.

1. Diese *Lehrerin* fährt in ihren Ferien nach Frankreich. (jung)
2. Welches *Auto* gehört ihr? (rot) *rotes*
3. Sie unternimmt diese *Reise* in den Süden mit einer Kollegin. (schön) *en*
4. Wer möchte nicht in jener *Landschaft* sein? (wunderbar) *en*
5. Die *Städte* im Süden sind sehr interessant. (klein) *en*
6. Sie besuchen so manchen *Markt*. (interessant) *en*
7. Auch fahren sie nach Marseille und Paris. Solche *Städte* sind zu der Zeit voll von Touristen. (berühmt) *en*

B. Der Ingenieur. Ellen tells about Silvia's friend, who is an engineer. Make her account smoother linguistically by combining each pair of sentences as in the model.

▶ Ich erzähle euch eine Geschichte. Sie ist toll.
Ich erzähle euch eine tolle Geschichte.

1. Silvia hat einen Ingenieur kennengelernt. Er ist nett und reich. *en en*
2. Sein *B*eruf gefällt ihm. Er ist interessant. *er*
3. Er wohnt in einem Haus. Es ist alt und schön. *en en*
4. Das Haus ist an einem See. Er ist groß. *en*
5. Silvias Augen haben den Ingenieur fasziniert°. Sie sind hübsch. *en*   fascinated
6. Er hat ein Boot. Es ist neu. *es*
7. Mit dem Boot fahren sie auf den See hinaus. Er ist still. *en*
8. In dem See ist eine Insel. Sie ist klein. *en*
9. Dort machen sie ein Picknick. Es ist fein. *es*

C. Weißt du? A friend of yours is visiting you. Your friend has lots of questions about your city. Answer according to the model, using the cues.

▶ Weißt du, wo hier ein guter Zahnarzt ist? (Adresse)
Ja, ich kann dir die Adresse eines guten Zahnarztes geben.

1. Kennst du auch eine gute Ärztin? (Telefonnummer)

2. Weißt du, wo ein billiges Restaurant ist? (Adresse)
3. Kennst du eine große Buchhandlung hier? (Name)
4. Kennst du eine erstklassige Musiklehrerin? (Telefonnummer)
5. Weißt du, wo das nächste Reisebüro ist? (Adresse)
6. Kennst du ein billiges Hotel in Berlin? (Name)

D. Frühstück. Monika and Kathrin are going to have breakfast together. Answer Monika's questions in the positive, using the cued adjectives as in the model.

▶ Trinkst du gern Kaffee? (stark)
Ja, ich trinke gern starken Kaffee.

1. Trinkst du Tee? (schwarz)
2. Möchtest du ihn mit Zucker? (braun)
3. Hast du schon Zucker auf dem Tisch? (braun)
4. Ist noch Käse im Kühlschrank? (französisch)
5. Sind auch Brötchen da? (frisch)
6. Willst du Musik hören zum Frühstück? (schön)

E. Wie war's? Matthias has returned from a trip to several large cities. Take Matthias's part and answer his friend's questions about the trip, using the cues in parentheses.

▶ Hast du Studenten kennengelernt? (viele / amerikanisch)
Ja, ich hab' viele amerikanische Studenten kennengelernt.

1. Warst du in Museen? (einige / berühmt)
2. Hast du auch Ausstellungen gesehen? (andere / ausgezeichnet)
3. Hast du Konzerte gehört? (einige / interessant)
4. Waren die Konzerte teuer? (alle / gut)
5. Warst du bei Freunden? (mehrere / alt)
6. Hast du Leute kennengelernt? (viele / nett)

F. Bekannte und Verwandte. Give the German equivalents.

Franz: Do you still have relatives in Switzerland?
Anni: Yes, we have many relatives there.
Franz: My relatives live in Austria. But my father has a good friend°   **Bekannter**
    in Switzerland. He lives in a small village on a high mountain.
Anni: In Switzerland there are many high mountains.
Franz: Yes, I was there once and spent a few wonderful days with good friends.

G. Der wievielte?   Answer the questions about dates by using the cued words.

1. Wann feiert man in der Bundesrepublik den Tag der deutschen Einheit? (am 17. Juni)
2. Wann feiert man den Tag der Arbeit? (am 1. Mai)
3. Wann öffnet man in Deutschland die Weihnachtsgeschenke? (am 24. Dezember)
4. Wann kommt der Nikolaus? (am 6. Dezember)
5. Welcher Tag im Dezember ist der Zweite Weihnachtstag? (der 26.)
6. Welcher Sonntag im Mai ist Muttertag? (der 2.)
7. Wann haben Sie Geburtstag? (am ?)
8. Den wievielten haben wir heute? (den ?)

H. Eine verrückte Geschichte.   Complete the sentences with the German equivalent of the English cues.

1. Gestern hat mir Evelyn die _____ Geschichte erzählt: (following)
2. „Letzten Freitag kaufte ich einen _____ Wagen. (used)
3. Später aß ich mit Kai und Uwe zu Abend. Wir aßen _____ Fisch und _____ Kartoffeln. (fried / boiled)
4. Kai schaute durch das _____ Fenster und rief: (closed)
5. ,Schaut! Da ist eine _____ Untertasse° am Himmel!' (flying)   saucer
6. Wir schauten ihn mit _____ Gesichtern an und dachten, er ist verrückt. (surprised)
7. Es war nur das Spiegelbild° einer _____ Kerze°.“ (burning)   reflection / candle

I. Das neue Haus.   Herr Rüb has a new house and is being asked rather silly questions about it. He replies in kind. Answer for Herr Rüb according to the model.

▶ Ist das Arbeitszimmer so klein wie das Bad?
Ja, es ist sogar kleiner als das Bad.
Und die Küche?
Sie ist am kleinsten.

1. Ist das Eßzimmer so warm wie das Schlafzimmer? Und das Wohnzimmer?
2. Ist der Keller so groß wie das Erdgeschoß? Und der Garten?
3. Sind die neuen Stühle so bequem wie die Sessel? Und das Sofa?
4. Ist die Küche so toll wie das Eßzimmer? Und das Badezimmer?
5. War der Kühlschrank so teuer wie die Spülmaschine? Und die Stereoanlage?
6. Ist der neue Briefträger° so nett wie der alte? Und die neuen Nachbarn?   mailman
7. Finden Sie diese Fragen so dumm wie die Ihrer Nachbarn? Und diese Frage?

J. Freizeit.   Answer the questions on leisure time using the comparative and superlative as in the model.

▶ Flüsse und Wälder finde ich schön.
Und Berge?   *Berge finde ich noch schöner.*
Und das Meer?   *Das Meer finde ich am schönsten.*

1. Ich gehe gern ins Theater. Und ins Kino? Und in ein Rockkonzert?
2. Der Eintrittspreis° fürs Kino ist hoch. Und der fürs Theater?   price of admission
Und der für ein Rockkonzert?
3. Der neue Film von Schlöndorff soll gut sein. Und der von Margarethe von Trotta? Und das neue Stück im Stadttheater?
4. Der Tennisplatz ist nah. Und das Schwimmbad? Und der Sportplatz?
5. Abends esse ich viel. Und mittags? Und zum Frühstück?

K. Fotos.   Herr Untermeier shows some photographs to his two friends who are very competitive and try to go him one better.

▶ Das ist mein schneller Wagen.
Herr Meier: *Ich habe einen viel schnelleren Wagen.*
Herr Obermeier: *Ich habe den schnellsten Wagen.*

1. Das ist mein großes Haus.
2. Das ist mein schöner Garten.

3. Das ist mein teurer Swimming-Pool.
4. Das ist mein gemütliches Wohnzimmer.
5. Das ist mein gutes Fahrrad.
6. Das ist mein hübscher Hund.
7. Das sind meine reichen Freunde.

L. Die Reise.   Karolin is back from a long trip through Europe. She compares the different countries and cities. Give her account in German.

1. In France there was the best food, in Paris the most elegant clothes.
2. But in Italy it was warmer than in France.
3. In Germany the mountains are high, but in Switzerland there are higher mountains.
4. In the mountains it rained more; at the sea there was more sun.
5. In the cities people were not so friendly as in the country.
6. I liked Austria best.

M. Persönliche Fragen.   Answer according to your preference.

1. Welches Fach finden Sie am schwersten?
2. Was trinken Sie am liebsten?
3. Welche Musik ist am schönsten?
4. Was essen Sie am liebsten?
5. Welche Sprache sprechen Sie am besten?
6. Wer in dieser Klasse spricht am meisten?
7. Wer kommt immer am spätesten?

N. Kurze Aufsätze

1. Write a paragraph in which you compare or contrast something.
2. Discuss the advantages and disadvantages of a modern invention, such as **Auto, Fernsehen, Computer, Flugzeug, Telefon.**

Kapitel 8

- General subjunctive
- Present-time subjunctive
- Modals in present-time subjunctive
- Past-time subjunctive
- Modals in past-time subjunctive (double infinitive construction)
- Uses of the subjunctive
- *Würde*-construction
- Uses of the *würde*-construction
- *Als ob* and *als wenn* constructions

---

1. Indicative and subjunctive

Indicative:	Ich **komme** nicht mit.	*I'm not coming along.*
	Was **hast** du **getan?**	*What did you do?*
Subjunctive:	Ich **käme** nicht mit.	*I wouldn't come along.*
	Was **hättest** du **getan?**	*What would you have done?*

In both English and German, the indicative mood is used to talk about real conditions or factual situations. The subjunctive mood is used to talk about unreal, hypothetical, uncertain, or unlikely events.

For example, the first subjunctive sentence above, *I wouldn't come along (even if I had been asked),* refers to a hypothetical situation because the person hasn't been asked.

Stellen Sie sich vor, Sie wären in Indien...

2. Present-time subjunctive

Wenn ich heute oder morgen Zeit **hätte, käme** ich mit.	*If I had time today or tomorrow, I would come along.*

The present-time subjunctive is used to talk about hypothetical situations in present or future time.

3. Verb endings in present-time general subjunctive

ich käme	wir kämen
du kämest	ihr kämet
er/es/sie käme	sie kämen
Sie kämen	

The subjunctive endings above are used for all verbs, strong and weak. In colloquial German, the endings -**est** and -**et** often contract to -**st** and -**t**.

4. Strong verbs in the general subjunctive

Infinitive	Simple past	Present-time subjunctive
gehen	ging	er/es/sie **ginge**
kommen	kam	er/es/sie **käme**
fahren	fuhr	er/es/sie **führe**
fliegen	flog	er/es/sie **flöge**

The present-time general subjunctive of strong verbs is formed by adding subjunctive endings to the simple past stem. An umlaut is added to the stem vowels **a**, **o**, and **u**.

5. Weak verbs in the general subjunctive

Infinitive	Simple past	Present-time subjunctive
sagen	sagte	er/es/sie **sagte**
arbeiten	arbeitete	er/es/sie **arbeitete**

The present-time general subjunctive forms of weak verbs are identical to the simple past-tense forms.

6. Irregular weak verbs in the general subjunctive

Infinitive	Simple past	Present-time subjunctive
brennen	brannte	er/es/sie **brennte**
kennen	kannte	er/es/sie **kennte**
rennen	rannte	er/es/sie **rennte**
nennen	nannte	er/es/sie **nennte**
bringen	brachte	er/es/sie **brächte**
denken	dachte	er/es/sie **dächte**
wissen	wußte	er/es/sie **wüßte**
haben	hatte	er/es/sie **hätte**

The present-time general subjunctive forms of irregular weak verbs are like the simple past-tense forms, but with the addition of an umlaut. Note that the present-time subjunctive forms of **brennen**, **kennen**, **rennen**, and **nennen** are written with an **e** instead of **ä**: **brennte, kennte, rennte, nennte.**

7. Modals in the general subjunctive

Infinitive	Simple past	Present-time subjunctive
dürfen	durfte	er/es/sie **dürfte**
können	konnte	er/es/sie **könnte**
müssen	mußte	er/es/sie **müßte**
mögen	mochte	er/es/sie **möchte**
sollen	sollte	er/es/sie **sollte**
wollen	wollte	er/es/sie **wollte**

The four modals that have an umlaut in the infinitive keep the umlaut in the present-time general subjunctive.

Beinahe hätte Sylvia ihren Urlaub in den Wind schreiben können. Jetzt liegt sie an ihrem Traumstrand.

Jeden Tag sagte sich Sylvia: Jetzt mußt Du endlich buchen. Aber immer kam was dazwischen . . .
Ihren Traumstrand hatte Sylvia längst entdeckt. Nun entdeckte sie Bildschirmtext und wählte sich die aktuellsten Urlaubsangebote einfach auf ihren Fernsehschirm. Btx-Reisebüros sind immer geöffnet. Das nützt nicht nur dem Urlauber, sondern auch dem Btx-Anbieter, den seine Kunden blitzschnell erreichen.

Btx eröffnet ganz neue Vertriebswege. Um bei Sylvia zu bleiben: Den schicken Bikini bestellte sie ebenfalls über Bildschirmtext. Bei einem großen Versandhaus. Auf Knopfdruck.

8. Past-time general subjunctive

Wenn ich genug Geld **gehabt hätte, hätte** ich einen Mercedes **gekauft**.

If I had had *enough money, I* would have bought *a Mercedes*.

Wenn sie das **gewußt hätte, wäre** sie **mitgekommen**.

If she had known *that, she* would have come *along*.

Past-time general subjunctive consists of the subjunctive forms **hätte** or **wäre** plus the past participle of the verb. It corresponds to the English construction *would have* plus the past participle.

9. Modals in past-time subjunctive

In past-time subjunctive, modals have two forms of the participle, a regular form (**gekonnt**) and a form identical to the infinitive (**können**).

Du **hättest** es **gekonnt**.

You could have done *it*.

The regular form of the participle has the **ge**-prefix and the ending **-t** (**gedurft, gekonnt, gemocht, gemußt, gesollt,** and **gewollt**). The regular form is used when the modal is the main verb, that is, without a dependent infinitive.

Ingrid **hätte** dir **helfen müssen**.

Ingrid would have had to help *you*.

Du **hättest** allein **fahren können**.

You could have driven *alone*.

When a modal is used with a dependent infinitive, an alternative past participle that is identical with the modal infinitive is used (**dürfen, können, mögen, müssen, sollen,** and **wollen**). This construction is often called the double infinitive construction. The auxiliary **haben** is always used with modals in the perfect tenses.

Ingrid sagte, daß sie dir **hätte helfen müssen**.
Ich finde, daß du allein **hättest fahren können**.

The double infinitive is always the last element in a clause, even in a dependent clause. The auxiliary verb **hätte** precedes the double infinitive.

10. Use of the subjunctive mood

Contrary-to-fact conditions:	Wenn ich reich **wäre, würde** ich einen Mercedes **kaufen.**	*If I were rich, I would buy a Mercedes.*
	Wenn du mich **gefragt hättest, hätte** ich es dir **gesagt.**	*If you had asked me, I would have told you.*
Wishes:	Wenn du nur **mitkommen könntest!**	*If only you could come along!*
	Ich **wollte (wünschte),** ich **hätte** das **gesehen!**	*I wish I had seen that.*
Hypothetical situations:	So ein Buch **läse** er nicht.	*He wouldn't read such a book.*
	Hättest du es **gelesen?**	*Would you have read it?*
Polite requests or questions:	**Würdest** du mir bitte das Brot **reichen?**	*Would you please pass me the bread?*
	Möchtet ihr eine Tasse Kaffee?	*Would you like a cup of coffee?*
	Könnten Sie das Fenster ein bißchen aufmachen?	*Could you open the window a little?*

The subjunctive mood is used to express contrary-to-fact conditions, wishes that cannot be realized, hypothetical situations, and polite requests or questions. Note that the past-time subjunctive is used in the same ways as the present-time subjunctive, except that in the past, there are usually no polite requests.

Möchten Sie mitkommen?	*Would you like to come along?*
Dürfte ich Sie etwas fragen?	*Could I ask you something?*
Ich **wollte,** ich hätte mehr Zeit!	*I wish I had more time!*

The subjunctive form of the modals is often used to express polite requests or wishes. The expression **ich wollte** is used frequently to introduce wishes.

11. The *würde*-construction

Ich **würde** das nicht sagen.	*I would not say that.*
Würdest du ihm helfen?	*Would you help him?*

The **würde**-construction consists of a form of **würde** plus the infinitive and is equivalent in meaning to the English construction *would* plus the infinitive.

HOCHTAUNUS STRASSE

. . . wer würde sich da nicht wohl fühlen?

Forms of the *würde*-construction

ich **würde** es machen	*wir* **würden** es machen
du **würdest** es machen	*ihr* **würdet** es machen
er/es/sie **würde** es machen	*sie* **würden** es machen
Sie **würden** es machen	

The verb **würde** is the general subjunctive form of **werden**. It is formed by adding an umlaut to **wurde**, the simple past of **werden**.

12. Uses of the *würde*-construction

a. Contrary-to-fact conditions

Wenn ich genug Geld hätte, **würde** ich einen Mercedes **kaufen.**

If I had enough money, I would buy a Mercedes.

Wenn es heute schön wäre, **würde** ich Tennis **spielen.**

If it were nice today, I would play tennis.

b. Wishes

Wenn sie nur lauter **sprechen würde!**

If only she would speak louder.

Wenn es nur **regnen würde!**

If only it would rain!

c. Hypothetical situations

Das **würde** ich nicht **machen.**

I wouldn't do that.

Würdest du das **glauben?**

Would you believe that?

d. Polite requests or questions

Würden Sie einen Augenblick **warten?**

Would you wait a moment?

Würdest du mir eine Zeitung **mitbringen?**

Would you bring me back a newspaper?

The **würde**-construction is used in the conclusion of a contrary-to-fact condition, in wishes that cannot be realized, hypothetical conclusions, and polite requests or questions.

13. Contrary-to-fact conditions

	Condition	Conclusion
Present-time:	**Wenn** ich Zeit **hätte,**	**würde** ich **mitkommen.**
	Wenn ich Zeit **hätte,**	**käme** ich **mit.**
Past-time:	**Wenn** ich Zeit **gehabt hätte,**	**wäre** ich **mitgekommen.**

A contrary-to-fact statement has two clauses: the condition and the conclusion. The condition is usually expressed as a **wenn**-clause. Contrary-to-fact conditions describe a situation that does not exist or will not take place. The speaker simply speculates on how something could or would be under certain circumstances or conditions. To speculate about how conditions could be in the present or future, a German speaker uses the present-time subjunctive in the condition and the present-time subjunctive or a **würde**-construction in the conclusion. To speculate about how conditions could have been in the past, a speaker uses the past-time subjunctive in both the condition and the conclusion.

When the condition (**wenn**-clause) begins a sentence, the **wenn** may be omitted, in which case the verb comes first.

Condition	Conclusion
Hätte ich Zeit,	käme ich mit.

14. The *würde*-construction versus the subjunctive of the main verb

a. The **würde**-construction is regularly used in informal usage in the conclusion of contrary-to-fact conditions in present time.

Wenn ich Zeit hätte, **würde** ich **mitkommen.**

b. The **würde**-construction is used in place of the subjunctive form of weak verbs in the conclusion when the sentence could be otherwise interpreted as indicative past.

Immer wenn Dieter arbeitete, **verdiente** er viel.	*Whenever Dieter was working, he earned a lot.*
Wenn Dieter arbeitete, **würde** er gut **verdienen.**	*If Dieter were working, he would earn a lot.*

c. The general subjective is preferred to the **würde**-construction for **sein, haben,** and the modals in both conditions and conclusions.

Wenn Christel nicht so fleißig **wäre, hätte** sie mehr Freizeit und
   könnte ein Hobby haben.

d. The subjunctive of the main verb is generally preferred in the **wenn**-clause. However, in colloquial German the **würde**-construction is sometimes used in the **wenn**-clause.

Wenn du mir helfen **würdest, würde** ich die Arbeit machen.

15. Clauses introduced by *als ob* and *als wenn*

Present-time subjunctive:	Er sieht aus, **als ob** (**als wenn**) er krank wäre.	*He looks as if he were ill.*
	Er sah aus, **als ob** (**als wenn**) er krank wäre.	*He looked as if he were ill.*
Past-time subjunctive:	Er tut, **als ob** (**als wenn**) er krank gewesen wäre.	*He acts as if he had been ill.*
	Er tat, **als ob** (**als wenn**) er krank gewesen wäre.	*He acted as if he had been ill.*

Constructions with **als ob** and **als wenn** (*as if, as though*) express suppositions and comparisons. If the **als ob/als wenn**-clause refers to the same time as the main clause, the present-time subjunctive is used. If the **als ob/als wenn**-clause refers to something that took place before the action of the main clause, the past-time subjunctive is used.

Er sieht aus, **als** wäre er krank.
Tun Sie, **als** wären Sie zu Hause!

The conjunction **als** can be used without **ob** or **wenn** to mean *as if.* In this case, the verb follows **als** directly.

Übungen

A. Auf dem Fest. Two people are gossiping at a party. They spend a lot of time saying how other people would behave differently. Restate their sentences in present-time subjunctive.

▶ Erika kommt nicht mit ihrem Freund.
  Erika käme nicht mit ihrem Freund.

1. Hans-Peter spricht nicht mit so vielen Leuten.
2. Ich ziehe so eine bunte Hose nicht an.

3. Ernst ißt auf einer Party nicht so viel.
4. Ich tue das nicht.
5. Mit kurzen Haaren sieht Lucie nicht besser aus.
6. Barbara unterhält sich nicht so laut über ihr Privatleben. *unterhielte*
7. Meiers bleiben nicht länger.
8. Wir gehen nicht so spät.
9. Ich trinke nicht soviel Saft.
10. Du fährst nicht mit dem Wagen nach Hause. *führest*

B. The next day one of the people at the party runs into a friend and relates all the comments made the night before. Restate the sentences in *Übung A* in past-time subjunctive.

▶ Erika kommt nicht mit ihrem Freund.
Erika wäre nicht mit ihrem Freund gekommen.

C. Faule Ausreden°.   You are about to play a critical tennis match.   excuses
Express the wish that a number of things were different. Start each sentence with **wenn**.

▶ Es ist furchtbar heiß.
Wenn es nur nicht so furchtbar heiß wäre!

1. Die Sonne scheint so hell.
2. Der Wind ist so stark.
3. Mein linker Fuß tut so weh.
4. Ich habe so einen Durst.
5. Die Bälle sind so weich.
6. Mein Partner kommt zum Spiel.
7. Ich habe so große Angst.
8. Wir fangen in fünf Minuten schon an.

D. Das Picknick.   You have planned a picnic with your friends. In discussing it say that the person in parentheses would do the right thing. Follow the model.

▶ Ich hoffe, Volker hat die Kamera dabei. (du)
Du hättest natürlich die Kamera dabei.

1. Ich hoffe, Susi denkt an den Wein. (ich)
2. Ich hoffe, Peter hat Zeit. (ich)
3. Ich hoffe, Karla und Paula bringen die Gitarre mit. (wir)
4. Ich hoffe, alle kennen den Weg. (wir)

5. Ich hoffe, Brigitte weiß, daß sie Uwe abholen soll. (du)
6. Ich hoffe, Erwin bringt den Fußball mit. (du)
7. Ich hoffe, Müllers haben ihren Hund dabei. (wir)
8. Ich hoffe, alle wissen, wann wir uns treffen wollen. (wir)
9. Ich hoffe, alle denken an einen Regenschirm. (ich)

E. Wir hätten's anders gemacht.   Your picnic turned out to be a flop. Express the belief that things could have been very different. Restate the sentences in *Übung D* in past-time subjunctive.

▶ Hoffentlich hat Volker die Kamera dabei. (du)
  Du hättest natürlich die Kamera dabei gehabt.

F. Das wäre schön.   Alexander describes how he would spend the summer if he could. Express his thoughts in German. Use the general subjunctive of the main verb.

1. There would be no work.
2. I would sleep a lot.
3. My friends would always have time for me.
4. In the afternoons we would sit in the café and eat a lot of° cake.   **eine Menge**
5. Often I would go for a walk and would go biking.
6. Sometimes I would watch TV or write a letter.
7. I would like such a life.
8. That would be nice.

G. Ich nicht.   You don't approve at all of Ingrid's lifestyle. Describe all the things she does that you definitely would not do. Use the **würde**-construction.

▶ Ingrid schläft jeden Nachmittag.
  Ich würde nicht jeden Nachmittag schlafen.

1. Sie ißt nur Schokolade zum Frühstück.
2. Sie trinkt jeden Tag zehn Tassen Kaffee.
3. Sie duscht dreimal am Tag.

4. Sie telefoniert stundenlang mit ihrer Nachbarin.
5. Sie geht jede Woche zum Friseur.
6. Sie fährt so furchtbar Auto.
7. Sie sieht jeden Abend fern.
8. Sie geht immer nach Mitternacht ins Bett.
9. Sie redet dauernd über andere Leute.

H. Wenn nur! Holger is going to have an important exam and is studying hard. While at his desk he dreams about how it would be if conditions were different. Finish his sentences using the **würde**-construction.

▶ Wenn ich mit der Arbeit fertig wäre, ... (ins Kino gehen)
Wenn ich mit der Arbeit fertig wäre, würde ich ins Kino gehen.

1. Wenn das Examen nicht wäre, ... (ins Schwimmbad gehen)
2. Wenn ich nicht so viel arbeiten müßte, ... (die Zeitung lesen)
3. Wenn ich reich wäre, ... (nicht mehr arbeiten)
4. Wenn ich Zeit hätte, ... (in die Berge fahren)
5. Wenn wir auf dem Land wohnen könnten, ... (den ganzen Tag im Garten sitzen)
6. Wenn das Wetter besser wäre, ... (spazierengehen)
7. Wenn ich nicht studieren müßte, ... (ein herrliches Leben führen)

I. Wäre ich nur! Say again what Holger is dreaming about. This time omit **wenn.**

▶ Wenn ich mit der Arbeit fertig wäre, ... (ins Kino gehen)
Wäre ich mit der Arbeit fertig, würde ich ins Kino gehen.

J. Du bist unmöglich! You are fed up with your roommate's habits. Discuss them with your roommate and tell him/her how you would like things changed. Use **nicht** before the italicized words. Use the **würde**-construction in sentences 1–7.

▶ Du machst morgens *soviel* Lärm.
Ich wollte, du würdest morgens nicht soviel Lärm machen.

der Lärm
noise

1. Deine Sachen liegen *in der ganzen* Wohnung herum.
2. Dein schmutziges Geschirr steht *tagelang*° in der Küche.   for days
3. Du spielst *immer* so fürchterliche Platten.
4. Du läßt *immer* die Haustür offen.
5. Du benutzt *immer* mein Handtuch.
6. Du telefonierst *dauernd.*
7. Ich höre *immer* dein Schnarchen° durch die Wand.   snoring
8. Deine Freunde sind *immer* so unfreundlich zu mir.
9. Du hast *dauernd* schlechte Laune.

K. Die Heimfahrt. After an evening with friends you are ready to leave. Soften the tone of your statements and make your requests seem more polite by restating the modals in present-time subjunctive.

▶ Ich muß jetzt eigentlich gehen.
  Ich müßte jetzt eigentlich gehen.

1. Ich soll um elf zu Hause sein.
2. Ich muß die Bahn um Viertel nach bekommen.
3. Das müssen unsere Freunde eigentlich verstehen.
4. Ich kann ja ein Taxi nehmen.
5. Darf ich mal telefonieren?
6. Oder darf ich Sie um etwas bitten?
7. Können Sie mich vielleicht nach Hause fahren?

L. Ein Unfall. Chris has had a car accident. Torsten, with marvelous hindsight, tells him how he could have avoided it. Take Torsten's role and restate the sentences in past-time subjunctive.

▶ Du mußt schneller reagieren.
  Du hättest schneller reagieren müssen.

1. Das darf nicht passieren.
2. Du mußt besser aufpassen.
3. Und es darf nicht regnen.
4. Du mußt vorsichtiger° sein.   more careful
5. Aber auch der andere soll langsamer fahren.
6. Die Straße darf eben nicht naß sein.
7. Naja, es kann viel schlimmer ausgehen°.   turn out
8. Und ich will heute dein Auto benutzen.
   —Aber das ist ja nun kaputt.

M. Die Erkältung. You don't feel well and your friend, Marianne is trying to help diagnose your symptoms. Describe what your symptoms feel like. Use **als ob** or **als wenn** with the cues in parentheses.

▶ Fühlst du dich so schlecht? (ich bin krank)
  Ja, ich fühle mich so schlecht, als ob ich krank wäre.

1. Läuft deine Nase? (ich habe eine Erkältung)
2. Tut dir der Kopf weh? (er will explodieren)
3. Brennt dein Hals? (ich habe Feuer gegessen)
4. Brummen° deine Ohren? (ein kaputtes Radio ist darin)   ring
5. Tun dir die Augen weh? (ich habe zuviel ferngesehen)
6. Bist du müde? (ich habe zwei Nächte nicht geschlafen)

N. Schade!   Give the German equivalents.

Andrea: Could you help me, please?
   Rudi: I would like to (do that). If I only had time. You look as if
          you were ill.
Andrea: I wish I felt better.
   Rudi: Maybe you should go to bed.
Andrea: I wish I hadn't eaten the fish.
   Rudi: You should have asked me. Too bad. We could have gone to
          a nice restaurant tonight.

O. Kurze Aufsätze

1. Suppose you could live exactly as you wished or be what you
   wished to be; describe what your life would be like.
2. If you could change general things in the world, what would you
   change so that, in your opinion, it would be a better place to
   live?

Kapitel 9

- Future tense
- Uses of the future tense
- Reflexive pronouns
- Reflexive with parts of the body and clothing
- Reflexive verbs and verbs used reflexively
- *Selbst, selber, einander*

1. Future tense

Ich **werde** eine Reise **machen.**	*I'm going to take a trip.*
Wirst du das wirklich **machen?**	*Are you really going to do that?*
Glaubst du, daß Ute wirklich **mitkommen wird?**	*Do you think that Ute will really come along?*

In German, the future tense consists of the present tense of **werden** plus a dependent infinitive. The infinitive is in final position except in a dependent clause. In a dependent clause, the auxiliary **werden** is in last position and follows the infinitive.

2. Future tense of modals

Du **wirst** bestimmt nicht **schlafen können.**	*You'll surely not be able to sleep.*
Ich **werde** die Bücher **lesen müssen.**	*I'll have to read the books.*

In the future tense, a modal is in the infinitive form and is in final position. The modal follows the dependent infinitive.

Ich glaube nicht, daß du **wirst schlafen können.**
Ich fürchte, daß ich die Bücher **werde lesen müssen.**

In a dependent clause, the auxiliary **werden** precedes the dependent infinitive and the modal infinitive, both of which are in final position. The modal is always the last element.

3. Use of the future tense

Assumption:	Er wird uns sicher glauben.	He'll surely believe us.
Determination:	Ich werde es machen.	I shall do it.

The future tense is regularly used to express an assumption or a determination to do something.

Present probability:	Er wird **sicher** müde sein.	He's surely tired.
	Das wird **wohl** stimmen.	That's probably correct.
	Das wird **schon** in Ordnung sein.	That's probably O.K.

The future tense can express the probability of something taking place in the present time. Adverbs such as **sicher, wohl,** and **schon** are often used.

4. Use of present tense to express future time

Ich **komme bald** wieder.	*I'll come again soon.*
Wir **fahren morgen** nach Koblenz.	*We're going to Koblenz tomorrow.*

In German, the present tense is used to express future time if the sentence contains a clear reference to future time.

Inge **wird** alles selber **machen.**	*Inge will do everything herself.*
Detlev **wird** ihr nicht **helfen.**	*Detlev will not help her.*

When a sentence or the context does not contain a clear reference to future time, the future tense is used to indicate future time.

5. Reflexive pronouns

Ich wasche **mich.**	*I wash (myself).*
Ich kaufe **mir** eine Schallplatte.	*I'm buying myself a record.*

A reflexive pronoun is a pronoun that indicates the same person or thing as the subject. A reflexive pronoun may be either in the accusative or dative case, depending on its function.

Nominative (subject):	ich	du	er/es/sie	wir	ihr	sie	Sie
Accusative reflexive:	mich	dich	sich	uns	euch	sich	sich
Dative reflexive:	mir	dir	sich	uns	euch	sich	sich

The first and second person reflexive pronouns are identical to the personal pronouns. The pronoun **sich** is used for all third person reflexives and for the **Sie**-form.

6. Accusative reflexive pronouns

Direct Object:	Ich ziehe **mich** an.	*I'm getting dressed.*
Object of Preposition:	Er macht es für **sich** selbst.	*He's doing it for himself.*

A reflexive pronoun is in the accusative case when it functions as direct object or as the object of a preposition that requires the accusative case.

7. Dative reflexive pronouns

Indirect Object:	Ich kaufe **mir** eine Jacke.	*I'm buying myself a jacket.*
Dative Verb:	Ich kann **mir** nicht helfen.	*I can't help myself.*
Object of Preposition:	Sprichst du von **dir?**	*Are you speaking of yourself?*

A reflexive pronoun is in the dative case when it functions as an indirect object, the object of a dative verb, or the object of a preposition that requires the dative case.

8. Verbs with either accusative or dative reflexive pronouns

Accusative:	Ich wasche **mich**.	*I wash (myself).*
Dative:	Ich wasche **mir** die Hände.	*I wash my hands.*

Some verbs can be used with either accusative or dative reflexive pronouns. The dative is used if there is also an accusative object.

9. Reflexive with parts of body and clothing

Ich muß **mir** die Zähne putzen.   *I have to brush my teeth.*

Zieh **dir** die Schuhe aus!   *Take off your shoes.*

German often uses a definite article and a dative reflexive pronoun in referring to parts of the body and articles of clothing. The dative reflexive pronoun shows that the accusative object belongs to the subject of the sentence. English uses a possessive adjective.

10. Reflexive verbs and verbs used reflexively

Ich habe mich erkältet.   *I caught a cold.*

Benimm dich bitte!   *Please behave.*

Some verbs always have reflexive pronouns. They are called reflexive verbs.

Ich fühle mich nicht wohl.   *I don't feel well.*

Erinnerst du dich daran?   *Do you remember it?*

Er rasiert sich.   *He's shaving.*

Wir interessieren uns dafür.   *We're interested in it.*

Wundert ihr euch darüber?   *Are you surprised about it?*

Zieh dich an!   *Get dressed.*

Setzen Sie sich!   *Sit down.*

Beeil dich!   *Hurry up.*

Many German verbs are regularly used reflexively. Their English equivalents are not reflexive. These verbs are noted in the end vocabulary as follows: **(sich) fühlen.**

Die Frau **erinnert** Marta an ihre Mutter.	*The woman reminds Marta of her mother.*
Marta **erinnert sich** an ihre Mutter.	*Marta remembers her mother.*

Some verbs change their meanings when used reflexively.

11. Intensifiers *selber* and *selbst*

Ich fühle mich **selber (selbst)** nicht wohl.	*I don't feel well myself.*

The intensifiers **selbst** or **selber** may be used after a reflexive pronoun to emphasize the reflexive meaning. The pronouns **selbst** and **selber** are interchangeable.

12. Reciprocal use of reflexives

Wann sehen sie **sich** wieder?	*When will they see each other again?*

Reflexive pronouns may have a reciprocal meaning. The subject is normally in the plural.

Wir schreiben **uns** oft.	
Wir schreiben **einander** oft.	*We write each other often.*

The pronoun **einander** may be used instead of the reflexive to express a reciprocal action.

Übungen

A. Sommerferien. You and Sylvia are discussing summer vacation plans. Restate your conversation, using the future tense.

▶ Fährst du mit deiner Familie nach Frankreich?
  Wirst du mit deiner Familie nach Frankreich fahren?

1. Nein, dieses Jahr fahre ich nicht mit meinen Eltern.
2. Du bleibst doch nicht die ganze Zeit zu Hause, oder?
3. Nein, ich besuche meine Freundin in Florenz.
4. Sie studiert an der Akademie, und ich wohne dann bei ihr.
5. Sie zeigt mir Florenz und die Toscana°.   Tuscany
6. Das ist bestimmt schön!

B. Was machen deine Freunde am Wochenende? Your friends are going to have a big party on the weekend. Susan asks what they told you about it. Tell her, putting the information in the future tense.

▶ Peter sagt, daß er ein Fest macht.
  Peter sagt, daß er ein Fest machen wird.

1. Karola meint, daß es gutes Essen gibt, wie immer auf Peters Festen.
2. Paul sagt, daß er auch auf das Fest kommt.
3. Anneliese behauptet, daß Peter sogar eine Band einlädt.
4. Ich bin sicher, daß die Leute viel lachen und tanzen.
5. Ich glaube bestimmt, daß es ziemlich laut wird.
6. Ich fürchte, daß die Nachbarn die Polizei rufen.
7. Glaubst du, daß du hingehst?
8. Ich muß sagen, daß ich leider keine Zeit habe.

C. Keiner hat Zeit. You feel like going out tonight and have tried to call a few friends. But either they were not at home or they didn't have time. Finally you reach Sibylle and together you speculate about the others. Use the future tense + **wohl** to express what they are probably doing.

▶ Wo ist Rainer im Moment? (beim Sport)
  Er wird im Moment wohl beim Sport sein.

1. Für was arbeitet Gabi diese Woche? (für ihr Seminar)
2. Zu wem geht Maria heute? (zu Daniela)
3. An wen schreibt Meike? (an ihren Freund)
4. Wo sind Kurt und Karla? (im Schwimmbad)
5. Wie lange bleibt Claudias Besuch? (das ganze Wochenende)
6. Wo spielt Jan heute abend? (im Jazz-Club)
7. Rufst du noch jemand anders an? (nein, niemand mehr)
8. Wohin gehst du nun? (zu dir)

D. Kurze Gespräche. Give the German equivalent of the English sentences. Use the present tense to express future time when the sentence contains a clear reference to future time. Otherwise use the future tense.

1. —Where are you going to be next summer?
   —We'll go to Austria in June.
2. —What will become of° Jörg?   **aus**
   —I don't know. We'll see.
3. —Tomorrow we are going to visit Aunt Marlies.
   —Until when will you have to work tomorrow?
4. —Are you going to visit your friends?
   —Yes, they said that they will be home.

E. Ein alter Freund. Karin is a student at the University of Munich and likes to meet with friends in Schwabing, a suburb of Munich frequented by artists and students. Yesterday she met an old friend there whom she hadn't seen for several years. Take her part as she tells about the experience. Use the tenses indicated.

▶ wir / sich begegnen / gestern / in Schwabing (present perfect)
   Wir sind uns gestern in Schwabing begegnet.

1. du / sich erinnern an / Frank / ? (present)
2. wir / sich verstehen / immer / gut (present perfect)
3. aber dann / wir / sich sehen / lange nicht (present perfect)
4. ihr / sich kennenlernen / doch auch mal (present perfect)
5. gestern im Café an der Uni / ich / sich wundern / (present perfect): „Mensch, das ist doch der Frank!"
6. ich / sich unterhalten / lange / mit ihm (present perfect)
7. er / sich interessieren / sehr / für meine Arbeit (present)
8. morgen abend / wir / wollen / sich treffen (present)
9. ich / sich freuen / sehr darauf (present)

F. Das Geburtstagsfest. Karola is telling about a scene for a new play. The main character is talking about her planned birthday. Take her part and tell about the preparations, according to the model.

▶ Sie kommt heim und zieht sich den Mantel aus.
   Ich komme heim und ziehe mir den Mantel aus.

1. Sie hat sich vorgestellt, daß sie sich an ihrem Geburtstag keine Arbeit macht.
2. Sie will sich ihr Geburtstagsdiner nicht selbst kochen. Dazu hat sie keine Lust.

3. Also hat sie den Partyservice angerufen und hat sich viele gute
   Delikatessen° bestellt.   special foods
4. Von ihren Freunden hat sie sich nur Blumen und gute Laune
   gewünscht.
5. Sie will sich ein sehr elegantes Kleid anziehen.
6. Sie wünscht sich, daß es ein sehr lustiges Geburtstagsfest wird.

G. Duschen? Nö. Erich is being questioned by his elder sister
Birgit about his hygiene. Complete their conversation.

▶ Wie oft _____ du _____ die Haare? (sich kämmen)
  Wie oft kämmst du dir die Haare?

1. Erich: Ich _____ _____ nicht gern die Haare. (sich kämmen)
2. Birgit: Wie oft _____ du _____ die Zähne? (sich putzen)
   Erich: Dreimal täglich, öfter als duschen.
3. Birgit: Du _____ _____ nicht jeden Morgen? (sich duschen)
4. Erich: Nö. Keine Zeit. Ich muß _____ ja schließlich auch
   _____ und _____ _____ _____. (sich rasieren / sich Kaffee
   kochen)
5. Birgit: Du _____ _____ manchmal? (sich baden)
6. Erich: Ja, das hab' ich echt gern. Abends. Da muß ich _____
   nicht so _____. (sich beeilen)
7. Da kann ich _____ _____ _____. (sich eine tolle Musik
   anhören)
8. Da _____ ich _____ des Lebens. (sich freuen)
9. Aber hör mal—ich finde das nicht so wichtig. Können wir
   _____ über was anderes _____? (sich unterhalten)

H. Alles ärgert mich. Sonja is speaking with Jochen about her job. Complete their conversation with the German equivalent of the English cues. Notice that some verbs are reflexive and some are not.

1. Jochen: Was _____ so? (is making you angry)
2. Sonja: Ich _____, weil ich den Job nicht bekommen habe. (am angry)
3. Jochen: Ah, ich _____, daß du davon gesprochen hast. (remember)
   Du hast mich angerufen, als ich gerade meine Wäsche gewaschen habe.
4. Sonja: Weißt du, meine alte Arbeit _____ nicht mehr. (interests me)
5. Jochen: Wofür _____ denn? (are you interested)
6. Sonja: Ich weiß nicht. Ich _____ in der Firma nicht wohl. (feel)
7. Jochen: Und dein Chef _____ immer. (annoys you)
8. Sonja: Ach, _____ an ihn! (don't remind me)

I. Selbst (selber) / einander. Complete the sentences with **selbst (selber)** or **einander.**

1. Mein Vater kocht sich sein Mittagessen immer _____.
2. Sie erzählten _____ viele lustige Geschichten.
3. Mehr kann ich dir über den Film nicht erzählen. Du mußt ihn dir schon _____ ansehen.
4. Sie schauten _____ in die Augen und mußten plötzlich lachen.
5. Hier ist Herr Bender. Möchten Sie sich _____ mit ihm unterhalten?
6. Ich sehe meine Freundin oft. Wir besuchen _____ fast täglich.

J. Nichts als Probleme. Three girls have a brief conversation after class. Each is concerned with her own problems. Express their conversation in German.

1. Marion: I have to hurry up. I'm going to meet Paul at 8.
2. Julia: I'm amazed at Bernd. He behaved as if he didn't know me. I think he didn't remember me.
3. Dagmar: I don't feel so well. I think I've caught a cold. How stupid! But I don't want to get upset°.

sich ärgern

K. Kurze Aufsätze. Describe to a friend how you manage to sleep late in the morning. Describe your streamlined 15-minute morning schedule. Use these reflexive verbs and others of your choice: **sich anziehen, sich kämmen, sich die Zähne putzen.**

Kapitel 10

- Passive voice
- Expressing agent and means
- Dative verbs in passive voice
- Impersonal passive construction
- Modals and the passive infinitive
- Actional and statal passive
- Substitutes for passive voice
- Summary of uses of *werden*

1. The passive voice

Active voice:	**Ein Physiker** schreibt den Artikel.	A physicist *is writing the article.*
Passive voice:	Der Artikel wird **von einem Physiker** geschrieben.	*The article is being written* by a physicist.
	Der Artikel wird bald geschrieben.	*The article will be written soon.*

German and English sentences are either in active voice or passive voice. In active voice a sentence has a subject that performs the action of the verb. In passive voice the subject is passive; it performs no action. The action of the verb is performed by some other agent. The subject (**Physiker**) of an active sentence corresponds to the agent (**Physiker**) in a passive sentence. The direct object (**Artikel**) in an active sentence corresponds to the subject (**Artikel**) in a passive sentence. The agent is often omitted in a passive sentence, as if the corresponding active sentence has no subject.

The passive is used very often in technical and scientific writing, where an impersonal style is frequently preferred. In everyday conversation the active voice is used more frequently by speakers of German. (See substitutes for the passive voice, *Section 8.*)

113

2. Tenses in the passive voice

Present:	Die Arbeit **wird gemacht.**	*The work is being done.*
Simple past:	Die Arbeit **wurde gemacht.**	*The work was done.*
Present perfect:	Die Arbeit **ist gemacht worden.**	*The work has been done.*
Past perfect:	Die Arbeit **war gemacht worden.**	*The work had been done.*
Future:	Die Arbeit **wird gemacht werden.**	*The work will be done.*

The passive voice consists of the auxiliary **werden** plus the past participle of the main verb. Passive voice can occur in any tense. Note that in the present perfect and past perfect tenses the participle **worden** is used instead of the form **geworden**.

Present-time subjunctive:	Die Arbeit **würde gemacht.**	The work would be done.
Past-time subjunctive:	Die Arbeit **wäre gemacht worden.**	The work would have been done.

The passive voice also occurs in the subjunctive.

3. Expressing agent and means

Die Zeitung wird **von Studentinnen** geschrieben.

The newspaper is being written by students.

Die Nachbarn wurden **durch die Musik** gestört.

The neighbors were disturbed by the music.

A sentence in the passive voice often indicates by what agent or means an action is performed. The person who causes an event to happen is known as an agent. The *agent* (**Studentinnen**) is the object of the preposition **von** and thus in the dative case. The *means* (**Musik**) by which an event happens is usually impersonal and is the object of the preposition **durch** and thus in the accusative case.

4. Dative verbs in the passive voice

Active voice:	Ich glaubte **ihm** nicht.	*I didn't believe him.*
Passive voice:	**Ihm** wurde nicht geglaubt.	*He was not believed.*
	Es wurde **ihm** nicht geglaubt.	

The dative object in an active sentence remains unchanged when used in a passive sentence. The resulting passive sentence has no subject. **Es** may be used as a *dummy* or *apparent* subject.

5. Impersonal passive constructions

Active voice:	Alle essen um zwölf.	*Everyone eats at twelve.*
Passive voice:	Jetzt wird gegessen.	*Now's the time to eat.*
	Es wird jetzt gegessen.	

A passive construction without a subject or agent is called an impersonal passive construction. The pronoun **es** begins an impersonal passive construction if no other words precede the verb. **Es** is a *dummy* or *apparent* subject.

6. Modals and the passive infinitive

Unser Wagen **kann** nicht mehr **repariert werden.**
Our car can't be fixed anymore.

Müssen die Fenster **geputzt werden?**
Do the windows have to be cleaned?

The passive infinitive consists of a past participle plus **werden.** Since modals cannot be put into the passive voice, they are sometimes used with a passive infinitive.

7. Actional and statal passive

Das Auto **wird** jetzt **repariert.**   *The car is being repaired now.*
Das Auto **ist** schon **repariert.**   *The car is already repaired.*

The actional passive expresses the act of something being done. The statal passive expresses the state or condition that results from that action. Statal passive is not really a true passive construction. In English, the verb *to be* is used for both actional and statal passive. In German, the verb **werden** plus past participle is used for actional passive; the verb **sein** plus past participle is used for statal passive. Statal passive is never used when an agent is expressed. Actional and statal passive are not interchangeable.

8. Substitutes for the passive voice

The passive voice is used less frequently in German than in English. In German, other constructions are frequently substituted for the passive voice. Following are four possible substitutes. Not all can be used for a single passive sentence.

a. *Man as subject*

So etwas tut **man** nicht.	*That's not done.*
Von hier kann **man** den See sehen.	*You can see the lake from here.*

The pronoun **man** plus an active voice construction is often used as a substitute for the passive voice, when no agent is expressed. English equivalents for the pronoun **man** are *one, you, we, they,* or *people.*

b. *sein ... zu* + infinitive

Das **ist** leicht **zu lernen.**	*That is easy to learn.*
Diese Aufgabe **ist** noch **zu machen.**	*This assignment still has to be done.*

A form of **sein ... zu** + infinitive is often used in German instead of a passive verb phrase. The **sein ... zu** + infinitive construction expresses the possibility *(leicht zu lernen)* or necessity *(noch zu machen)* of doing something.

c. *sich lassen* + infinitive

Das **läßt sich machen.**	*That can be done.*
Das Radio **läßt sich** nicht **reparieren.**	*The radio can't be fixed.*

A form of **sich lassen** + infinitive can be used in place of a passive verb phrase. This construction expresses the possibility of something being done.

d. Reflexive constructions

Solche Sachen **verkaufen sich** leicht.

Such things can be sold easily.

Das Buch **liest sich** leicht.

The book is easy to read.

A reflexive construction expresses the possibility of doing something and may sometimes be used in place of a passive verb phrase.

9. Summary of the uses of *werden*

a. Main verb

Herr Meier **wird** alt.

Mr. Meier is growing old.

Jutta **wurde** müde.

Jutta was getting tired.

Volker **ist** wieder krank **geworden.**

Volker has become ill again.

Werden as a main verb is equivalent to the English *to grow, get,* or *become.*

b. Auxiliary verb in future tense

Wir **werden** im Café **essen.**

We'll eat in the café.

Frau Lange **wird** wohl krank **sein.**

Mrs. Lange is probably ill.

Werden is used with a dependent infinitive to form the future tense. The future tense also expresses present probability.

c. Auxiliary verb in the passive voice

Bei Eberts **wird** jeden Samstag **gefeiert.**

There's a party at the Eberts every Saturday.

Letzten Samstag **wurde** viel **gelacht.**

Last Saturday there was a lot of laughing.

Wir **sind** auch **eingeladen worden.**

We were also invited.

Werden is used with a past participle to form the passive voice. Passive voice can occur in any tense.

Übungen

A. Wer macht die Hausarbeit? Restate the sentences in the tenses indicated.

► Der Haushaltsplan° wird von uns allen gemacht. (simple past)   housekeeping schedule
   Der Haushaltsplan wurde von uns allen gemacht.

1. Das Essen wird von meinem Vater gekocht. (present perfect)
2. Die Gartenarbeit wird von meinem Bruder gemacht. (simple past)
3. Die Wäsche wird von meiner Schwester gewaschen. (simple past)
4. Eingekauft wird von mir. (simple past)
5. Die Fenster werden von uns allen geputzt. (future)
6. Der Küchenplan wird von der ganzen Familie diskutiert. (present perfect)
7. Jeder wird von jedem kritisiert. (future)
8. Das Geld wird von meiner Mutter verdient. (present perfect)

B. Am Sonntag. Helga describes a Sunday in her home town. Change the sentences from active to passive. Keep the same tense.

► Früher brachte der Bäcker die frischen Brötchen ins Haus.
   Früher wurden die frischen Brötchen vom Bäcker ins Haus gebracht.

1. Heute toasten wir die Brötchen vom Samstag. (omit agent)
2. Der Vater wäscht das Auto.
3. Nicht die Mutter, sondern mein Bruder kocht das Mittagessen.
4. Beim Spaziergang grüßen wir die Nachbarn freundlich. (omit agent)

5. Im Café bedient° uns ein italienischer Kellner.   serves
6. Das Abendessen essen wir zu Hause. (omit agent)
7. Am Abend sehen wir fern. (omit agent)

C. Ein Essen für die Gäste.   Tell in German about all the things you did last night for your guests.

1. The meat was put in wine°.   in Wein legen
2. Then it was fried.
3. The rice was cooked (for) twenty minutes.
4. The salad was prepared too.
5. Apples were cut.
6. The sweet cream was beaten.
7. Flowers were put° on the table.   stellen
8. And the guests were picked up at the station.

D. Beim Friseur.   Identify the phrases with **werden**: (a) tense of main verb, (b) future or present probability, or (c) tense of passive voice. Then give the English equivalents of the sentences.

▶ Meine Haare werden gewaschen.
   present passive; My hair is being washed.

1. Sie werden kurz geschnitten.
2. Ich werde so schön aussehen.
3. Mich wird wohl keiner mehr erkennen.
4. Durch die Sonne werden meine Haare immer sehr hell.
5. Hinten werden sie wohl lang bleiben.
6. Von der Friseuse wird mir eine Tasse Kaffee gebracht.
7. Am Schluß wird mein Haar mit dem Haartrockner in Form gebracht.

E. Ein Unfall.   People are still talking about a recent accident. Restate the sentences beginning with **es** and give the English equivalents.

▶ Dem anderen Fahrer konnte nichts bewiesen werden.
   Es konnte dem anderen Fahrer nichts bewiesen werden.
   Nothing could be proved against the other driver.

1. Ihm wurde aber auch nicht geglaubt.
2. Nach dem Unfall ist viel diskutiert worden.
3. Uns wurde erklärt, daß wir zu schnell gefahren wären.
4. Beiden Fahrern wurde geraten, etwas vorsichtiger° zu fahren.   more carefully
5. Später ist beschlossen worden, die Polizei nicht zu rufen.
6. Schließlich ist nicht mehr über die Sache gesprochen worden.

F. Abreise°.   Mr. and Mrs. Knoll are leaving for a trip. They are a   departure
little bit nervous and check to be sure everything has been taken
care of.

▶ Die Fahrkarten müssen noch abgeholt werden.
   Die Fahrkarten sind (doch/schon) abgeholt.

1. Der Fotoapparat muß noch abgeholt werden.
2. Die Koffer müssen noch gepackt werden.
3. Das Geschirr muß noch gespült werden.
4. Die Betten müssen noch gemacht werden.
5. Die Fenster müssen geschlossen werden.
6. Das Taxi muß bestellt werden.

G. Ein autofreier Sonntag.   For the protection of the environment
some cities are planning a day free of car traffic. The city planner
says what can, must, and will be done. Restate using the cued modal
and passive infinitive.

▶ Alle Leute werden informiert. (müssen)
   Alle Leute müssen informiert werden.

1. Autos werden nicht gefahren. (dürfen)
2. Fahrräder werden benutzt. (können)
3. Die Straßen werden vom Autoverkehr frei gehalten. (sollen)
4. Auch Motorräder werden zu Hause gelassen. (müssen)
5. Energie wird gespart. (müssen)
6. Die Polizisten werden in Urlaub geschickt. (können)
7. Auf den Straßen wird getanzt. (dürfen)
8. Statt Benzin wird an den Tankstellen Limonade verkauft.
   (sollen)

H. Die Fahrradtour.   Dagmar and Ulrike are going on a biking trip
for a few days. They check their last preparations. Tell what they do
in German.

1. The bicycles are well prepared.
2. The water bottle must not be forgotten.
3. It is already packed°.   einpacken
4. The sandwiches are already made.
5. But they still have to be packed.
6. The inn in Bad Tölz still has to be called.
7. The neighbors are already informed°.   informieren
8. Only the keys still have to be taken to the neighbors.

I. In einem andern Land. John is visiting Austria for the first time. Tell him how Sundays are often spent. Restate the sentences using **man**.

▶ Sonntags wird nicht gearbeitet.
Sonntags arbeitet man nicht.

1. Sonntags wird lange geschlafen.
2. Manchmal wird im Gasthaus zu Mittag gegessen.
3. Sonntagnachmittags wird ein Spaziergang gemacht.
4. Danach wird Kaffee getrunken.
5. Dazu werden viele Stücke Kuchen gegessen.
6. Bei schönem Wetter wird viel radgefahren.
7. Abends wird ferngesehen.

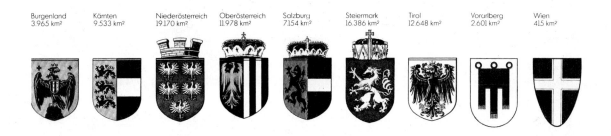

| Burgenland | Kärnten | Niederösterreich | Oberösterreich | Salzburg | Steiermark | Tirol | Vorarlberg | Wien |
| 3.965 km² | 9.533 km² | 19.170 km² | 11.978 km² | 7.154 km² | 16.386 km² | 12.648 km² | 2.601 km² | 415 km² |

Österreich ist ein aus neun Bundesländern - Burgenland, Kärnten, Niederösterreich, Oberösterreich, Salzburg, Steiermark, Tirol, Vorarlberg und Wien - bestehender Bundesstaat mit einer Bodenfläche von 83.850 km².

J. Reise nach Wien. Mr. and Mrs. Münz are planning a trip to Vienna. They are at the travel agency asking all sort of questions. You, the agent, respond according to the cues using **sein** plus **zu** plus infinitive.

▶ Können wir das Stadtzentrum vom Hotel aus leicht erreichen? (ja)
Ja, das Stadtzentrum ist vom Hotel aus leicht zu erreichen.

1. Können wir den Wienerwald vom Hotel aus sehen? (nein)
2. Können wir die Oper leicht finden? (ja)
3. Müssen wir die Fahrkarten schon jetzt bezahlen? (ja)
4. Müssen wir die Plätze für die Donaufahrt° bei Ihnen reser-   trip on the Danube
   vieren? (ja)
5. Müssen wir morgen alle Papiere mitbringen? (ja)
6. Können Sie die Stadtrundfahrt° in Wien empfehlen°? (nein)   sightseeing tour / recommend

K. Was ist das?   Jan has received a birthday gift but he won't tell his friends what it is. So they ask him all sorts of questions. Answer for Jan using **sich lassen** plus infinitive.

▶ Kann man das Ding gut gebrauchen? (ja)
Ja, das Ding läßt sich gut gebrauchen.

1. Kann man das Ding essen? (nein)
2. Kann man das Ding draußen benutzen? (ja)
3. Kann man es auch im Haus benutzen? (ja)
4. Kann man Freunde damit unterhalten? (ja)
5. Kann man es leicht herumtragen? (ja)
6. Kann man Musik damit machen? (ja)
   — Ist es ein Kassettenrecorder?
   — Ja.

L. Umzug° nach Großbritannien.   The Schneiders are moving   move
from Germany to Great Britain. They discuss their move with
friends. Restate their comments using reflexive constructions.

▶ Die alte Wohnung ist leicht zu verkaufen.
Die alte Wohnung verkauft sich leicht.

1. Eine neue Wohnung ist sicher schnell zu finden.
2. Die britische Kultur ist aus ihrer Geschichte zu erklären.
3. Die englischen Zeitungen sind leicht zu lesen.
4. Denn die englische Sprache ist leicht zu lernen.
5. Gute Freunde sind aber nicht so leicht zu finden.
6. Geld verdient man auch nicht so leicht im Ausland.
7. Es ist fraglich, wie es der Familie gefallen wird.

M. Auf deutsch bitte!

1. I was given this letter. (**man**)
2. It must be written immediately. (passive)
3. I'm sorry, but such a letter isn't easy to write. (**sein ...   zu +** infinitive)
4. It's understood that you get an hour off tomorrow. (reflexive)
5. That's easy to say, I know. (**sich lassen**)
6. But the work must be done. (passive)

N. Kurze Aufsätze.   In chapter 3 you described a process; now
describe it again, this time using the passive voice.

Kapitel 11

- Relative clauses
- Relative pronouns
- Indirect discourse
- Time relationship between direct and indirect statements
- Indirect questions
- Indirect commands
- Special subjunctive
- Special subjunctive in wishes, commands, and requests

1. Relative clauses

Wer ist der Gast, **der an dem Tisch sitzt?**

Who's the guest (who is) sitting at the table?

Meinst du die Frau, **die ihre Brille gerade geputzt hat?**

Do you mean the woman who just cleaned her glasses?

A relative clause provides additional information about a previously mentioned noun. The clause is introduced by a relative pronoun that refers back to the noun, which is the antecedent. In English the relative pronoun may be omitted. In German it must be stated.

Since a relative clause is a dependent clause, the finite verb is in final position. In writing, a comma separates the relative clause from the main clause.

heihoff
internationale damenmoden

schmiedestr. 2 2000 hamburg 1
(0 40) 32 69 27

Mode über die man spricht.
Mitten in Hamburg nahe der
Petrikirche. Für alle Frauen,
die besonderen Wert auf
Exclusivität und gepflegte
Atmosphäre legen.

123

2. Forms of relative pronouns

	Masculine	Neuter	Feminine	Plural
Nominative:	der	das	die	die
Accusative:	den	das	die	die
Dative:	dem	dem	der	denen
Genitive:	dessen	dessen	deren	deren

The forms of the relative pronouns are the same as the definite article, except for the dative plural and all genitive forms.

Masculine:	Wer ist *der Mann*, **der** an dem Tisch sitzt?
Neuter:	Wer ist *das Kind*, **das** an dem Tisch sitzt?
Feminine:	Wer ist *die Frau*, **die** an dem Tisch sitzt?
Plural:	Wer sind *die Leute*, **die** an dem Tisch sitzen?

The *gender* (masculine, neuter, feminine) and *number* (singular and plural) of a relative pronoun are determined by the gender and number of the antecedent.

Nominative:	Ist das der Mann, **der** nebenan wohnt?	*Is that the man who lives next door?*
Accusative:	Ist das der Mann, **den** wir gestern gesehen haben?	*Is that the man whom we saw yesterday?*
Dative:	Ist das der Mann, von **dem** Sie gesprochen haben?	*Is that the man about whom you spoke?*
Genitive:	Ist das der Mann, **dessen** Frau Schweizerin ist?	*Is that the man whose wife is Swiss?*

The *case* of the relative pronoun depends on its function in the relative clause. For example, a relative pronoun used as a subject (**der**) is in the nominative case, and a relative pronoun used as a direct object (**den**) is in the accusative case.

3. The indefinite relative pronouns *wer* and *was*

Wer zu spät kommt, bekommt
    nichts zu essen.

Whoever *comes late gets*
    nothing to eat.

Wen du einlädst, ist mir gleich.

Whomever *you want to invite is okay with me.*

Was er von seinem Leben erzählte, war interessant.

What(ever) *he told about his life was interesting.*

The interrogative pronouns **wer (wen, wem, wessen)** and **was** can be used as relative pronouns to refer to nonspecific persons or things.

Ich glaube nicht alles, **was** in der Zeitung steht.

I don't believe everything that's in the newspaper.

Das war das Beste, **was** ich tun konnte.

That was the best (that) I could do.

Er hat nicht die Wahrheit gesagt, **was** uns nicht überraschte.

He didn't tell the truth, which didn't surprise us.

The relative pronoun **was** is also used to refer to an antecedent that is an indefinite pronoun (**alles, etwas, nichts, viel, wenig**) or a neuter superlative noun (**das Beste, das Schönste**). **Was** can also be used to refer to an entire clause.

Er hat nicht die Wahrheit gesagt, **worüber** wir uns wundern.

The adverb **wo(r)-** is used with a preposition (instead of **was +** preposition) to refer to an entire clause.

FLEISCH FÜR KENNER UND GENIESSER

Wer
Gutes will,
der geht zu

Mandel

Dielinger Straße 44
Ecke Krahnstraße

4. Indirect discourse in German: statements

Direct discourse:	Uwe sagte: „Ich bin müde."	*Uwe said: "I'm tired."*
Indirect discourse:	Uwe sagte, **daß er** müde **wäre**.	*Uwe said that he was tired.*
	Uwe sagte, **er wäre** müde.	*Uwe said he was tired.*

Direct discourse or *direct quotation* is used to report the exact words of another person. *Indirect discourse* is used to report the substance of a message, not the exact words.

The pronouns change in indirect discourse to correspond to the perspective of the speaker. Uwe speaks of himself and says "**ich**." You report his message, and refer to Uwe as **er**.

The conjunction **daß** may or may not be stated in indirect discourse. When **daß** is stated, the finite verb (that is, the verb that agrees with the subject) is in last position; when it is omitted, the finite verb is in second position.

Karin sagte, sie **könnte** nicht mitkommen.	*Karin said she couldn't come along.*

The verbs in indirect discourse are in the subjunctive. By using the subjunctive in indirect discourse, the speaker indicates that she/he does not take responsibility for the accuracy of the original statement. Although subjunctive is required for indirect discourse in formal writing, indicative is used more and more in colloquial German by some speakers, especially when the verb in the introductory statement is in the present tense:

Karin sagt, sie **kann** nicht mitkommen.	*Karin says she can't come along.*

Indirect discourse occurs in three time categories: present, past, and future. The time used depends on the tense used in the direct quotation.

5. Indirect discourse in present time

Direct discourse:	Dieter sagte: „Ich **bin** krank."	*Dieter said: "I'm ill."*
Indirect discourse:	Dieter sagte, er **wäre** krank.	*Dieter said he was ill.*

In German, when the direct statement or quotation is in the present tense, the present-time subjunctive is used in the indirect quotation. The introductory statement can be in any tense and does not affect the time category of the indirect quotation. The present-time subjunctive shows that the action or event was happening at the same time the speaker was telling about it. Dieter was ill when he commented on it.

Ingrid sagte, sie **machte** es allein.
            sie **würde** es allein **machen.**

In colloquial German the **würde**-construction is often used in place of the present-time subjunctive of the main verb. It is, however, not generally used with the verbs **haben** and **sein** or modals:

Ingrid sagte, sie **wäre allein.**
            sie **müßte** alles allein machen.
            sie **hätte** kein Geld.

6. Indirect discourse in past time

Direct discourse:	Lore sagte: „Ich **habe** gestern **angerufen.**"	*Lore said, "I called yesterday."*
Indirect discourse:	Lore sagte, sie **hätte** gestern **angerufen.**	*Lore said she had called yesterday.*

In German, when a past tense (simple past, present perfect, past perfect) is used in the direct quotation, the past-time subjunctive is used in the indirect quotation. The introductory statement can be in any tense and does not affect the time category of the indirect quotation. The past-time subjunctive shows that the action or event happened at a time prior to the moment when the statement was made. In the example above, Lore called the day before she talked about it.

7. Indirect discourse in future time

Direct discourse:	Heinz sagte: „Ich **werde** es später **machen.**"	*Heinz said, "I'll do it later."*
Indirect discourse:	Heinz sagte, er **würde** es später **machen.**	*Heinz said he would do it later.*

In German, when future tense is used in the direct quotation, the **würde**-construction is used in the indirect quotation. The introductory statement can be in any tense and does not affect the time category of the indirect quotation. The **würde**-construction shows that the action or event was to happen at a time that had not yet occurred when the statement was made. In the example above, Heinz said he hadn't done it yet but would do so later.

Time relationship between direct and indirect statements

Introductory statement	Direct statement	Indirect statement	Time relationship of indirect statement to introductory statement
Any tense	Present tense	Present-time subjunctive	Occurs at same time
Any tense	Past, present perfect, past perfect	Past-time subjunctive	Has already occurred
Any tense	Future	**würde** + infinitive	Has not occurred, but will occur

8. Indirect general questions

Werner fragte Ingrid: „**Hast** du den Schlüssel **gefunden?**"

Werner asked Ingrid, "Did you find the key?"

Werner fragte Ingrid, **ob** sie den Schlüssel **gefunden hätte.**

Werner asked Ingrid if (whether) she had found the key.

A general indirect question, which requires a yes-no answer, is introduced by **ob** *(if, whether).* The verb is in the subjunctive and is in last position.

9. Indirect specific questions

Werner fragte Ingrid:„Wo **hast** du den Schlüssel **gefunden?**"

Werner asked Ingrid, "Where did you find the key?"

Werner fragte Ingrid, **wo** sie den Schlüssel **gefunden hätte.**

Werner asked Ingrid where she had found the key.

An indirect specific question, which elicits specific information, is introduced by an interrogative that functions like a subordinating conjunction. The verb is in the subjunctive and is in last position.

Questions in indirect discourse, like statements, may occur in present, past or future time.

10. Indirect commands

Direct:	Kai sagte zu mir: „**Komm** doch **mit**!"	*Kai said to me, "Come along."*
Indirect:	Kai sagte mir, ich **sollte** doch **mitkommen**.	*Kai told me that I should come along.*
		Kai told me to come along.

In German, an indirect command uses the subjunctive form of the modal **sollen** + infinitive. The English equivalents can be expressed in two ways: with **should** plus the main verb, or with an infinitive (e.g. *to come along*).

    Sagen is used with **zu** to introduce direct quotations. **Sagen** may be used without **zu** to introduce indirect quotations.

11. Special subjunctive

Special subjunctive:	Der Polizist behauptet, er **habe** es **gesehen**.
General subjunctive:	Der Polizist behauptet, er **hätte** es **gesehen**.

German has a special subjunctive that is usually used in formal writing, such as newspapers and literature, as well as in certain kinds of wishes, and commands. The meaning of special and general subjunctive is the same.

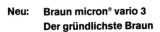

**Und fast alle dachten,
die Braun Rasur
sei nicht zu verbessern**

Neu: **Braun micron® vario 3
Der gründlichste Braun**

BRAUN

12. Present-time special subjunctive

ich gehe	wir gehen
du gehest	ihr gehet
er/es/sie gehe	sie gehen
Sie gehen	

The present-time special subjunctive is composed of the infinitive stem plus subjunctive endings: **-e, -est, -e, -en, -et, -en.**

Use of the special subjunctive is generally limited to the third person singular since only that form is clearly distinct from the indicative.

Infinitive	Special subjunctive er/es/sie-form	Indicative er/es/sie-form
schlafen	**schlafe**	schläft
geben	**gebe**	gibt
sehen	**sehe**	sieht
müssen	**müsse**	muß
haben	**habe**	hat
sein	**sei**	ist
werden	**werde**	wird

Verbs that have vowel changes in the second and third person singular forms of the indicative do not undergo vowel change in the special subjunctive.

13. Special subjunctive of *sein*

ich **sei**	*wir* **seien**
du **sei(e)st**	*ihr* **sei(e)t**
er/es/sie **sei**	*sie* **seien**
Sie **seien**	

Sein is the only verb that occurs with some frequency in the special subjunctive form in indirect discourse, since the forms are clearly different from the indicative. Note that **sei** does not have the -e ending characteristic of the **ich** and **er/es/sie**-forms in the special subjunctive.

14. Past-time special subjunctive

Ein Kritiker meinte, das Orchester **habe** endlich gut **gespielt.**	*A critic said the orchestra had finally played well.*
Eine Polizistin sagte, die Demonstration **sei** friedlich **gewesen.**	*A policewoman said the demonstration had been peaceful.*

Past-time special subjunctive consists of the special subjunctive forms of the auxiliaries **haben** or **sein** plus the past participle of the main verb.

15. Future-time special subjunctive

Die Präsidentin erklärte, man **werde** die politschen Probleme **lösen können.**	*The president declared one would be able to solve the political problems.*
Der Beamte sagte, er **werde** die Frage morgen **beantworten.**	*The official said he would answer the question tomorrow.*

Future-time special subjunctive consists of the special subjunctive forms of the auxiliary **werden** plus a dependent infinitive.

16. Special subjunctive in wishes, commands, requests

Certain wishes:	Gott **gebe** es!	May God grant that.
	Möge er noch lange leben!	May he live long.
	Gott **sei** Dank!	Thank God.
Certain commands and wishes:	**Nehmen** wir als Beispiel ...	Let's take as an example . . .
	Essen wir!	Let's eat!
	So **sei** es!	So be it!
	Seien wir froh, daß alles vorbei ist.	Let's be glad it's all over.

The special subjunctive is used in certain standard wishes, commands, or requests.

17. Special vs. general subjunctive in indirect discourse

Special subjunctive and general subjunctive are equivalent in meaning. There are no specific rules that govern the use of the special vs. the general subjunctive, but here are some guidelines to help you.

a. The special subjunctive is used mainly in indirect discourse in formal German. The general subjunctive is more common in colloquial German.

b. The special subjunctive is generally used only in the **er/es/sie-**form, which is clearly different from the indicative.

c. The special subjunctive is always replaced by general subjunctive when the special subjunctive forms are identical to the indicative forms. Compare the following sentences:

Indicative and special subjunctive	Sie sagte, die Kinder **haben** es gemacht.
General subjunctive	Sie sagte, die Kinder **hätten** es gemacht.

Übungen

A. Der falsche Koffer. On their way to Salzburg, Karin and her friend change trains in Munich. Identify each relative clause in their conversation. Give the gender, case, and function of each relative pronoun and identify the antecedent.

▶ Die Tafel, die die Abfahrtszeiten° anzeigt, hängt dort drüben.   departure times
   die die Abfahrtszeiten anzeigt; feminine nominative, subject;
   antecedent is Tafel.

1. Gerti: Wo ist der Zug, mit dem wir weiterfahren müssen?
2. Karin: Keine Ahnung! Komm, wir schauen auf dem Plan nach, der dort hängt.
3. Gerti: Mensch, Karin, das ist doch gar nicht unser Koffer, den du da in der Hand hast.
4. Karin: O je! Gehört er dem Herrn, dessen Kinder die ganze Zeit so geschrien haben?
5. Gerti: Nein, ich glaube, der Frau, die uns ihre Zeitung gegeben hat. Schau, da drüben sitzt sie.
6. Karin: Au ja! Das ist mein Koffer, auf dem sie sitzt.

B. Verschiedene Interessen.   Think of your own friends and relatives and answer with *yes* or *no*.

▶ Meine Tante kennt viele gute Geschichten.
Ich habe auch eine Tante, die viele gute Geschichten kennt.
Ich habe keine Tante, die ...

1. Mein Freund schreibt ein Buch nach dem andern.
2. Mein Bruder spielt gern mit Computern.
3. Meine Schwester ist im Fahrradclub.
4. Meine Cousine fährt immer nach Italien.
5. Mein Onkel malt wunderschöne Bilder.
6. Meine Freundin gibt ihr ganzes Geld für Kleider aus.
7. Mein Nachbar interessiert sich für Musik aus fremden Ländern.
8. Meine Großeltern haben eine tolle Bibliothek.

C. Die gute alte Zeit.   John and Greg spent their junior year in Heidelberg. Some years later they return and the memories from the good old days come back. Fill in the blanks with the appropriate relative pronouns.

1. John: Ist das nicht das Hotel, in _____ wir die erste Nacht verbracht haben?
2. Greg: Ja, und da ist die Marktfrau, bei _____ wir unser Obst gekauft haben.
3. John: Laß uns durch die Straße gehen, in _____ wir im Sommersemester gewohnt haben.
4. Greg: Das ist eine gute Idee! Und ich möchte wieder in dem Gasthaus einen Kaffee trinken, in _____ wir samstags immer gegangen sind.
5. John: Sieh mal, dort! Das ist doch der, _____ wir im Hauptseminar° kennengelernt haben, nicht?   advanced seminar
6. Greg: Richtig. Ich möchte auch wieder den Spaziergang zum Schloß machen, auf _____ wir Barbara kennengelernt haben.
7. John: Gut. Und was ist wohl aus dem kleinen Café geworden, _____ wir damals immer besucht haben?

D. Ein produktiver Mensch.   Complete the information about the journalist Peter Schreiber. Use the genitive form of the relative pronoun.

1. Wie heißt der Autor, _____ Bücher du so gern liest?
2. Er ist ein Journalist, _____ Namen jeder kennt: Peter Schreiber.

3. Er schreibt für eine Zeitschrift, _____ Berichte immer sehr interessant sind.
4. Er spielt auch in einer Rockband, _____ Schallplatten recht gut sind.
5. Meine Schwester, _____ Freund auch in der Band spielt, kommt heute abend mit ihm zu mir.
6. Er spielt immer ein Lied für mich, _____ Melodie ich sehr gern mag.

E. Das Müller'sche Volksbad°.   Combine the sentences using relative pronouns in place of the italicized words.   *public swimming pool*

▶ In München gibt es ein Schwimmbad. *Sein* Baustil° ist wunderschön.   *style of architecture*
In München gibt es ein Schwimmbad, dessen Baustil wunderschön ist.

1. Ich wollte in ein Schwimmbad gehen. *Es* ist sehr alt.
2. Freunde hatten mir davon erzählt. *Ihnen* gefällt das Bad sehr.
3. Ich war schon neugierig auf das Bad. Ein bekannter Architekt hat *es* gebaut.
4. Meine Badetasche war sehr schwer. Ich packte *sie* ganz voll.
5. An der Haltestelle traf ich einen Freund. *Sie* ist vor meinem Haus. Ich erzählte *ihm* davon.
6. Mein Freund ging mit. *Sein* liebster Sport ist Schwimmen.
7. Wir fuhren mit der Straßenbahn. *Sie* hält genau vor dem Schwimmbad.
8. An der Tür hing eine Tafel: Heute geschlossen. *Sie* war zu.

F. Schön war's.   Louise and Eva are coming back from a wonderful trip and tell their friends about it. Complete the sentences with the appropriate prepositions and relative pronouns.

▶ Das war eine schöne Zeit, <u>_an_</u> <u>_die_</u> ich mich gern erinnern werde.

1. Das Leben in dem Land, _____ _____ wir gefahren sind, ist ganz anders als hier.
2. Es war eine sehr interessante Reise, _____ _____ ich am liebsten ein ganzes Buch schreiben würde.
3. Am schönsten war der große alte Baum, _____ _____ wir immer gefrühstückt haben.
4. Das Zimmer, _____ _____ wir geschlafen haben, war schön hell.

5. Wir haben uns auch die Schlösser angesehen, _____ _____ ihr uns erzählt habt.
6. Bald hole ich die Fotos ab, _____ _____ ich mich schon sehr freue.

G. Medizinstudium. Complete the sentences with a form of **wer, was,** or the compound **wo(r)** + preposition.

▶ Meine Freundin studiert Medizin, _worüber_ sie sehr glücklich ist.

1. _____ ihr damals zur Medizin geraten hat, war ihre Mutter.
2. Das war das Beste, _____ sie tun konnte.
3. Denn das Medizinstudium ist etwas, _____ sie sich schon immer gewünscht hatte.
4. _____ in diesem Studium nicht hart arbeitet, wird nie Ärztin.
5. Bald macht sie Examen, _____ sie noch eine Menge lernen muß.
6. Später wird sie die Praxis° ihres Vaters übernehmen°, _____   practice/take over
sie sich schon sehr freut.

H. Kein schlechter Job. Tell a friend what Lore said about the conditions at a restaurant where she works. Use present-time general subjunctive.

▶ Mein Job gefällt mir ganz gut.
  Lore sagt, ihr Job gefiele ihr ganz gut.

1. Die Musik ist immer ziemlich laut dort.
2. Man kann da ganz gut Geld verdienen.
3. Ich muß mich immer gut anziehen.
4. Die Kollegen sind alle jung und sehr nett.
5. Ich kann so lange dort arbeiten, wie ich will.
6. Freitagabends und samstags ist es immer knallvoll°.   full to bursting
7. Da muß ich ganz schön rennen.
8. Aber es macht auch Spaß.

Gut Essen und Trinken in Bonn und Umgebung

I. Reise nach Österreich. Report what you and your friends asked Hans about his trip to Austria. Use past-time general subjunctive.

▶ Bist du mit dem Zug gefahren?
Wir fragten ihn, ob er mit dem Zug gefahren wäre.

1. Wie war es in Österreich? *wie gewesen wäre / sei*
2. Bist du allein gefahren? *ob er allein gefahren wäre / sei*
3. Welche Städte hast du besucht? *besucht hätte / habe*
4. Warst du auch in Salzburg? *gewesen wäre / sei*
5. Bist du dort ins Mozarthaus gegangen? *gegangen wäre / sei*
6. Bist du auch im Gebirge gewandert?
7. Wo hat es dir am besten gefallen? *hätte / habe*
8. Warum bist du nicht länger geblieben? *geblieben wäre / sei*
9. Wie hat dir das österreichische Essen geschmeckt? *hätte / habe*
10. Hast du den Dialekt verstanden? *hätte / habe*

J. Vor dem Rennen. Jürgen is going to participate in a track meet. Tell your friends what he said about his feelings and plans concerning the upcoming event. Use future-time general subjunctive.

▶ Ich werde bestimmt eine gute Zeit laufen.
Jürgen sagte, er würde bestimmt eine gute Zeit laufen.

1. Ich werde vorher viel trainieren müssen.
2. Ich werde jeden Tag zehn Kilometer laufen.
3. Meine Beine werden sehr stark werden.
4. Ich werde bald neue Sportschuhe brauchen.
5. Ich werde hoffentlich gewinnen.
6. Ich werde aber nicht traurig sein, wenn ich nicht gewinne.
7. Alle meine Freunde werden kommen.
8. Danach werden wir bestimmt zusammen feiern.

K. Vor der Prüfung. Stefan is very nervous about his exam tomorrow. Philipp has given him advice about being ready. Take Stefan's role as he tells his roommate about the advice. Use general subjunctive.

▶ Geh früh ins Bett!
Philipp hat gesagt, ich sollte früh ins Bett gehen.

1. Mach dir keine Sorgen!
2. Schlaf genug!
3. Steh nicht zu spät auf!

4. Iß ein gutes Frühstück!
5. Bleib ruhig!
6. Sei pünktlich!
7. Werd nicht nervös!
8. Denk an etwas Schönes!

L. Beim Arzt. Lutz is seeing the doctor because he had a little accident. Report the conversation he had with the doctor to his girlfriend.

▶ Arzt: Wie geht es Ihnen?
Der Arzt fragte, wie es ihm ginge.
Lutz: Es geht mir schlecht.
Lutz antwortete, es ginge ihm schlecht.   ~~gebe~~

1. Arzt: Was ist los?   *los wäre /sei* ~~wäre u.~~ ~~wehgeten u.~~
2. Lutz: Ich habe mir am Fuß wehgetan.   ~~hätte~~ ~~wehgetan~~
3. Arzt: Wie ist das passiert?   *passiert wäre /sei*
4. Lutz: Ich bin vom Fahrrad gefallen.   *gefallen wäre /sei*
5. Arzt: Oh, das sieht nicht gut aus. (Der Arzt sagte, …)   *sehe /sähe*
6. Lutz: Kann ich bald wieder richtig gehen?   *gehen könnte*
7. Arzt: Na, das wird eine Zeit dauern.   *dauern werde /würde*
8. Lutz: Das ist doof°.   *wäre/sei*   stupid
9. Arzt: Bewegen Sie den Fuß nicht! Er muß ruhig liegen.   *bewegen solle / bewegen sollte* ~~er müsse~~ */müßte* ~~liegen~~
10. Lutz: Oh je! Das wird mir schwer fallen°. Ich tanze doch so gern.   **schwer fallen:** find difficult
   fallen würde *tanze* ~~werde~~ *tanzte*

M. Mehr Umweltschutz°. As a reporter you attend a conference on   environmental protection
the environment. Report the remarks of one of the speakers in your newspaper article. Use special subjunctive.

▶ Man muß mehr öffentliche Verkehrsmittel° benutzen.   public transportation
Der Redner sagte, man müsse mehr öffentliche Verkehrsmittel benutzen.

1. Die Luft soll reingehalten werden.
2. Es muß mehr Energie gespart werden.
3. Jeder soll weniger Auto fahren.
4. Jeder einzelne trägt Verantwortung° für die Zukunft°.   responsibility / future
5. Wir haben schon zuviel Zeit verloren. (use general subjunctive)
6. Unsere Seen sind schmutzig.
7. In den Flüssen sind schon viele Fische gestorben.
8. Es darf nicht länger gewartet werden.

N. Kurze Aufsätze

1. You are helping write material for a quiz show. Describe an historical person so that contestants must guess his or her name. Use at least 3 relative pronouns.
2. You have interviewed a famous person. Report in a short newspaper article what this person said. Use indirect discourse.

Kapitel 12

- Infinitives without *zu*
- Double infinitive construction with *hören, sehen, lassen*
- Meanings of *lassen*
- Objective and subjective use of modals
- Infinitives with *zu*
- Expressions *um ... zu, anstatt ... zu,* and *ohne ... zu*
- Pre-noun inserts

1. Infinitives without *zu*

Ich **muß** jetzt **frühstücken.**	*I have to eat breakfast now.*
Ich **höre** die Kinder in der Küche **reden.**	*I hear the children talking in the kitchen.*
Ich **sehe** sie jeden Morgen **wegfahren.**	*I see them drive off every morning.*
Sie **läßt** uns das allein **machen.**	*She's letting us do that alone.*

Like modal auxiliaries (see Kapitel 1, p. 8), the verbs **hören, sehen,** and **lassen** can take a dependent infinitive without **zu.**

2. Double infinitive constructions with modals, *hören, sehen, lassen.*

Hast du das **gewollt?**	*Did you want that?*
Ich **habe** es nicht **schreiben wollen.**	*I didn't want to write it.*
Ich **habe** die Nachbarn **gehört.**	*I heard the neighbors.*

139

Ich **habe** die Nachbarn **wegfahren hören.**	*I heard the neighbors drive off.*
Ich **hatte** das Auto nicht **gesehen.**	*I hadn't seen the car.*
Ich **hatte** das Auto nicht **kommen sehen.**	*I hadn't seen the car coming.*
Sie **hätte** uns allein **gelassen.**	*She would have left us alone.*
Sie **hätte** uns das allein **machen lassen.**	*She would have let us do that alone.*

When modals, **hören, sehen** and **lassen** are used with a dependent infinitive they form the perfect tenses with a double infinitive (see Kapitel 8, p. 94). The auxiliary verb **haben** is always used.

3. The double infinitive construction in subordinate clauses

Ich weiß, daß sie **hatte kommen wollen.**	*I know that she had wanted to come.*
Er sagte, daß er es allein **hätte tun können.**	*He said that he could have done it alone.*

In a dependent clause containing a double infinitive, the auxiliary **haben** is not at the end, where it usually is in a dependent clause. Rather the auxiliary precedes the double infinitive. (see p. 94)

4. Meaning of *lassen*

Lassen is one of the most commonly used verbs in German. Some basic meanings follow:

a. *to leave*

Laß die Teller im Schrank!	*Leave the plates in the cupboard.*
Wo **habe** ich meinen Schirm **gelassen?**	*Where did I leave my umbrella?*

b. *to permit*

Laß mich den Brief lesen!	*Let me read the letter.*
Ich **lasse** dich fahren.	*I'll let you drive.*
Lassen Sie mich Ihnen helfen.	*Let me help you.*

c. *let's*

Gerd, **laß** uns jetzt arbeiten!	*Gerd, let's work now.*
Kinder, **laßt** uns gehen!	*Children, let's go.*
Frau Meier, **lassen Sie** uns anfangen!	*Mrs. Meier, let's begin.*

The imperative form of **lassen** plus the pronoun **uns** is often used in place of the first person plural imperative: **Arbeiten wir! Gehen wir! Fangen wir an!**

d. *to cause something to be done or have something done*

Sie **ließen sich** ein Haus bauen.	*They had a house built.*
Er **läßt sich** die Haare schneiden.	*He's having his hair cut.*
Sollen wir den Elektriker kommen **lassen**?	*Should we send for the electrician?*

Der läßt Sie nicht im Stich.

BRIDGESTONE
Ihre Sicherheit liegt uns am Herzen

5. Objective and subjective use of modals

Objective:	Inge **muß** schwer **arbeiten.**	*Inge has to work hard.*
	Du **sollst** das nicht **sagen.**	*You mustn't say that.*
Subjective:	Gabi **muß** sehr jung **sein.**	*Gabi must be very young.*
	Daniel **soll** sehr intelligent **sein.**	*Daniel is supposed to be very intelligent.*

Modal auxiliaries can be used either objectively or subjectively. When used objectively, they define a situation objectively as seen or understood by the speaker. (It's a fact that Inge has to work hard.) When used subjectively, they express the opinion of the speaker about a situation. (The speaker assumes that Gabi is very young.)

6. Subjective statements in present time

Objective:	Sie **will** jetzt **gehen.**	*Sie intends to leave now.*
Subjective:	Er **will** ein großer Musiker **sein.**	*He claims to be a great musician.*

In present time, modal constructions used subjectively have the same form as those used objectively.

7. Subjective statements in past time

Objective:	Sie **mußte** schwer **arbeiten.**	*She had to work hard.*
	Sie **hat** schwer **arbeiten müssen.**	*She had to work hard.*
Subjective:	Sie **muß** schwer **gearbeitet haben.**	*She must have worked hard.*
	Sie **mußte** schwer **gearbeitet haben.**	*She had to have worked hard.*

In past time, forms of modals used subjectively differ from forms used objectively. In past time the modal of the subjective statement is either in the present (**muß**) or simple past (**mußte**), and the main verb is in the past-infinitive form (**gearbeitet haben**).

8. Objective and subjective meanings of modals

a. dürfen

Objective: permission; prohibition (in the negative)

Sie darf heute **mitkommen.** *She's allowed to come along today.*

Das darfst du nicht **machen.** *You mustn't do that.*

Subjective: uncertain assumption (in subjunctive **dürfte**)

Er dürfte recht **haben.** *He might be right.*

b. können

Objective: ability

Sie **kann** gut Tennis **spielen.**   *She can play tennis well.*

Subjective: fair degree of certainty; impossibility

Morgen **kann** das Wetter   *Tomorrow the weather could*
  besser **werden.**   *get better.*
Er **kann** das nicht **gesagt**   *He surely can't have said that.*
  haben.

c. mögen

Objective: liking, personal preference

Magst du klassische Musik?   *Do you like classical music?*

Subjective: possibility that is likely; an estimation

Das **mag** wahr **sein.**   *That may be true.*
Wir **mochten** eine Stunde   *We may have waited an hour.*
  gewartet haben.

d. müssen

Objective: compulsion; obligation; absolute necessity

Mit sechs **müssen** Kinder in die   *At the age of six children have*
  Schule.   *to go to school.*
Du **mußt** mir **helfen.**   *You have got to help me.*

Subjective: indicates a firm belief; uncertainty (in subjunctive
müßte)

Er **muß** sehr reich **sein.**   *He must be very rich.*
Wenn Sie dort waren, **müssen**   *If you were there, you must*
  Sie es **gesehen haben.**   *have seen it.*
Sie **müßte** eigentlich schon   *She ought to have arrived*
  angekommen sein.   *already.*

e. sollen

Objective: obligation; an order, command, or request

Du **sollst** das nicht **machen.**   *You mustn't do that.*
Ich **soll** Thomas helfen.   *I'm supposed to help Thomas*
                                   (he asked me to).

Subjective: introduces a doubting question (in subjunctive **sollte**); the speaker has heard something but does not vouch for the truth of the statement:

Er **soll** sehr intelligent **sein.**	*He is said to be very intelligent.*
Sie **soll** es gesagt **haben.**	*She is supposed to have said it.*
Sollten Sie das wirklich nicht **wissen?**	*Don't you really know that?*

f. wollen

Objective: wish, desire, intention

Er **will** immer Geld von mir **haben.**	*He always wants money from me.*
Ich **will** nächstes Jahr nach Europa **reisen.**	*I intend to go to Europe next year.*

Subjective: expresses doubt about the claim of the assertion.

Er **will** viermal in Europa **gewesen sein.**	*He claims to have been in Europe four times.*
Sie **will** es nicht **gesagt haben.**	*She claims she didn't say it.*
Und Sie **wollen** so klug **sein?**	*And you claim to be so smart?*

9. Infinitives with *zu*

Nicole versuchte **zu arbeiten.**	*Nicole tried to work.*
Es fängt an **zu regnen.**	*It's beginning to rain.*
Ich bat ihn, hier **zu bleiben.**	*I asked him to stay here.*

Dependent infinitives used with most verbs are preceded by **zu** and are in last position.

Haben Sie Lust, den Film **zu sehen?**	*Do you feel like seeing the film?*
Es ist Zeit, nach Hause **zu gehen.**	*It's time to go home.*

A number of expressions using the verb **haben (Lust haben)** or **sein (es ist Zeit)** are followed by the infinitive with **zu.** An infinitive construction that contains other sentence elements such as objects, prepositional phrases, or adverbs is called an *infinitive clause* (**den Film zu sehen, nach Hause zu gehen**). In writing, an infinitive clause is set off by commas.

Ich habe vor, alle meine Freunde einzuladen.	*I plan to invite all my friends.*
Es ist Zeit anzufangen.	*It's time to begin.*

When a separable-prefix verb is in the infinitive form, the **zu** comes between the prefix and the base form of the verb. The construction is written as one word.

10. Expressions *um ... zu, anstatt ... zu, ohne ... zu*

Sie fuhr nach Bonn, **um** das Beethovenhaus **zu sehen.**	*She went to Bonn in order to see Beethoven's house.*
Wir werden sie anrufen, **anstatt** einen Brief **zu schreiben.**	*We'll call her instead of writing a letter.*
Er ist weggegangen, **ohne** ein Wort **zu sagen.**	*He left without saying a word.*

The prepositions **um, anstatt,** and **ohne** may combine with **zu** to introduce an infinitive clause.

11. Pre-noun inserts

Relative clause	Sie wollte das Kind, das vor Müdigkeit eingeschlafen war, nicht stören.
Pre-noun insert	Sie wollte das **vor Müdigkeit eingeschlafene** Kind nicht stören.
Relative clause	Er hat sich zu einem Menschen entwickelt, der mechanisch denkt.
Pre-noun insert	Er hat sich zu einem **mechanisch denkenden** Menschen entwickelt.

In German, relative clauses which follow nouns can be replaced by special constructions that precede nouns. These constructions can be called *pre-noun inserts.* They function like relative clauses but without a relative pronoun and a main verb. Instead they have a participle that immediately precedes the noun it modifies, and the participle has an adjective ending. The participle can be a past participle (**eingeschlafen**) or a present participle (**denkend**).

Pre-noun inserts are found mainly in formal writing such as scholarly works, especially scientific articles.

Denken Sie an unser **schwer zu lösendes** Problem.	*Think of our problem that is difficult to solve.*

Pre-noun inserts with a present participle preceded by **zu** indicate something that can (not) or should (not) be done. This construction is similar to a form of **sein** + **zu** + infinitive (see substitutes for passive voice, Kapitel 10, p. 116).

Übungen

A. Der Nachbar hat's gut.   Herr Kleinmann is jealous of his neighbor who apparently has an easy life. Give the English equivalents.

1. Ich sehe meinen Nachbarn oft im Garten sitzen.
2. Abends sehe ich ihn fröhlich von der Arbeit nach Hause kommen.
3. Oft höre ich ihn etwas im Hause reparieren.
4. Bei der Arbeit höre ich ihn singen.
5. Im teuersten Geschäft läßt er sich die Anzüge machen.
6. Manchmal höre ich ihn Klavier spielen.
7. Ich lasse mir jetzt auch ein schönes Haus bauen.

Man muß ja
nicht gleich bauen
wollen.

B. Sommerabend.   Last night was a beautiful summer evening. Tell what you saw and heard.

▶ Die Kinder spielten im Garten, nicht wahr? (sehen)
  Ja, ich sah sie im Garten spielen.

1. Peter übte gestern abend Cello, nicht wahr? (hören)
2. Er saß am offenen Fenster. (sehen)
3. Er zählte manchmal ganz laut. (hören)
4. Er spielte eine Menge Brahms. (hören)
5. Später packte er das Cello weg. (sehen)
6. Dann spazierte er im Garten. (sehen)
7. Dabei sang er leise Lieder. (hören)

C. Wir haben uns neu eingerichtet.   Frau Haller has gone over to a friend's house who has redecorated recently. She finds out how and why things happened. Give the English equivalents.

1. Die Vorhänge habe ich von meiner Mutter nähen lassen.
2. Die Spülmaschine habe ich billig von meiner Schwester kaufen können.
3. Den Spiegel habe ich mir aus Italien mitbringen lassen.
4. Den alten Tisch habe ich einfach nicht wegwerfen mögen.
5. Um die Stühle zu bekommen, habe ich lange telefonieren müssen.
6. Einen neuen Fernseher hatte ich eigentlich gar nicht kaufen wollen, aber mein Mann wollte absolut einen haben.
7. Die Gartenmöbel sind gar nicht neu; wir haben die alten einfach neu anmalen° lassen.   paint

D. Spielverderber°.   Daniel is being asked by his friends why he   spoil sport
was in such a strange mood last night at the party. Take his part. Use the present perfect tense of the modal.

▶ Warum bist du nicht früher gekommen? (können)
  Ich habe nicht gekonnt.

1. Warum bist du nicht mit dem Auto gekommen? (dürfen)
2. Warum hat dir dein Vater sein Auto nicht gegeben? (wollen)
3. Warum hast du den ganzen Abend nicht getanzt? (mögen)
4. Warum ist deine Freundin nicht mitgekommen? (können)
5. Warum hast du Bernd nicht die Hand gegeben? (mögen)
6. Warum bist du nicht bis zum Ende geblieben? (wollen)

E. Abenteuerreise°.   Rainer and his friends made an adventurous   adventure trip
and expensive trip during the summer. Karl was going to come along

but couldn't. By the time Erich hears about it, Rainer has already returned.

▶ Rainer: Karl konnte die Reise nicht machen.
   Erich: Ich hätte die Reise machen können.

1. Er konnte wohl nicht genug Geld zusammenkriegen.
2. Er durfte auch nicht so lange von der Arbeit wegbleiben.
3. Er konnte seine Familie nicht so lange allein lassen.
4. Er mochte wohl auch nicht drei Wochen mit uns zusammen sein.
5. Er mochte wohl auch nicht so gefährlich leben.
6. Kurz und gut°: Er wollte nicht mitmachen.   in a word

F. Kurze Gespräche.   Give the English equivalents.

1. —Ich habe mein Mathebuch bei meinen Eltern gelassen.
   —Dann laß uns doch zusammen bei mir arbeiten.
2. —Jutta läßt mich nicht an meinem Papier schreiben.
   —Laß dich von ihr nicht aus der Ruhe bringen°.   aus ... bringen: upset
3. —Wann wollen Sie das Haus bauen lassen?
   —Wir werden Sie wissen lassen, wenn die Pläne fertig sind.
4. —Laß uns heute abend ins Kino gehen.
   —Ach, laß mich in Ruhe°!   peace

G. Beim Tapezieren°.   Gert, Mirko, Niki, and Jörg are remodeling   wall papering
their apartment. They are working hard. Give their remarks in
German.

1. Leave the table there!
2. Let me do that!
3. He has me do his work!
4. Where did you leave the knife?
5. Do we have to send for an ambulance°?   der Krankenwagen
6. Let me hold that!
7. Let's have something to drink!

H. Jazz.   Lore and Conny are considering going to a jazz concert.
Give their conversation in English.

1. Lore: Hast du gehört, McCoy Tyner soll heute abend im „Domi-
         cile" spielen.
2. Conny: Echt? Da muß ich hin!
3. Lore: Ja, er soll nur zwei Abende in der Stadt sein.
4. Conny: Der muß ja wirklich super sein.
5. Lore: Willst du mit?

6. Conny: Ja. Ich muß nur noch fertig tippen°.   type
7. Lore: Soll ich dich dann abholen?
8. Conny: Gern. Das dürfte ein ziemlich toller Abend werden.

I. Die neue Bekanntschaft°. Eva has a new boyfriend. Tell a   acquaintance
friend what you have heard about him. Instead of the introductory
statement, use the cued modal.

▶ Ich glaube nicht, daß sie sich schon lange kennen. (können)
Sie können sich noch nicht lange kennen.

1. Ich habe gehört, daß Evas neuer Freund gut aussieht. (sollen)
2. Ich glaube, er ist Sportler. (müssen)
3. Kann sein, daß sie ihn beim Tennis kennengelernt hat. (mögen)
4. Ich glaube nicht, daß er viel älter ist als sie. (können)
5. Man behauptet, daß er sehr reich ist. (sollen)
6. Ich glaube, daß er sehr in sie verliebt° ist. (müssen)   in love
7. Man sagt, daß sie sehr glücklich ist. (sollen)
8. Kann sein, daß damit alles in Ordnung ist. (dürfen)

J. Translate the sentences you made in *Übung I.*

K. Eine Verwechslung°. Anna and Inge are discussing Ernst who   case of mistaken identity
can't remember who people are. He even confuses his friends. Give
their conversation in English.

1. Anna: Ernst will dich gestern abend im Theater gesehen haben.
2. Inge: Aber das kann ich doch gar nicht gewesen sein.
3. Anna: Ich weiß, das dürfte deine Schwester gewesen sein.
4. Inge: Ich konnte an dem Abend überhaupt nicht weggehen.
5. Anna: Richtig, du mußtest ja dein Papier schreiben.
6. Inge: Übrigens, das Stück soll wirklich gut sein.
7. Anna: Ich will es mir auch noch ansehen.
8. Inge: Das solltest du wirklich tun.
9. Anna: Vielleicht will Ernst mitgehen.

L. Griechenland.   Wolfgang is planning a trip and is discussing it
with Manuela.

▶ Es ist schon lange mein Wunsch (in den Süden fahren)
Es ist schon lange mein Wunsch, in den Süden zu fahren.

1. W.: Jetzt habe ich endlich Zeit (eine Reise machen).
   M.: Und wohin?

2. W.: Ich habe große Lust (nach Griechenland fahren). Athen muß (sehr interessant sein).
3. M.: Aber es soll auch (furchtbar viel Verkehr geben).
4. W.: Vielleicht sollte ich (lieber ans Meer fahren).
5. M.: Es wäre ganz gut (die Sprache ein bißchen lernen). Meinst du nicht?
6. W.: Ja, es wäre schön (mit den Leuten reden können).
7. M.: Hast du vor (lange bleiben)?
8. W.: Ich möchte schon (zwei Monate bleiben).
9. M.: Glaubst du (genug Geld haben)?
10. W.: Hm, das Leben dort scheint (nicht sehr teuer sein).
    M.: Na denn, gute Reise!

M. Wien.   Your cousin, who has somewhat unusual ideas, went to Vienna. Tell what he did, combining sentences using **um ... zu, ohne ... zu, statt ... zu.**

▶ Er fuhr mit seinem alten Auto. Er fuhr nicht mit dem Zug.
Er fuhr mit seinem alten Auto, statt mit dem Zug zu fahren.

1. Er fuhr nach Wien. Er reservierte kein Hotelzimmer.
2. Er mußte lange suchen. Er fand ein hübsches Zimmer in einer kleinen Pension°.   small hotel
3. Er war eine Woche in Wien. Er sah kein einziges Mal den Stephansdom an.
4. Er saß jeden Tag im Café. Er ging nicht in ein Museum.
5. Er verbrachte eine Woche in Wien. Er sah kein einziges Bild.
6. Er ging dauernd ins Kino. Er ging überhaupt nicht ins Theater.
7. Er ist wohl nach Wien gefahren. Er wollte nur im Café sitzen und die herrlichen Torten essen.

N. Atomenergie.   Scientists and scholars are discussing nuclear energy. Give the English equivalents.

1. Eine oft gestellte Frage wurde hier diskutiert.
2. Nun ist also der größte anzunehmende Unfall passiert.
3. Wir stehen vor einem schon lange bekannten Problem.
4. Wir befinden uns in einer oft diskutierten Situation.
5. Es stellen sich viele schwer zu beantwortende Fragen.
6. Viele nicht immer zu akzeptierende Antworten wurden angeboten.
7. Meine eigene, leider meistens mißverstandene Meinung ist:
8. Die bis heute als umweltfreundlich geltende Atomenergie muß neu durchdacht werden.

O. Kurze Aufsätze

1. International Scholarship: You must write several paragraphs about yourself; in your paragraphs include answers or comments on at least three of the following points:
   a. Was war schon immer Ihr Wunsch?
   b. Was würden Sie besonders schön oder interessant finden? Erklären Sie!
   c. Wozu haben Sie keine Zeit?
   d. Was finden Sie wichtig? Und was finden Sie schwer?
   e. Was macht Ihnen Spaß? Erklären Sie!
2. Tell about a dream.

Appendix: Grammatical Tables

1. Personal pronouns

Nominative:	ich	du	er	es	sie	wir	ihr	sie	Sie
Accusative:	mich	dich	ihn	es	sie	uns	euch	sie	Sie
Dative:	mir	dir	ihm	ihm	ihr	uns	euch	ihnen	Ihnen

2. Reflexive pronouns

	ich	du	er / es / sie	wir	ihr	sie	Sie
Accusative:	mich	dich	sich	uns	euch	sich	sich
Dative:	mir	dir	sich	uns	euch	sich	sich

3. Interrogative pronouns

Nominative:	wer	was
Accusative:	wen	was
Dative:	wem	
Genitive:	wessen	

4. Relative and demonstrative pronouns

	Singular			Plural
Nominative:	der	das	die	die
Accusative:	den	das	die	die
Dative:	dem	dem	der	denen
Genitive:	dessen	dessen	deren	deren

5. Definite articles

	Singular			Plural
Nominative:	der	das	die	die
Accusative:	den	das	die	die
Dative:	dem	dem	der	den
Genitive:	des	des	der	der

6. *Dieser*-words

	Singular			Plural
Nominative:	dieser	dieses	diese	diese
Accusative:	diesen	dieses	diese	diese
Dative:	diesem	diesem	dieser	diesen
Genitive:	dieses	dieses	dieser	dieser

The **dieser**-words are **dieser, jeder, jener, mancher, solcher,** and **welcher.**

7. Indefinite articles and *ein*-words

	Singular			Plural
Nominative:	ein	ein	eine	keine
Accusative:	einen	ein	eine	keine
Dative:	einem	einem	einer	keinen
Genitive:	eines	eines	einer	keiner

The **ein**-words include **kein** and the possessive adjectives: **mein, dein, sein, ihr, unser, euer, ihr,** and **Ihr.**

8. Plural of nouns

Category	Singular	Plural	Type	Notes
1	das Zimmer	**die Zimmer**	Ø (no change)	Masc. and neut. nouns ending in
	der Mantel	**die Mäntel**	¨ (umlaut)	-el, -en, -er
2	der Tisch	**die Tische**	-e	
	der Stuhl	**die Stühle**	¨e	
3	das Bild	**die Bilder**	-er	Stem vowel e or i cannot take umlaut
	das Buch	**die Bücher**	¨er	Stem vowel **a, o, u** takes umlaut
4	die Uhr	**die Uhren**	-en	
	die Lampe	**die Lampen**	-n	
	die Freundin	**die Freundinnen**	-nen	
5	das Radio	**die Radios**	-s	Mostly foreign words

9. Masculine N-nouns

	Singular	Plural
Nominative:	der Herr	die Herren
Accusative:	den Herrn	die Herren
Dative:	dem Herrn	den Herren
Genitive:	des Herrn	der Herren

Some other masculine N-nouns are **der Automat, der Bauer, der Journalist, der Junge, der Jurist, der Kollege, der Mensch, der Nachbar, der Neffe, der Patient, der Polizist, der Soldat, der Student, der Tourist.**

A few masculine N-nouns add -ns in the genitive: **der Name** > **des Namens; der Gedanke** > **des Gedankens; der Glaube** > **des Glaubens.**

10. Preceded adjectives

	Singular			Plural
	Masculine	Neuter	Feminine	
Nom.:	der **alte** Tisch ein **alter** Tisch	das **alte** Buch ein **altes** Buch	die **alte** Uhr eine **alte** Uhr	die **alten** Bilder keine **alten** Bilder
Acc.:	den **alten** Tisch einen **alten** Tisch	das **alte** Buch ein **altes** Buch	die **alte** Uhr eine **alte** Uhr	die **alten** Bilder keine **alten** Bilder
Dat.:	dem **alten** Tisch einem **alten** Tisch	dem **alten** Buch einem **alten** Buch	der **alten** Uhr einer **alten** Uhr	den **alten** Bildern keinen **alten** Bildern
Gen.:	des **alten** Tisches eines **alten** Tisches	des **alten** Buches eines **alten** Buches	der **alten** Uhr einer **alten** Uhr	der **alten** Bilder keiner **alten** Bilder

11. Unpreceded adjectives

	Masculine	Neuter	Feminine	Plural
Nominative:	kalter Wein	kaltes Bier	kalte Milch	alte Leute
Accusative:	kalten Wein	kaltes Bier	kalte Milch	alte Leute
Dative:	kaltem Wein	kaltem Bier	kalter Milch	alten Leuten
Genitive:	kalten Weines	kalten Bieres	kalter Milch	alter Leute

12. Nouns declined like adjectives

a. Nouns preceded by definite articles or **dieser**-words

	Masculine	Neuter	Feminine	Plural
Nominative:	der Deutsche	das Gute	die Deutsche	die Deutschen
Accusative:	den Deutschen	das Gute	die Deutsche	die Deutschen
Dative:	dem Deutschen	dem Guten	der Deutschen	den Deutschen
Genitive:	des Deutschen	des Guten	der Deutschen	der Deutschen

b. Nouns preceded by indefinite article or **ein**-words

	Masculine	Neuter	Feminine	Plural
Nominative:	ein Deutscher	ein Gutes	eine Deutsche	keine Deutschen
Accusative:	einen Deutschen	ein Gutes	eine Deutsche	keine Deutschen
Dative:	einem Deutschen	einem Guten	einer Deutschen	keinen Deutschen
Genitive:	eines Deutschen	—	einer Deutschen	keiner Deutschen

Other nouns declined like adjectives are **der / die Angestellte, Bekannte, Erwachsene, Fremde, Jugendliche, Verwandte.** Note: **der Beamte** but **die Beamtin.**

13. Comparison of irregular adjectives and adverbs

Base form:	gern	gut	hoch	nah	viel
Comparative:	lieber	besser	höher	näher	mehr
Superlative:	liebst-	best-	höchst-	nächst-	meist-

14. Prepositions

With accusative	With dative	With either accusative or dative	With genitive
bis	aus	an	(an)statt
durch	außer	auf	trotz
entlang	bei	hinter	während
für	entgegen	in	wegen
gegen	gegenüber	neben	diesseits
ohne	mit	über	jenseits
um	nach	unter	oberhalb
wider	seit	vor	unterhalb
	von	zwischen	innerhalb
	zu		außerhalb

15. Verbs and prepositions with special meanings

achten auf (+ *acc.*)	aufhören mit	bestehen aus
antworten auf (+ *acc.*)	beginnen mit	bitten um

blicken auf (+ *acc.*)
danken für
denken an (+ *acc.*)
diskutieren über (+ *acc.*)
sich erinnern an (+ *acc.*)
erkennen an (+ *dat.*)
erzählen von or über
   (+ *acc.*)
fliehen vor (+ *dat.*)
fragen nach
sich fürchten vor (+ *dat.*)
sich gewöhnen an (+ *acc.*)
halten für

halten von
helfen bei
hoffen auf (+ *acc.*)
sich interessieren für
klettern auf (+ *acc.*)
lachen über (+ *acc.*)
leiden an (+ *dat.*)
riechen nach
schicken nach
schimpfen auf (+ *acc.*)
schreiben an (+ *acc.*)
schreiben über (+ *acc.*)
sorgen für

sprechen über (+ *acc.*) or
   von
sterben an (+ *dat.*)
suchen nach
teilnehmen an (+ *dat.*)
warten auf (+ *acc.*)
sich wenden an (+ *acc.*)
werden aus
wohnen bei
zeigen auf (+ *acc.*)
zweifeln an (+ *dat.*)

16. Dative verbs

antworten	erlauben	gehören	nützen	schmecken
befehlen	fehlen	gelingen	passen	verzeihen
begegnen	folgen	glauben	passieren	weh tun
danken	gefallen	helfen	raten	
dienen	gehorchen	leid tun	schaden	

The verbs **glauben, erlauben,** and **verzeihen** may take an impersonal accusative object: **ich glaube es; ich erlaube es.**

17. Present tense

		lernen[1]	arbeiten[2]	tanzen[3]	geben[4]	lesen[5]	fahren[6]	laufen[7]	auf·stehen[8]
	ich:	lerne	arbeite	tanze	gebe	lese	fahre	laufe	stehe...auf
	du:	lernst	arbeitest	tanzt	gibst	liest	fährst	läufst	stehst...auf
er / es / sie:		lernt	arbeitet	tanzt	gibt	liest	fährt	läuft	steht...auf
	wir:	lernen	arbeiten	tanzen	geben	lesen	fahren	laufen	stehen...auf
	ihr:	lernt	arbeitet	tanzt	gebt	lest	fahrt	lauft	steht...auf
	sie:	lernen	arbeiten	tanzen	geben	lesen	fahren	laufen	stehen...auf
	Sie:	lernen	arbeiten	tanzen	geben	lesen	fahren	laufen	stehen...auf
Imper. sg.:		lern(e)	arbeite	tanz(e)	gib	lies	fahr(e)	lauf(e)	steh(e)...auf

1. The endings are used for all verbs except the modals, **wissen, werden,** and **sein.**
2. A verb with stem ending in **-d, -t,** or **-m, -n** preceded by another consonant (except **-l** or **-r**) has an **e** before the **-st** and **-t** endings.

3. The **-st** ending of the 2nd person contracts to **-t** when the verb stem ends in a sibilant (**-s, -ss, -ß, -z** or **-tz**). Thus the 2nd and 3rd persons are identical.
4. Some strong verbs have a stem-vowel change **e > i** in the 2nd and 3rd person singular and the imperative singular.
5. Some strong verbs have a stem-vowel change **e > ie** in the 2nd and 3rd person singular and the imperative singular. The strong verbs **gehen, heben,** and **stehen** do not change their stem vowel.
6. Some strong verbs have a stem-vowel change **a > ä** in the 2nd and 3rd person singular.
7. Some strong verbs have a stem-vowel change **au > äu** in the 2nd and 3rd person singular.
8. In the present tense, separable prefixes are separated from the verb and are in last position.

18. Simple past tense

	Weak verbs		Strong verbs
	lernen[1]	arbeiten[2]	geben[3]
ich:	lernte	arbeitete	gab
du:	lerntest	arbeitetest	gabst
er / es / sie:	lernte	arbeitete	gab
wir:	lernten	arbeiteten	gaben
ihr:	lerntet	arbeitetet	gabt
sie:	lernten	arbeiteten	gaben
Sie:	lernten	arbeiteten	gaben

1. Weak verbs have the past-tense marker **-te** plus endings.
2. A weak verb with stem endings in **-d, -t,** or **-m, -n** preceded by another consonant (except **-l** or **-r**) has a past-tense marker **-ete** plus endings.
3. Strong verbs have a stem-vowel change plus endings.

19. Auxiliaries *haben, sein, werden*

ich:	habe	bin	werde
du:	hast	bist	wirst
er / es / sie:	hat	ist	wird
wir:	haben	sind	werden
ihr:	habt	seid	werdet
sie:	haben	sind	werden
Sie:	haben	sind	werden

20. Modal auxiliaries: present, simple past, and past participle

	dürfen	können	mögen	müssen	sollen	wollen
ich:	darf	kann	mag	muß	soll	will
du:	darfst	kannst	magst	mußt	sollst	willst
er / es / sie:	darf	kann	mag	muß	soll	will
wir:	dürfen	können	mögen	müssen	sollen	wollen
ihr:	dürft	könnt	mögt	müßt	sollt	wollt
sie:	dürfen	können	mögen	müssen	sollen	wollen
Sie:	dürfen	können	mögen	müssen	sollen	wollen
Simple past:	durfte	konnte	mochte	mußte	sollte	wollte
Past participle:	gedurft	gekonnt	gemocht	gemußt	gesollt	gewollt

21. Verb conjugations: strong verbs *sehen* and *gehen*

a. Indicative

	Present		Simple past	
ich:	sehe	gehe	sah	ging
du:	siehst	gehst	sahst	gingst
er / es / sie:	sieht	geht	sah	ging
wir:	sehen	gehen	sahen	gingen
ihr:	seht	geht	saht	gingt
sie:	sehen	gehen	sahen	gingen
Sie:	sehen	gehen	sahen	gingen

	Present perfect				Past perfect			
ich:	habe		bin		hatte		war	
du:	hast		bist		hattest		warst	
er / es / sie:	hat		ist		hatte		war	
wir:	haben	gesehen	sind	gegangen	hatten	gesehen	waren	gegangen
ihr:	habt		seid		hattet		wart	
sie:	haben		sind		hatten		waren	
Sie:	haben		sind		hatten		waren	

	Future			
ich:	werde		werde	
du:	wirst		wirst	
er / es / sie:	wird		wird	
wir:	werden	sehen	werden	gehen
ihr:	werdet		werdet	
sie:	werden		werden	
Sie:	werden		werden	

b. Imperative

	Imperative	
Familiar singular:	Sieh!	Geh(e)!
Familiar plural:	Seht!	Geht!
Formal:	Sehen Sie!	Gehen Sie!

c. Subjunctive

	Present-time subjunctive			
	General subjunctive		Special subjunctive	
ich:	sähe	ginge	sehe	gehe
du:	sähest	gingest	sehest	gehest
er / es / sie:	sähe	ginge	sehe	gehe
wir:	sähen	gingen	sehen	gehen
ihr:	sähet	ginget	sehet	gehet
sie:	sähen	gingen	sehen	gehen
Sie:	sähen	gingen	sehen	gehen

Past-time subjunctive							
General subjunctive				**Special subjunctive**			
ich:	hätte		wäre		habe		sei
du:	hättest		wärest		habest		seiest
er / es / sie:	hätte		wäre		habe		sei
wir:	hätten	gesehen	wären	gegangen	haben	gesehen	seien	gegangen
ihr:	hättet		wäret		habet		seiet
sie:	hätten		wären		haben		seien
Sie:	hätten		wären		haben		seien

Future-time subjunctive							
General subjunctive				**Special subjunctive**			
ich:	würde		würde		werde		werde
du:	würdest		würdest		werdest		werdest
er / es / sie:	würde		würde		werde		werde
wir:	würden	sehen	würden	gehen	werden	sehen	werden	gehen
ihr:	würdet		würdet		werdet		werdet
sie:	würden		würden		werden		werden
Sie:	würden		würden		werden		werden

d. Passive voice

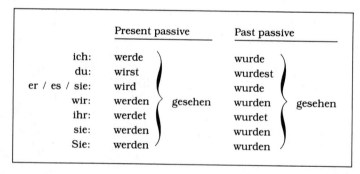

	Present passive		Past passive	
ich:	werde		wurde	
du:	wirst		wurdest	
er / es / sie:	wird		wurde	
wir:	werden	gesehen	wurden	gesehen
ihr:	werdet		wurdet	
sie:	werden		wurden	
Sie:	werden		wurden	

	Present perfect passive	Past perfect passive
ich:	bin	war
du:	bist	warst
er / es / sie:	ist	war
wir:	sind	waren
ihr:	seid	wart
sie:	sind	waren
Sie:	sind	waren

ich: bin ⎫
du: bist ⎪
er / es / sie: ist ⎬ gesehen worden
wir: sind ⎪
ihr: seid ⎪
sie: sind ⎪
Sie: sind ⎭

war ⎫
warst ⎪
war ⎬ gesehen worden
waren ⎪
wart ⎪
waren ⎪
waren ⎭

Future passive

ich: werde ⎫
du: wirst ⎪
er / es / sie: wird ⎬ gesehen werden
wir: werden ⎪
ihr: werdet ⎪
sie: werden ⎪
Sie: werden ⎭

22. Principal parts of strong and irregular weak verbs

The following list includes all the strong verbs and irregular weak verbs used in this book. Compound verbs like **hereinkommen** and **hinausgehen** are not included since the principal parts of those compound verbs are identical to the basic forms **kommen** and **gehen**. Inseparable prefix verbs like **beweisen** are included only when the basic verb (**weisen**) is not listed elsewhere in the table. Basic English equivalents are given for all verbs in this list. For additional meanings consult the German-English end vocabulary.

Infinitive	Present-tense vowel change	Simple past	Past participle	General subjunctive	Meaning
backen	bäckt	backte	gebacken	backte	*to bake*
beginnen		begann	begonnen	begönne (begänne)	*to begin*
befehlen	befiehlt	befahl	befohlen	beföhle (befähle)	*to command*
beißen		biß	gebissen	bisse	*to bite*
betrügen		betrog	betrogen	betröge	*to deceive*

Infinitive	Present-tense vowel change	Simple past	Past participle	General subjunctive	Meaning
beweisen		bewies	bewiesen	bewiese	to prove
biegen		bog	gebogen	böge	to bend
sich bewerben	bewirbt	bewarb	beworben	bewürbe	to apply for
bieten		bot	geboten	böte	to offer
binden		band	gebunden	bände	to bind
bitten		bat	gebeten	bäte	to request
bleiben		blieb	ist geblieben	bliebe	to remain
braten	brät	briet	gebraten	briete	to roast
brechen	bricht	brach	gebrochen	bräche	to break
brennen		brannte	gebrannt	brennte	to burn
bringen		brachte	gebracht	brächte	to bring
denken		dachte	gedacht	dächte	to think
entscheiden		entschied	entschieden	entschiede	to decide
empfehlen	empfiehlt	empfahl	empfohlen	empföhle	to recommend
erschrecken	erschrickt	erschrak	erschrocken	erschräke	to be frightened
essen	ißt	aß	gegessen	äße	to eat
fahren	fährt	fuhr	ist gefahren	führe	to drive; to travel
fallen	fällt	fiel	ist gefallen	fiele	to fall
fangen	fängt	fing	gefangen	finge	to catch
finden		fand	gefunden	fände	to find
fliegen		flog	ist geflogen	flöge	to fly
fliehen		floh	ist geflohen	flöhe	to flee
fließen		floß	ist geflossen	flösse	to flow
fressen	frißt	fraß	gefressen	fräße	to eat (of animals)
frieren		fror	gefroren	fröre	to freeze
geben	gibt	gab	gegeben	gäbe	to give
gehen		ging	ist gegangen	ginge	to go
gelingen		gelang	ist gelungen	gelänge	to succeed
gelten	gilt	galt	gegolten	gälte	to be worth
genießen		genoß	genossen	genösse	to enjoy
geschehen	geschieht	geschah	ist geschehen	geschähe	to happen
gewinnen		gewann	gewonnen	gewönne (gewänne)	to win
gießen		goß	gegossen	gösse	to pour
gleichen		glich	geglichen	gliche	to resemble
graben	gräbt	grub	gegraben	grübe	to dig
greifen		griff	gegriffen	griffe	to grab
haben	hat	hatte	gehabt	hätte	to have
halten	hält	hielt	gehalten	hielte	to hold
hängen		hing	gehangen	hinge	to hang
heißen		hieß	geheißen	hieße	to be called

Infinitive	Present-tense vowel change	Simple past	Past participle	General subjunctive	Meaning
helfen	hilft	half	geholfen	hülfe	to help
kennen		kannte	gekannt	kennte	to know
klingen		klang	geklungen	klänge	to sound
kommen		kam	ist gekommen	käme	to come
kriechen		kroch	ist gekrochen	kröche	to crawl
laden	lädt	lud	geladen	lüde	to load
lassen	läßt	ließ	gelassen	ließe	to let, permit
laufen	läuft	lief	ist gelaufen	liefe	to run
leiden		litt	gelitten	litte	to suffer
leihen		lieh	geliehen	liehe	to lend
lesen	liest	las	gelesen	läse	to read
liegen		lag	gelegen	läge	to lie
lügen		log	gelogen	löge	to tell a lie
messen	mißt	maß	gemessen	mäße	to measure
nehmen	nimmt	nahm	genommen	nähme	to take
nennen		nannte	genannt	nennte	to name
pfeifen		pfiff	gepfiffen	pfiffe	to whistle
raten	rät	riet	geraten	riete	to advise
reiben		rieb	gerieben	riebe	to rub
reißen		riß	gerissen	risse	to tear
reiten		ritt	ist geritten	ritte	to ride
rennen		rannte	ist gerannt	rennte	to run
riechen		roch	gerochen	röche	to smell
rufen		rief	gerufen	riefe	to call
schaffen		schuf	geschaffen	schüfe	to create
scheinen		schien	geschienen	schiene	to shine
schieben		schob	geschoben	schöbe	to push
schießen		schoß	geschossen	schösse	to shoot
schlafen	schläft	schlief	geschlafen	schliefe	to sleep
schlagen	schlägt	schlug	geschlagen	schlüge	to hit
schließen		schloß	geschlossen	schlösse	to shut
schneiden		schnitt	geschnitten	schnitte	to cut
schreiben		schrieb	geschrieben	schriebe	to write
schreien		schrie	geschrie(e)n	schriee	to cry out, scream
schreiten		schritt	ist geschritten	schritte	to step
schweigen		schwieg	geschwiegen	schwiege	to be silent
schwimmen		schwamm	ist geschwommen	schwömme (schwämme)	to swim
sehen	sieht	sah	gesehen	sähe	to see
sein	ist	war	ist gewesen	wäre	to be
senden		sandte	gesandt	sendete	to send
singen		sang	gesungen	sänge	to sing
sinken		sank	ist gesunken	sänke	to sink

Infinitive	Present-tense vowel change	Simple past	Past participle	General subjunctive	Meaning
sitzen		saß	gesessen	säße	*to sit*
spinnen		spann	gesponnen	spönne	*to spin*
sprechen	spricht	sprach	gesprochen	spräche	*to speak*
springen		sprang	ist gesprungen	spränge	*to spring*
stechen	sticht	stach	gestochen	stäche	*to sting, stick*
stehen		stand	gestanden	stände (stünde)	*to stand*
stehlen	stiehlt	stahl	gestohlen	stähle	*to steal*
steigen		stieg	ist gestiegen	stiege	*to climb*
sterben	stirbt	starb	ist gestorben	stürbe	*to die*
stinken		stank	gestunken	stänke	*to stink*
stoßen	stößt	stieß	gestoßen	stieße	*to push*
streichen		strich	gestrichen	striche	*to paint*
streiten		stritt	gestritten	stritte	*to quarrel*
tragen	trägt	trug	getragen	trüge	*to carry, wear*
treffen	trifft	traf	getroffen	träfe	*to meet*
treiben		trieb	getrieben	triebe	*to drive*
treten	tritt	trat	ist getreten	träte	*to step; to kick*
trinken		trank	getrunken	tränke	*to drink*
tun	tut	tat	getan	täte	*to do*
verderben	verdirbt	verdarb	verdorben	verdürbe	*to spoil*
vergessen	vergißt	vergaß	vergessen	vergäße	*to forget*
verlieren		verlor	verloren	verlöre	*to lose*
verzeihen		verzieh	verziehen	verziehe	*to pardon*
wachsen	wächst	wuchs	ist gewachsen	wüchse	*to grow*
waschen	wäscht	wusch	gewaschen	wüsche	*to wash*
wenden		wandte	gewandt	wendete	*to turn*
werden	wird	wurde	ist geworden	würde	*to become*
werfen	wirft	warf	geworfen	würfe	*to throw*
wiegen		wog	gewogen	wöge	*to weigh*
wissen	weiß	wußte	gewußt	wüßte	*to know*
ziehen		zog	gezogen	zöge	*to pull, move*
zwingen		zwang	gezwungen	zwänge	*to compel*

German-English Vocabulary

The German-English end vocabulary includes all words used in *Kaleidoskop* except common function words such as articles, pronouns, and possessive adjectives; days of the week; names of the months; numbers; obvious cognates; and words that are glossed in the margins but not used in exercises.

Words included in the basic list of 1,200 are marked with an asterisk (*). These words occur in the three standard frequency lists: *Das Zertifikat Deutsch als Fremdsprache* (Deutscher Volkshochschul-Verband and Goethe-Institut), *Grundwortschatz Deutsch* (Heinz Oehler), and *Grunddeutsch: Basic (Spoken) German Word List* (J. Alan Pfeffer).

Nouns are listed in this vocabulary with their plural forms: **die Aufgabe, -n**. No plural entry is given if the plural is rarely used or nonexistent. If two entries follow a noun, the first one indicates the genitive and the second one the plural: **der Vorname, -ns, -n**. For strong and irregular weak verbs, the vowel changes of the principal parts are given in parentheses. The present-tense vowel change is followed by a semicolon and the stem vowels in the simple past and past participle. Forms with consonant changes are written out in their entirety. All verbs take **haben** in the perfect tenses except those marked with [ist]: **fahren (ä; u, [ist] a)**. Separable prefix verbs are indicated with a raised dot: **auf·stehen**. Adjectives and adverbs that take umlaut in the comparative and superlative are noted as follows: **warm (ä)**.

The symbol ~ indicates repetition of a key word or phrase. Where appropriate, noun compounds or adjectives derived from nouns or verbs follow the main entries.

The following abbreviations are used in this vocabulary:

acc. accusative	*conj.* conjunction	*gen.* genitive
adj. adjective	*dat.* dative	*inf.* infinitive
adv. adverb	*decl.* declined	*pl.* plural
coll. colloquial		

*ab off, down, away; ~ und zu now and then

ab·bauen to remove; to demolish

ab·biegen (o, [ist] o) to turn off; to diverge

die Abbiegung, -en turn

ab·brechen (i, a, o) to break off

*der Abend, -e evening; am ~ in the evening

*das Abendessen, - supper

das Abendkleid, -er evening dress

*abends in the evening, evenings

das Abenteuer, - adventure

*aber but, however

*ab·fahren (ä; u, [ist] a) to depart; to drive off

die Abfahrt, -en departure

ab·fallen (ä; ie, [ist] a) to fall off

ab·fliegen (o, [ist] o) to fly off, take off (of an airplane)

ab·geben (i; a, e) to deliver; to release

ab·hängen von (i, a) to depend on

abhängig (von) dependent (on)

ab·hauen to take off

*ab·holen to fetch; to pick up

das Abitur final comprehensive examination at Gymnasium

ab·lehnen to refuse, reject

ab·machen to loosen, detach; to arrange

ab·nehmen (nimmt ab; a, abgenommen) to remove; to accept

ab·putzen to clean

ab·reisen ([ist]) to leave, to depart

ab·rüsten to disarm

der Absatz, ̈e paragraph

*ab·schaffen to get rid of, to abolish

der Abschied, -e departure, farewell; zum ~ at departure

ab·schließen (o, o) to close; to conclude

die Abschlußprüfung, -en final examination

ab·schneiden (schnitt ab, abgeschnitten) to cut off

der Abschnitt, -e section, paragraph

die Abschrift, -en copy

die Absicht, -en intention, purpose

absolut absolute

sich ab·spielen to take place

ab·springen (a, [ist] u) to jump down

ab·stauben to dust

ab·stoßen (ö; ie, o) to repel

absurd absurd

die Abteilung, -en division; compartment

*ab·trocknen to dry off; to dry dishes

abwärts downward

ab·waschen (ä; u, a) to wash dishes

sich ab·wenden (a, [ist] a) to turn away

ab·zahlen to pay off

der Abzählreim, -e counting rhyme

*ach oh

achten to esteem, respect; to pay attention

acht·geben (i; a, e) to pay attention

die Achtung attention; esteem, respect

adäquat adequate

das Adjektiv, -e adjective

*die Adresse, -en address

der Advent, -e advent

das Adverb, -ien adverb

der Agent, -en, -en agent

*aggressiv aggressive

ähnlich (+ dat.) similar; das sieht ihm ~ that's just like him

die Ähnlichkeit, -en similarity

die Ahnung, -en presentiment, idea; keine ~ no idea

akademisch having university training

*aktiv active

die Aktivität, -en activity

aktuell current, contemporary

*akzeptieren to accept

alarmiert alarmed

der Alkohol alcohol

*alle all, everybody

*allein(e) alone

alleinstehend single

allerbest best of all

allerdings of course; to be sure

*alles everything

*allgemein general

alliiert allied

allmählich gradual

der Alltag, -e daily life

alltäglich commonplace; daily

die Alpen Alps

*als when; than

*als ob as if

*also thus, therefore

*alt(ä) old

das Alter age, old age

alternativ alternative

*(das) Amerika America, USA

*der Amerikaner, - (m)/die Amerikanerin, -nen (f) American

*amerikanisch American

die Ampel, -n traffic light

das Amt, ̈er office; appointment

*an (+ dat./acc.) at, on, to

analysieren to analyze

*an·bieten (o, o) to offer

der Anblick, -e sight, view

an·blicken to look at

andauernd lasting, continuous

*andere other; different

andererseits on the other hand

*ändern to change

*anders different

anderswo elsewhere

die Änderung, -en alteration, change

an·drehen to turn on

die Anekdote, -n anecdote

an·erkennen (a, a) to acknowledge

*der Anfang, ̈e beginning, start

*an·fangen (ä; i, a) to start, to begin

anfangs in the beginning

an·fassen to touch

angeblich alleged

das Angebot, -e offer

angeführt quoted, cited

angegeben indicated; provided

an·gehen (ging an, [ist] angegangen) to begin; to concern; **das geht mich nichts an** that doesn't concern me

an·gehören (+ *dat.*) to belong to

die Angelegenheit, -en matter, affair

der/die Angelernte, -n semi-skilled worker (*noun decl. like adj.*)

***angenehm** (+ *dat.*) pleasant

der/die Angestellte (*noun decl. like adj.*) employee; official

an·greifen (i, i) to attack

der Angriff, -e attack

***die Angst, ̈e** fright, anxiety; **~ haben vor** (+ *dat.*) to be frightened of

ängstlich (wegen) anxious, uneasy (about)

an·halten (ä; ie, a) to stop; to hold

an·hören to listen to, to hear

an·klagen to accuse

***an·kommen (kam, [ist] o)** to arrive

die Anlage, -n establishment

an·legen to apply; to invest; to establish

der Anlernberuf, -e job requiring on-the-job training

an·machen to attach; to light (fire)

an·malen to paint

***an·nehmen (nimmt an; a, angenommen)** to accept; to assume; **Schritt ~** to fall into step

die Anordnung, -en arrangement; regulation, order

die Anredeform, -en form of address

an·reden to address, speak to

der Anruf, -e phone call

***an·rufen (ie, u)** to call up, to telephone

die Anschaffung, -en acquisition

an·schauen to look at, to contemplate

anscheinend apparently

***an·sehen (ie; a, e)** to look at

die Ansicht, -e view, opinion; **die Ansichtskarte, -n** picture post card

an·sprechen (i; a, o) to speak to; to please

die Anstalt, -en establishment; preparation

anständig decent

***anstatt** (+ *gen.*) instead of

an·stellen to employ

(sich) an·strengen to exert; **anstrengend** exhausting

die Anstrengung, -en exertion; effort

die Anthologie, -n collection of literary works

antiamerikanisch anti-American

der Antiamerikanismus anti-Americanism

***die Antwort, -en** answer

***antworten** to answer; **antworten auf** (+ *acc.*) to reply to

die Anzeige, -n advertisement, notice

an·zeigen to advertise; to report; to show

***an·ziehen (zog an, angezogen)** to get dressed; to attract

***der Anzug, ̈e** suit, clothes

an·zünden to light

***der Apfel, ̈** apple

der Apfelkuchen, - apple cake

***die Apotheke, -n** pharmacy

***der Apotheker, -** (*m*)/**die Apothekerin, -nen** (*f*) pharmacist

***der Apparat, -e** apparatus, appliance

***der Appetit** appetite; **appetitlich** appetizing

applaudieren to applaud

der Applaus applause

das Äquivalent, -e equivalent

***die Arbeit, -en** work; exam; **an die ~ gehen** to begin to work; **sich an die ~ machen**

to start; **der Arbeitgeber, -** employer; **der Arbeitnehmer, -** employee; **das Arbeitsamt, ̈er** employment office; **die Arbeitsgruppe, -n** study group; **der Arbeitshandschuh, -e** work glove; **die Arbeitskraft, ̈e** worker; **der/die Arbeitslose** (*noun decl. like adj.*) unemployed worker; **der Arbeitsmarkt, ̈e** job market; **der Arbeitsplatz, ̈e** place of work; **die Arbeitsstunde, -n** working hour; **die Arbeitsteilung, -** division of work; **die Arbeitsvorbereitung, -en** preparation for a job; **die Arbeitswelt** world of work; **die Arbeitszeit** working hours; **das Arbeitszimmer, -** study

***arbeiten** to work

***der Arbeiter, -** (*m*)/**die Arbeiterin, -nen** (*f*) worker; **die Arbeiterschaft** workers, working class

arbeitsam hard-working

arbeitsfrei to be off from work

arbeitslos unemployed

der Architekt, -en, -en (*m*)/**die Architektin, -nen** (*f*) architect

(das) Argentinien Argentina

der Ärger vexation, anger

ärgerlich (über + *acc.*) irritable, angry (about, over)

***ärgern** to annoy; **sich ~** to become angry

das Argument, -e reason, proof

***arm** poor

der Arm, -e arm; **auf den ~ nehmen** to tease

ärmlich poor; poorly

arrogant arrogant

das Arsenal, -e arsenal

***die Art, -en** manner; kind, species

die Arthritis arthritis

***der Artikel, -** article; goods

***der Arzt, ̈e** (*m*)/**die Ärztin, -nen** (*f*) medical doctor die Arzthelferin, -nen doctor's assistant

der Aspekt, -e aspect

der Asphalt, -e asphalt

der Assistent, -en, -en (m) die Assistentin, -nen (f) assistant

assoziieren to associate

das Asthma asthma

der Atem breath, respiration

atemlos out of breath

athletisch athletic

*atmen to breathe

das Atom, -e atom; das Atomkraftwerk, -e nuclear power plant; der Atomphysiker, - nuclear physicist

attraktiv attractive

*auch also, too, likewise; indeed

*auf (+ dat./acc.) on, upon; upward; open

auf·bauen to erect; to set up

auf·bleiben (ie, [ist] ie) to stay up

auf·brechen (i; a, o) to break open

auf·drehen to turn up; to turn on

der Aufenthalt, -e stay; residence

auf·essen (i; a, e) to eat up

auf·fahren (ä; u, [ist] a) to start up

*auf·fallen (ä; ie, [ist] a) to be noticeable, to attract attention

auf·fliegen (o, [ist] o) to blow off

auf·fordern to order, to command

*die Aufgabe, -n task; assignment

auf·geben (i; a, e) to give up; to deliver

aufgeschlossen open-minded

aufgetakelt rigged up

auf·halten (ä; ie, a) to stop; to open

auf·hängen to hang (up), to suspend

auf·heben (o, o) to pick up; to cancel

*auf·hören to stop, quit

auf·kochen to boil up; to boil

auf·lösen to dissolve, break up

*auf·machen to open

*aufmerksam (auf + acc.) attentive (to)

die Aufmerksamkeit attention, attentiveness

auf·nehmen (nimmt auf; a, aufgenommen) to take a photograph; to take up

*auf·passen (paßt auf; paßte auf, aufgepaßt) to pay attention

auf·räumen to clear away

aufrecht erect; ~ erhalten to maintain

sich auf·regen to get excited

die Aufregung, -en excitement, irritation

der Aufreißer, - playboy

auf·rufen (ie, u) to call up

auf·rüsten to build up arms

die Aufrüstung, -en (re)arming

der Aufsatz, ⸗e composition

auf·schauen to look up

auf·schließen (o, o) to open, to unlock

auf·schreiben (ie, ie) to write down

auf·sehen (ie; a, e) to look up

auf·setzen to set up; to put on

auf·springen (a, [ist] u) to jump up

*auf·stehen (stand auf, [ist] aufgestanden) to get up, to rise, to stand open

auf·steigen (ie, [ist] ie) to rise

auf·stellen to put up; to arrange

auf·suchen to seek out

auf·treten (i; a, [ist] e) to appear, to rise

auf·wachen to wake up

aufwärts upward

*das Auge, -n eye

*der Augenblick, -e moment, instant

augenblicklich at present

*aus (+ dat.) out of, from

aus·bauen to complete; to improve

aus·bilden to educate

die Ausbildung, -en education; die Ausbildungsabschluß-prüfung, -en final exam

aus·brechen (i; a, [ist] o) to escape, to break out

der Ausbruch, ⸗e escape

aus·denken (dachte aus, ausgedacht) to imagine; to make up

*der Ausdruck, ⸗e expression; ausdruckslos expressionless

aus·drücken to express

auseinander·nehmen (nimmt auseinander; a, auseinan-dergenommen) to take apart

aus·fahren (ä; u, [ist] a) to drive out

*der Ausflug, ⸗e excursion

aus·füllen to fill out

*aus·geben (i; a, e) to spend; to give out

aus·gehen (ging aus, ist ausgegangen) to go out; to turn out

ausgeschlossen impossible

*ausgezeichnet excellent

aus·graben (ä; u, a) to unearth

aus·halten (ä; ie, a) to endure, stand; to suffer

aus·kommen (a, [ist] o) to get along

die Auskunft, ⸗e information

*das Ausland foreign country; der Ausländer, -(m)/die Ausländerin, -nen (f) foreigner, alien; ausländisch foreign

aus·machen to put out; to plan, arrange; es macht mir nichts aus it doesn't matter

die Ausnahme, -n exception

aus·packen to unpack

das Auspuffrohr, -e exhaust pipe

aus·rechnen to calculate

die Ausrede, -n excuse; faule Ausreden lame excuses

aus·reden to utter, finish speaking

aus·reichen to suffice

aus·rufen (ie, u) to exclaim; to call out

sich aus·ruhen to rest

aus·schieben (o, o) to shove out

aus·schließen (schloß aus, ausgeschlossen) to exclude

der Ausschuß, -üsse committee

*aus·sehen (ie; a, e) to look, to appear; aussehend: gut ~ good looking

das Aussehen appearance

aus·sein (ist aus; war aus, [ist] ausgewesen) to be switched off

außen outside

*außer (+ dat.) except

*außerdem besides, moreover

außergewöhnlich exceptional

*außerhalb (+ gen.) outside, beyond

außerordentlich exceptional

äußerst extreme

die Äußerung, -en utterance, expression

die Aussicht, -en view, perspective; prospect

die Aussprache, -n pronunciation

aus·sprechen (i; a, o) to pronounce

aus·stehen (stand aus, ausgestanden) to endure

*aus·steigen (ie, [ist] ie) to get out (of vehicle); to drop out

der Aussteiger, - (m)/die Aussteigerin, -nen (f) drop-out

aus·stellen to exhibit

die Ausstellung, -en exhibition

aus·stoßen (ö; ie, o) to expel, throw out; to utter

der Austausch exchange; der Austauschler, - exchange student

aus·üben to exercise; to exert

aus·wählen to choose, to select

aus·wandern ([ist]) to emigrate

ausweichend evasive

der Ausweis, -e identification card

das Ausweispapier, -e identification papers

auswendig from memory

*aus·ziehen (zog aus, ausgezogen) to undress; ~ (zog aus, [ist] ausgezogen) to move out

*das Auto, -s car; *die Autobahn, -en interstate highway, expressway

die Autobiographie, -n autobiography

*der Autobus, -se bus; der Autofahrer, - car driver; die Autostraße, -n highway, road for cars

der Automat, -en, -en machine that runs by itself; vending machine

automatisch automatic

der Autor, -en (m)/die Autorin, -nen (f) author

autoritär authoritarian

der/die Azubi (Auszubildende) (noun decl. like adj.) apprentice, trainee

*das Baby, -s baby

*backen (ä; backte, gebacken) to bake

*der Bäcker, - baker

die Bäckerei, -en bakery

*das Bad, ̈er bath; die Badewanne, -n bathtub; *das Badezimmer, - bathroom; die Badetasche, -n beach or swimming bag

*baden to bathe

*die Bahn, -en train; track; road

*der Bahnhof, ̈e train station; das Bahnhofsrestaurant, -s a restaurant inside a railway station

der Bahnpolizist, -en, -en railway policeman

*der Bahnsteig, -e platform

*bald (eher, ehest) soon; bald ... bald now ... now; ~ darauf a short time later

*der Ball, ̈e ball; dance

die Ballade, -n ballad

das Band, ̈er ribbon; tape

der Band, ̈e volume (book)

die Band, -s band

die Bandarbeit, -en assembly-line work

*die Bank, ̈e bench

*die Bank, -en bank

die Bar, -s bar, pub

der Bär, -en, -en bear

der Bart, ̈e beard

basiert based

die Basis, Basen basis

basteln to build, to work on a hobby

die Bastion, -en fortress, bastion

der Bau, -ten building; die Bauart, -en type of construction, design

der Bauch, ̈e belly, stomach

*bauen to build, to construct

*der Bauer, -n, -n (m)/die Bäuerin, -nen (f) farmer

*der Baum, ̈e tree

das Bayern Bavaria

beachten to observe

*der Beamte, -n, -n (m)/die Beamtin, -nen (f) official

beantworten to answer

der Becher, - goblet, mug

sich bedanken to thank

bedauern to pity

*bedeuten to mean; to point out; bedeutend significant; bedeutsam significant

*die Bedeutung, -en meaning; importance; bedeutungslos meaningless

bedienen to serve

die Bedingung, -en condition; restriction

bedrohen to threaten

die Bedrohung, -en threat

*sich beeilen to hurry

beeinflussen to influence

beenden to finish

der Befehl, -e order

befehlen (ie; a; o) (+ dat. of person) to command

befreien to free; rescue

die Befreiung, -en liberation

befürchten to fear

*begegnen ([ist]) (+ dat.) to meet

die Begegnung, -en meeting

begeistert enthusiastic

die Begeisterung, -en enthusiasm

der Beginn beginning

*beginnen (a, o) to begin

begleiten to accompany

begreifen (begriff, begriffen) to understand; to touch

der Begriff, -e conception, idea

begründen to justify; support

die Begrüßung, -en welcome; greeting

behalten (ä; ie, a) to keep, retain

behandeln to treat; to handle

*behaupten to assert

die Behauptung, -en claim, assertion

*bei (+ dat.) at; near

*beide both

bei·legen to enclose (in a letter)

*das Bein, -e leg; sich auf die Beine machen to leave

beinahe almost

*das Beispiel, -e example; zum ~ for example

beißen (biß, gebissen) to bite

*bekannt (für) familiar; well known (for); mir ~ known to me

*der/die Bekannte (noun decl. like adj.) acquaintance, friend

sich beklagen to complain

beknackt stupid; foolish

*bekommen (bekam, bekommen) to get, to receive

belästigt bothered, annoyed

belebt lively; crowded

beleidigen to insult

beliebt popular

bellen to bark

belohnen to reward

die Belohnung, -en reward

bemalen to paint; bemalt painted

*bemerken to mention; to notice; to realize

bemerkenswert remarkable

die Bemerkung, -en comment; observation

benachbart adjacent, neighboring

benachteiligen to put at a disadvantage

*sich benehmen (benimmt sich; a, sich benommen) to behave

das Benehmen behavior

*benutzen/benützen to use

*das Benzin gasoline

beobachten to observe

die Beobachtung, -en observation

*bequem comfortable

*bereit (zu) ready, prepared (for)

bereiten to prepare

bereits already

die Bereitschaft readiness to help

*der Berg, -e mountain

bergsteigen to climb mountains

*der Bericht, -e report

*berichten to report

*der Beruf, -e profession; die Berufsausbildung education for a profession; die Berufswahl choice of a profession; die Berufswelt world of work; der Berufswunsch, ⁻e preference of profession; die Berufsschule, -n vocational school

beruflich professional

berufstätig employed

der/die Berufstätige (noun decl. like adj.) someone with a job

beruhigen to comfort, to calm

*berühmt (wegen) famous (for)

beschäftigen to occupy

beschäftigt (mit) occupied (by, with)

die Beschäftigung, -en occupation; pursuit

beschämt (über + acc.) ashamed (about)

bescheiden modest

*beschließen (beschloß, beschlossen) to decide; to conclude

der Beschluß, ⁻sse decision

*beschreiben (ie, ie) to describe

die Beschreibung, -en description

sich beschweren to complain

besetzen to occupy

besetzt occupied; busy (telephone)

*besitzen (besaß, besessen) to own; to possess

*besonder special

*besonders especially

besorgt (um, für) anxious, concerned (about, over)

*besser better

bestehen (bestand, bestanden) to persist; to pass (exam); ~ (aus) to consist of; ~ (auf + acc.) to insist upon

besteigen (ie, ie) to climb

*bestellen to order

die Bestellung, -en order

bestimmen to determine

*bestimmt probably; sure; certain; particular; bestimmt zu destined for, determined for

bestrafen to punish

die Bestrafung, -en punishment

*besuchen to visit; to attend

*der Besuch, -e visit

der Besucher, - (m)/die Besucherin, -nen (f) visitor

beten to pray

betonen to emphasize

betrachten to observe; to regard; to consider

beträchtlich considerable

betreffen (i; a, o) to concern

betreten (i; a, e) to enter

der Betrieb, -e business, firm; der Betriebswirt, -e economist

betrügen (o, o) to deceive; to cheat

betrunken drunk

*das Bett, -en bed; Betten machen to make beds; das Bettuch, ⁻er sheet

beurteilen to judge

die Bevölkerung, -en population

*bevor *(conj.)* before
bevorzugen to favor, to prefer
*(sich) bewegen to move;
  beweglich flexible
die Bewegung, -en movement
der Beweis, -e proof
*beweisen (ie, ie) to prove
sich bewerben (i; a, o) to apply
der Bewerber, - *(m)*/die
  Bewerberin, -nen *(f)*
  candidate, applicant
die Bewerbung, -en application
bewußt conscious; aware
das Bewußtsein
  consciousness; awareness
*bezahlen to pay
die Bezahlung, -en payment
sich beziehen (o, o) to relate;
  to refer
die Beziehung, -en relation
bezug: in bezug auf *(acc.)* in
  regard to
die Bibel, -n Bible
*die Bibliothek, -en library
biegen (o, o) to bend
*das Bier, -e beer
*bieten (o, o) to offer; to show
*das Bild, -er picture; bildhaft
  clear as a picture; bildschön
  pretty as a picture
(sich) bilden to form; to
  educate
*billig cheap
*binden (a, u) to bind, tie
das Bio-Brot, -e organic bread
die Biographie, -n biography
die Birne, -n pear
*bis *(+ acc.)* until; as far as; by
  (time); ~ dann until then
  (later)
bisher so far; as yet; till now
bisherig previous
*bißchen: ein bißchen a little
*bitte please
*bitten (bat, gebeten) (um) to
  beg; to ask
bitter bitter; severe
blank shining
blasen (ä; ie, a) to blow
blaß (vor + *dat.)* pale
das Blatt, ̈er leaf; sheet of
  paper

blättern to turn over pages
*blau blue; ~ sein to be drunk
das Blei lead
*bleiben (ie, [ist] ie) to remain
*der Bleistift, -e lead pencil
der Blick, -e view; glance
blicken to look
blind blind
der Blitz, -e lightning; flash
blitzen to flash; lightning
der Block, ̈e block of countries
  like NATO or Warsaw Pact
blöd(e) dumb
blond blonde
bloß only; simply; bare
*blühen to bloom, flourish
*die Blume, -n flower; das
  Blumenbeet, -e flower bed;
  der Blumenladen, ̈ flower
  shop; der Blumenstrauß, ̈e
  bouquet
*die Bluse, -n blouse
das Blut blood
*der Boden, ̈ ground; floor;
  attic
die Bombe, -n bomb
*das Boot, -e boat
Bord: an ~ on board ship; das
  Bordklima atmosphere on
  shipboard
borgen to borrow; to lend
*böse (auf or über) (+ *acc.)*
  mean; angry (at, about); mir ~
  angry at me
der Boß, -sse boss
brackig brackish
*braten (ä; ie, a) to fry; to roast
*der Braten, - roast
brauchbar useful
*brauchen to need
*braun brown
*brechen (i; a, o) to break; to
  crush
*breit broad, wide
die Bremse, -n brake
bremsen to stop, apply the
  brakes
*brennen (a, a) to burn
das Brett, -er board
*der Brief, -e letter
*die Briefmarke, -n stamp
*die Brille, -n eyeglasses

*bringen (brachte, gebracht) to
  bring
britisch British
*das Brot, -e bread; sandwich
*das Brötchen, - roll
die Brote *(pl.)* sandwiches
*die Brücke, -n bridge
*der Bruder, ̈ brother
brünett brunette
der Brunnen, - well
brüsk harsh
*die Brust, ̈e breast; chest
brutal brutal
*das Buch, ̈er book; der
  Bücherwurm, ̈er book-
  worm; die Buchhandlung, -en
  bookstore
die Buche, -n beech tree
der Buchhalter, - *(m)*/die
  Buchhalterin, -nen *(f)*
  bookkeeper
der Buchstabe, -ns, -n letter
  (of alphabet)
das Budget, -s budget
bügeln to iron
die Bühne, -n stage
der Bund confederacy; der
  Bundeskanzler, - chancellor;
  das Bundesland, ̈er state;
  die Bundesregierung federal
  government; die
  Bundesstraße, -n highway;
  der Bundestag West German
  Parliament; die Bundeswehr
  army of the FRG
*die Bundesrepublik
  Deutschland Federal
  Republic of Germany
*bunt multi-colored
der Bürger, - citizen; die
  Bürgerinitiative, -n officially
  recognized citizens' action
  group; der Bürgermeister, -
  mayor
*das Büro, -s office; der/die
  Büroangestellte *(noun decl.
  like adj.)* office employee; die
  Bürofachkraft, ̈e office
  employee; der Bürokaufmann,
  die Bürokaufleute office
  clerk
*die Bürste, -n brush

*der Bus, -se   bus
*die Butter   butter; das
  Butterbrot, -e   sandwich
bzw. *abbreviation for*
  beziehungsweise
  respectively, relatively

*das Café, -s   café
*das Camping   camping out;
  *der Campingplatz, -e
  campground
das Cello, -s   cello
das Centrum, Centren   center;
  downtown
die Chance, -n   opportunity
der Charakter, -e   character;
  charakteristisch
  characteristic
charakterisieren   to
  characterize
*der Chef, -s *(m)*/die Chefin, -nen
  (f) boss
die Chemie   chemistry;
  chemiefrei   without
  chemicals
der Chor, ˚e   choir
der Club, -s   club
der Cognac, -s   cognac
das/die Cola, -s   cola drink
die Comics   comics
das Compositum, -a
  compound
*der Computer, -   computer
die Couch, -es   sofa; der
  Couchtisch, -e   coffee table
*die Cousine, -n   cousin *(f.)*

*da *(adv.)*   there; then; da
  drüben   over there
*da *(conj.)*   as; since
dabei   thereby; near; moreover
*das Dach, ˚er   roof
dadurch   thereby; by that
dafür   therefore; for this
dagegen   against it; on the
  other hand
*daher   therefore
*dahin   there; away; gone
dahinter   behind
*damals   at that time; then
*die Dame, -n   lady
*damit   in order that; with that

danach   after that; accordingly
daneben   beside it; besides;
  near
dank   thanks to
*der Dank   reward, thanks
*dankbar (für)   grateful (for); mir
  ~   grateful to me; die
  Dankbarkeit   gratitude
*danken (+ *dat. of person*)   to
  thank
*dann   then
daran   at, on; about
darauf   thereupon; afterward
daraus   therefrom
darin   inside, within
dar·stellen   to present; to
  describe
die Darstellung, -en
  presentation; description
darüber   over it; across it;
  about it
*darum   therefore; around it
darunter   under it; among
  them
*daß   that *(conj.)*
*dasselbe   the same
der Datenverarbeiter, -   data
  processor
das Datum, Daten   date
die Dauer   duration; auf die ~
  for a long time
*dauern   to last; dauernd
  continually
die Dauerstellung   permanent
  job
davon   of it; away
*dazu   to this; in addition; for
  this purpose
die Debatte, -n   debate
debattieren   to debate
*die Decke, -n   blanket; ceiling
decken   to cover; den Tisch ~
  to set the table
die Definition, -en   definition
die Delikatesse, -n   delicacy
demnächst   shortly, soon
die Demokratie, -n   democracy
demokratisch   democratic
der Demonstrant, -en, -en
  demonstrator; die
  Demonstration, -en
  demonstration

demonstrieren   to demonstrate
denkbar   thinkable, conceivable
*denken (dachte, gedacht)   to
  think; ~ an (+ *acc.*)   to think
  of
*denn   for, because
dennoch   yet, however
das Derby, -s   derby, horse race
*deren   whose
*derselbe   the same
*deshalb   therefore, for that
  reason
desillusionieren   to disillusion
*dessen   whose
*desto: je(mehr)...~ (besser)   the
  (more)...the (better)
*deswegen   for that reason,
  therefore
das Detail, -s   detail
deuten (auf) (+ *acc.*)   to point
  (to)
deutlich   distinct, clear
*deutsch   German;
  deutschsprachig   German-
  speaking
*der/die Deutsche (*noun decl.*
  like adj.)   German; auf
  deutsch   in German
die Deutsche Demokratische
  Republik (DDR)   German
  Democratic Republic
die Deutsche Kommunistische
  Partei (DKP)   German
  Communist Party
*(das) Deutschland   Germany
d.h. *abbreviation for* das heißt
  that is
der Dialekt, -e   dialect
der Dialog, -e   dialogue
die Diät, -en   diet; ~ essen   to
  diet
dicht   close; closed
der Dichter, -   poet, writer
*dick   big; thick; fat
der Dieb, -e   thief; diebisch
  thievish
dienen (+ *dat.*)   to serve
der Dienst, -e   service; ~
  leisten   to do a service
*dies   this
der Dieseltreibstoff, -e   diesel
  fuel

diesmal this time
*diesseits (+ *gen.*) on this side (of)
differenziert differentiated; exact
der Diktator, -en dictator
die Diktatur, -en dictatorship
diktieren to dictate
das Dilemma, -s dilemma
die Diminutivform, -en diminutive
das Diner, -s dinner
*das Ding, -e thing
der Dinosaurier, - dinosaur
der Diplomat, -en, -en diplomat
der Diplomsoziologe, -n, -n registered sociologist
direkt direct
*der Direktor, -en director
dirigieren to direct
*die Disco, -s disco
die Diskussion, -en discussion
*diskutieren über (+ *acc.*) to discuss
die Distanz, -en distance
die Disziplin discipline; disziplinlos undisciplined
diszipliniert disciplined
*doch however; still; surely
*der Doktor, -en medical doctor; PhD
*der Dom, -e cathedral; fair in Hamburg
die Donau Danube river
der Donner, - thunder
donnern to thunder
doof dumb, stupid
doppelt double
das Doppelzimmer, - double room
*das Dorf, ¨er village
*dorther from there
*dorthin to that place
die Dose, -n can
dösen to take a nap; to daydream
das Drama; Dramen drama
dramatisieren to dramatize
dran attached to; du bist dran it's your turn
drauf thereon; on top

*draußen outside
der Dreck filth, dirt
drehen to turn; sich drehen to spin around
drin inside
drinnen inside
das Drittel, - third
droben above; up there
die Droge, -n drug
*die Drogerie, -n drugstore
drohen (+ *dat.*) to threaten
*drüben over there
der Druck, -e pressure; printing
drucken to print
drücken to press
die Drucksache printed matter
dufte (*coll.*) great, excellent
*dumm (ü) stupid; foolish; der Dummkopf, ¨e fool; dummerweise foolishly, stupidly
*dunkel dark
*dünn thin, slender
*durch (+ *acc.*) *through, by means of;* durch und durch throughout; thoroughly
durcheinander in confusion
die Durchgangsstraße, -n through street
durch·lesen (ie; a, e) to read through
der Durchschnitt, -e average, mean
*dürfen to be permitted
*der Durst thirst
*durstig thirsty
die Dusche, -n shower
*(sich) duschen to take a shower
*das Dutzend, -e dozen
duzen to use informal address: (du)
der D-Zug, ¨e = Durchgangszug, ¨e train that doesn't stop at every train station

*eben even, smooth; exactly, precisely; just
ebenfalls equally; also
ebenso just as

*echt genuine, real; (*coll.*) very; really
*die Ecke, -n edge; corner; eckig square
der Effekt, -e effect
*egal equal, even; das ist mir ~ it's all the same to me
*ehe (*conj.*) before
die Ehe, -n marriage
das Ehepaar, -e married couple
eher earlier, sooner; rather
die Ehre, -n honor
ehren to honor
ehrlich honest, fair
*das Ei, -er egg
*eigen own; individual
die Eigenschaft, -en attribute, character
*eigentlich actually, really
die Eile haste, speed; eilig hasty; eilfertig eager
eilen (ist) to hurry
der Eimer, - bucket
ein: ein- und ausgehen to visit frequently
*einander one another
ein·bauen to build in
der Eindruck, ¨e impression
einerseits on the one hand
*einfach simple
die Einfachheit simplicity
ein·fallen (ä; fiel ein, [ist] eingefallen) to occur to; es fällt mir ein it occurs to me, it comes to mind
das Einfamilienhaus, ¨er single family house
der Einfluß, Einflüsse influence
die Einheit, -en unit; unity
einig agreed; united
*einige a few, several, some
sich einigen to agree upon
*ein·kaufen to shop
das Einkaufszentrum, -zentren shopping mall
das Einkommen, - income
*ein·laden (ä; u, a) to invite
die Einladung, -en invitation
die Einlaßkarte, -n ticket of admission
ein·machen to can, preserve

*einmal   once; nicht ~ not even
ein·packen   to pack
*einsam   lonely, solitary
ein·schlafen (ä; ie, [ist] a)   to
    fall asleep
ein·sehen (ie; a, e)   to
    understand; to perceive
einseitig   unilateral; biased
einst   formerly
*ein·steigen (ie, [ist] ie)   to get
    in, enter
die Einsteigerin, -nen   former
    housewife who takes a job
ein·stellen   to focus; to adjust;
    to hire
die Einstellung, -en   position;
    attitude
ein·treten (tritt ein; trat ein,
    [ist] eingetreten)   to enter; to
    happen
der Eintritt   entry; admission
ein·wandern ([ist])   to
    immigrate
ein·wickeln   to wrap up
der Einwohner, -   inhabitant
der Einzelfall, ·e   individual
    case
die Einzelheit, -en   detail
*einzeln   individual, single
das Einzelzimmer, -   single
    room
ein·ziehen (zog ein, ist
    eingezogen)   to move in
*einzig   only; unique
*das Eis   ice; ice cream; eisig
    icy
das Eisen   iron
*die Eisenbahn, -en   railroad;
    railroad train
der Eisschrank, ·e   refrigerator
sich ekeln   to be revolted
elegant   elegant
der Elektriker, - (m)/die
    Elektrikerin, -nen (f)
    electrician
elektrisch   electrical
Elektro-   electro-, electric(al);
    die Elektrofirma,
    Elektrofirmen   firm that
    produces electrical
    instruments; das
    Elektrogeschäft, -e   store

selling electrical supplies
elektronisch   electronic
der Ellbogen, -   elbow
*die Eltern (pl.)   parents;
    elterlich   parental
empfangen (ä; i, a)   to receive
empfehlen (ie; a, o)   to
    recommend
empfinden (a, u)   to feel,
    experience
*das Ende, -n   end; limit; zu ~
    over; das Endprodukt, -e   end
    product; die Endstation   the
    end of the line
enden   to end
*endlich   finally
die Endung, -en   ending
die Energie   energy; der
    Energieverbrauch   energy
    consumption
energisch   energetic
*eng   narrow
das Engagement   commitment
engagiert   committed
die Enge   narrowness
*(das) England   England; der
    Engländer, - (m)/die
    Engländerin, -nen (f)
    English person; englisch
    English
das Enkelkind, -er   grandchild
enorm   enormous
entdecken   to discover
entfernen   to remove,
    withdraw; entfernt   distant,
    removed
die Entfernung, -en   distance
entgegen (+ dat.)   against;
    opposite; toward
entgegengesetzt   opposite,
    opposed, contrary
entgegen·kommen (kam
    entgegen, [ist] o)   to come
    toward
enthalten (ä; ie, a)   to contain
sich entkleiden   to undress
*entlang (+ acc.)   along
entlassen (ä; ie, a)   to release;
    to fire
*entscheiden (ie, ie)   to decide
die Entscheidung, -en   decision
sich entschließen

(o, entschlossen)   to make
    up one's mind
*entschuldigen   to excuse
*die Entschuldigung, -en
    excuse
entsetzlich   terrible
die Entspannung   reduction of
    tension; relaxation
entsprechen (i; a, o) (+ dat.)
    to correspond; to comply with;
    entsprechend
    corresponding, according
entstehen (a, [ist] a)   to come
    about, to arise
*enttäuschen   to disappoint
*entweder ... oder   either . . . or
*(sich) entwickeln   to develop
die Entwicklung, -en
    development
entziffern   to decipher
die Episode, -n   episode
erarbeiten   to work out; to
    acquire
erblicken   to see, to discover
*die Erde, -n   earth; soil
*das Erdgeschoß, Erdgeschosse
    ground level floor
das Erdöl, -e   oil
der Erdrutsch, -e   landslide
sich ereignen   to take place
das Ereignis, -se   event
*erfahren (ä; u, a)   to experience;
    to hear about
*die Erfahrung, -en   experience
erfinden (a, u)   to invent; der
    Erfinder, -   inventor; die
    Erfindung, -en   invention
der Erfolg, -e   success;
    erfolgreich   successful
erforderlich   necessary,
    required
erfüllen   to fulfill; to come true
ergänzen   to complete
das Ergebnis, -se   result
ergreifen (ergriff, ergriffen)   to
    seize
erhalten (ä; ie, a)   to receive; to
    preserve, maintain
sich erheben (o, o)   to arise
erhellen   to shed light on
sich erholen   to recover
die Erholung   recuperation;

relaxation
*sich erinnern an (+ acc.) to remember; erinnern to remind
die Erinnerung, -en reminder, recollection
*sich erkälten to catch a cold
*die Erkältung, -en cold
*erkennen (a, a) to recognize
*erklären to explain; erklärbar explainable
*die Erklärung, -en explanation
sich erkundigen to inquire
erlauben to permit
die Erlaubnis permit
erleben to experience
das Erlebnis, -se experience
erlernen to acquire; to learn by study and experience
erlösen to set free
erneuern to renew
*ernst serious; ernsthaft serious
der Ernst seriousness, severity; das ist nicht dein ~ you aren't serious; ~ machen to really do it
eröffnen to open; to start
die Erosion, -en erosion
erraten (ä; ie, a) to guess
die Erregung agitation
*erreichen to achieve, to reach
erretten to rescue
der Ersatz substitute
*erscheinen (ie, [ist] ie) to seem; to appear; to be published
erschossen exhausted
erschrecken (i; erschrak, [ist] o) to be startled; to be terrified
erschrecken to startle (weak verb)
ersehen (ie; a, e) to learn; to infer; to understand
ersetzen to replace
ersparen to save
*erst first; not until; previously
erstaunen to surprise; erstaunt (über + acc.) surprised (at, by)
erstaunlich surprising;

erstaunlicherweise surprisingly
erstens first of all
erstklassig first-rate
erstmal first
erwachen ([ist]) to wake up
erwachsen grown up
*der/die Erwachsene (noun decl. like adj.) adult
erwähnen to mention
*erwarten to expect; to await
die Erwartung, -en expectation
erwecken to awaken
erwidern to reply
die Erwiderung, -en reply
*erzählen to tell, report
*die Erzählung, -en story
erziehen (erzog, erzogen) to rear; to educate
die Erziehung education
der or das Essay, -s essay
*essen (ißt; aß, gegessen) to eat; eßbar edible
*das Essen,- meal
*das Eßzimmer, - dining room
das Etablissement, -s establishment
die Ethik ethics
*etwa about, nearly
*etwas something; a little
*(das) Europa Europe; der Europäer, - (m)/die Europäerin, -nen (f) European; europäisch European
eventuell perhaps; probably
ewig eternal
*das Examen, Examina final examination at university
existent existent
die Existenz existence
das Experiment, -e experiment
experimentieren to experiment
der Experte, -n, -n expert
explodieren to explode
explosiv explosive; lively
der Export, -e export
exportieren to export

*die Fabrik, -en factory; der Fabrikbesitzer, - factory owner; der Fabrikdirektor, -en

factory manager
*das Fach, ⸚er subject; specialty; der Facharbeiter, - skilled worker; der Fachmann, ⸚er or -leute specialist; die Fachschule, -n technical school
der Faden, ⸚ thread
fähig able, capable
die Fähigkeit, -en capability
die Fahne, -n flag
*fahren (ä; u, [ist] a) to drive; to go
*der Fahrer, - (m)/die Fahrerin, -nen (f) driver
*die Fahrkarte, -n ticket (bus, train)
der Fahrkartenschalter, - ticket counter
der Fahrplan, ⸚e schedule (e.g., bus, train)
*das Fahrrad, ⸚er bicycle; der Fahrradweg, -e bike path
die Fahrschule, -n driving school
*die Fahrt, -en tour, trip
das Fahrzeug, -e vehicle
fair fair
das Faktum, Fakten fact
der Fall, ⸚e case; decline; im besten Falle at best
*fallen (ä; fiel, [ist] a) to fall
*falsch false; deceitful
die Falte, -n fold; wrinkle
falten to fold
*die Familie, -n family; der Familiensinn sense of family; das Familienauto, -s family car
der Fang, ⸚e catch
fangen (ä; i, a) to catch
*die Farbe, -n color; farbig colorful, colored
die Fassade, -n facade
fassen to grasp; to contain
*fast almost
*faul lazy; rotten
faulen to rot
faulenzen to be lazy; to do nothing
die Faust, ⸚e fist
*fehlen (+ dat.) to miss; to

be lacking
*der Fehler, - mistake;
fehlerhaft defective
die Feier, -n celebration; *der
Feiertag, -e holiday
*feiern to celebrate
*fein fine, delicate, thin; nice
*der Feind, -e enemy
der Feinmechaniker, -
specialist in fine mechanics
*das Feld, -er field
*das Fenster, - window
*die Ferien (pl.) vacation
*fern far, distant, away
die Ferne distance
ferner furthermore
das Ferngespräch, -e long
distance phone call; der
Fernsprecher, - telephone
*fern·sehen (ie; a, e) to watch
television
 *der Fernsehapparat, -e
television set; *der Fernseher, -
television set; der
Fernsehturm, -̈e television
tower
*das Fernsehen television
*fertig ready, done
*das Fest, -e festival; party;
feast; das Festspiel, -e
festival
*fest firm; compact, solid
fest·halten (ä; ie, a) to hold on;
to grasp firmly
das Festival, -s festival
fest·stellen to find out; to
confirm
die Fete, -n party
fett fat; greasy; thick
fettgedruckt boldface
feucht moist; humid
*das Feuer, - fire; light
(cigarette); das Feuerchen, -
campfire
die Feuerwehr, -en fire
department; der
Feuerwehrmann, -er (m)/die
Feuerwehrfrau, -en (f) fire-
fighter
das Feuerzeug, -e cigarette
lighter
die Fichte, -n fir tree; der

Fichtenbaum, -̈e fir tree
der Fiedler - fiddler
fies repulsive
der Filter, - filter
*der Film, -e film, movie
finanziell financial
*finden (a, u) to find, to
discover; to think
*der Finger, - finger; der
Fingernagel, -̈ fingernail;
lange ~ machen to steal; auf
die ~ schauen to observe
carefully; das Finger-
spitzengefühl intuition
finster dark
*die Firma, Firmen firm
*der Fisch, -e fish
der Fischer, - fisherman
*flach flat; even
die Flamme, -n flame
*die Flasche, -n bottle
der Fleck, -e or der Flecken, -
spot; place
*das Fleisch meat
*fleißig industrious
die Flexibilität, -en flexibility
die Fliege, -n fly
*fliegen (o, [ist] o) to fly
fliehen (o, [ist] o) to escape
*fließen (o, [ist] geflossen) to
flow
der Flohmarkt, -̈e flea market
die Flucht escape; der
Flüchtling, -e refugee
*der Flug, -̈e flight; *der
Flughafen, -̈ airport; *die
Flugkarte, -n plane ticket;
der Flugschein, -e pilot's
license; plane ticket
der Flügel, - wing
*das Flugzeug, -e airplane
*der Fluß, Flüsse river
flüstern to whisper
die Folge, -n consequence;
sequence; zur ~ haben to
result in
*folgen (+ dat.) to follow; to
obey; folgendes the
following; folgend the
following
die Folgerung, -en conclusion
fördern to foster, promote

die Form, -en form, shape
das Formular, -e form
formulieren to formulate
der Förster, - forester
*fort away; on, forward
fort·fahren (ä; u, [ist] a) to
continue; to drive away
der Fortschritt, -e progress;
improvement
fort·setzen to continue
die Fortsetzung, -en
continuation
*das Foto, -s photograph; das
Fotoalbum, Fotoalben photo
album; *der Fotoapparat, -e
camera
der Fotograf, -en, -en
photographer
fotografieren to take a picture;
fotografisch photographic
die Fotographie, -n
photography; photo
*die Frage, -n question; in ~
stellen to question; eine ~
stellen to ask a question
*fragen to ask
fragmentarisch incomplete
*(das) Frankreich France
*der Franzose, -n, -n (m)/die
Französin, -nen (f) French
person; französisch French
*die Frau, -en woman; Mrs.,
Ms.; wife
*das Fräulein, - unmarried
woman; Miss; waitress
*frei free; ~ haben to be off
from work; ~ sein to be
unoccupied
freigebig generous
*die Freiheit freedom
freilich of course
freiwillig voluntarily
die Freizeit leisure time
*fremd foreign; strange; das ist
mir ~ that is foreign to me
*der/die Fremde (noun decl.
like adj.) foreigner; stranger;
die Fremdsprache, -n foreign
language; das Fremdwort, -̈er
word borrowed from a foreign
language
*fressen (frißt; fraß, e) to

eat *(used for animals)*

*die Freude, -n joy; freudig joyful

die Freudigkeit, -en joyousness

*sich freuen to rejoice, be glad; sich freuen auf (+ *acc.*) to look forward to; sich freuen über (+ *acc.*) to be happy about

*der Freund, -e friend; ein fester ~ a steady boyfriend

*freundlich (gegen, zu) friendly (to)

die Freundlichkeit friendliness

die Freundschaft, -en friendship

der Frieden peace; die Friedensbewegung, -en peace movement; das Friedenslied, -er peace song

friedlich peaceful

frieren (o, o) to freeze

*frisch fresh; new

*der Friseur, -e *(m)* barber, hairdresser; *die Friseuse, -n (f)* hairdresser

frivol frivolous

*froh (über + *acc.*) glad (about)

*fröhlich happy, merry

die Fröhlichkeit gaiety

die Front, -en front

*früh early; früher formerly; earlier

das Frühjahr, -e spring

*der Frühling, -e spring

*das Frühstück, -e breakfast

*frühstücken to eat breakfast

*(sich) fühlen to feel

*führen to lead, to guide

*der Führerschein, -e driver's license

füllen to fill

*der Füller, - ink pen

fünfjährig five years old

der Funk broadcast; Funk- und Fernsehtechniker, - radio- and television technician

funktionieren to function

*für (+ *acc.*) for

die Furcht fear, anxiety

*furchtbar terrible

*fürchten to fear; fürchterlich terrible, frightful; furchtsam fearful, frightened

*der Fuß, -e foot

*der Fußball, -e soccer ball; soccer game; das Fußballmatch soccer game; das Fußballspiel, -e soccer game

*der Fußgänger, - pedestrian

füttern to feed

*die Gabel, -n fork

der Gang, -e walk, passage

*ganz complete, whole; quite

*gar entirely

*gar nicht not at all

*die Garage, -n garage

die Gardine, -n curtain

*der Garten, - garden; die Gartenarbeit gardening

das Gas, -e gas

*der Gast, -e guest; der Gastarbeiter, - foreign worker

*das Gasthaus, -er inn, hotel

*das Gebäude, - building

*geben (i; a, e) to give

das Gebet, -e prayer

*das Gebiet, -e region; subject

gebildet educated, cultured

*das Gebirge, - mountains

*geboren born

der Gebrauch, -e custom; use

*gebrauchen to use

gebraucht second hand, used

*die Geburt, -en birth; der Geburtsort, -e place of birth

*der Geburtstag, -e birthday

das Gedächtnis memory

*der Gedanke, -ns, -n thought; ich kann keinen klaren Gedanken fassen I can't get my thoughts together

die Gedankenfreiheit freedom of thought

das Gedicht, -e poem

die Geduld patience

geduldig patient

geehrt honored; dear *(in formal letter)*

*die Gefahr, -en danger; der ~

ins Auge sehen to face up to something; *gefährlich dangerous; gefährdet in danger

der Gefallen, - favor

*gefallen (ä; ie, a) (+ *dat.*) to please; sich etwas ~ lassen to consent, take it reluctantly

das Gefängnis, -se prison, jail

*das Gefühl, -e emotion; gefühllos unfeeling; gefühlvoll sentimental

*gegen (+ *acc.*) against

*die Gegend, -en area, region

gegeneinander against one another

der Gegensatz, -e contrast; gegensätzlich contrary, opposite

der Gegenstand, -e thing; subject

das Gegenteil, -e opposite

*gegenüber (+ *dat.*) opposite

gegenüber·stellen to juxtapose

die Gegenwart presence; present time; gegenwärtig present

die Gegenwirtschaft, -en alternative economy

gegrillt grilled

das Gehalt, -er salary

geheim secret; das Geheimnis, -se secret;

*gehen (ging, ist gegangen) to go; to work; das geht mich nichts an that doesn't concern me; das geht nicht that won't do; es geht darum it concerns that

der Gehilfe, -n, -n *(m)*/die Gehilfin, -nen *(f)* aid, helper

*gehorchen (+ *dat.*) to obey

*gehören (+ *dat.*) to belong

gelangweilt bored

*gelb yellow

*das Geld, -er money; das Geldstück, -e coin

das Gelee, -s jelly

*die Gelegenheit, -en opportunity

gelegentlich occasional

gelehrt scholarly, wise

*gelingen (a, [ist] u) (+ *dat.*) to
succeed

*gelten (i; a, o) to be of value; to
be valid; to be in effect

gemein mean; common; ein
gemeiner Hund low-down
fellow

die Gemeinde, -n community;
congregation

gemeinsam together

die Gemeinschaft, -en group;
community

*das Gemüse, - vegetable

*gemütlich comfortable, cozy;
good-natured

*genau exact, accurate; that's
right

genauso (wie) as well (as)

die Generation, -en
generation; der
Generationskonflikt, -e
generation gap

genießen (o, genossen) to
enjoy

der Genosse, -n, -n comrade

*genug enough

*das Gepäck luggage; das
Gepäckstück, -e piece of
luggage

*gerade straight; just;
geradeaus straight ahead

das Gerät, -e tool, instrument

geraten (ä; ie, [ist] a) to get
into; to come out

das Geräusch, -e noise

gerecht just, fair

das Gericht, -e court

gering small; insufficient

*gern (lieber, liebst-) gladly,
with pleasure

gerötet flushed

der Geruch, ¨e smell, fragrance

gesamt total, entire

der Gesang, ¨e song, singing

*das Geschäft, -e business;
Geschäfte machen to do
business; das Geschäftsleben
business world; der
Geschäftsmann, ¨er, -leute
(m)/die Geschäftsfrau, -en (f)
businessman, businesswoman

geschäftlich commercial; on
business

*geschehen (ie; a, [ist] e) to
happen

*das Geschenk, -e gift

*die Geschichte, -n story;
history

geschickt clever; skilled

*das Geschirr, -e dishes; die
Geschirrspülmaschine, -n
automatic dishwasher

der Geschmack taste

das Geschlecht, -er sex

die Geschwindig-
keitsbegrenzung, -en speed
limit

der Geselle, -n journeyman

*die Gesellschaft, -en society;
company; das Gesell-
schaftsspiel, -e party game

das Gesetz, -e law

*das Gesicht, -er face

gespannt (auf + *acc.*) curious
(about)

*das Gespräch, -e talk; ein ~
führen to converse

gesprächig talkative; sociable

die Gestalt, -en form, shape

die Geste, -n gesture

gestehen (gestand, gestanden)
to confess

*gestern yesterday

das Gesuchte that which is
searched for

*gesund healthy

*die Gesundheit health; das
Gesundheitswesen, - health
care system

das Getränk, -e drink,
beverage

das Getreide grain, crop

gewähren to allow

die Gewalt, -en force

gewaltig powerful

das Gewehr, -e gun, rifle

die Gewerkschaft, -en union

das Gewicht weight;
importance

gewillt: ~ sein to be willing

der Gewinn, -e gain, profit

*gewinnen (a, o) to gain, win

*gewiß sure, certain; probably

das Gewissen conscience

das Gewitter, - thunderstorm

sich gewöhnen an (+ *acc.*) to
get used to; gewohnt
accustomed

die Gewohnheit, -en habit

*gewöhnlich normally; common

gießen (o, gegossen) to pour

das Gift, -e poison

der Gipfel, - peak, top

*die Gitarre, -n guitar

der Gitarrist, -en, -en guitarist

glänzen to shine, gleam

*das Glas, ¨er glass

glatt smooth, even; polished

der Glaube, -ens, belief, faith

*glauben (+ *dat. of person*) to
believe

glaubhaft believable

*gleich soon; equal; ~ darauf
immediately afterwards; das
ist mir ~ it's all the same to
me

gleichberechtigt having equal
rights; die Gleichberech-
tigung equal rights

gleichen (i, i) (+ *dat.*) to be
equal; to be like

gleichfalls likewise

die Gleichheit equality; das
Gleichheitsprinzip, -ien
principle of equality

gleichmäßig steady

gleich-tun (a, a) to imitate

gleichwertig equivalent

gleichzeitig simultaneous

das Gleis, -e track

das Glied, -er limb; joint

die Glocke, -n bell

*das Glück luck, fortune; zum
~ luckily; der Glückwunsch,
¨e congratulations

*glücklich (über + *acc.*) happy
(about); glücklicherweise
fortunately

glühen to glow

das Gold gold

*der Gott, ¨er God; god; ~ sei
dank thank heavens gottlos
godless

das Grab, ¨er grave

graben (ä; u, a) to dig

der Grad, -e degree; rank

der/das Graffito, -i graffiti
*das Gramm, -e gram
*das Gras, ̈er grass
gräßlich horrible
gratulieren (+ *dat.*) to congratulate
*grau gray
grausam cruel
greifen (griff, gegriffen) to grasp
der Greis, -e old man
grell glaring; shrill
die Grenze, -n border; limit
(das) Griechenland Greece
griechisch Greek
grillen to grill
grinsen to grin
grob rude; rough
*groß (ö) great, big, tall
großartig excellent
(das) Großbritannien Great Britain
*die Größe, -n height; size
*die Großeltern *(pl.)* grandparents
die Großmacht, ̈e world power
*die Großmutter, ̈ grandmother
die Großstadt, ̈e city; die Großstadtszene city scene
größtenteils mostly
*der Großvater, ̈ grandfather
großzügig generous
grotesk grotesque
*grün green; im Grünen out in nature; ins Grüne into nature
*der Grund, ̈e reason; bottom
der Grundgedanke, -ns, -n fundamental or root idea
das Grundgesetz, -e Basic Law (of Federal Republic of Germany)
die Grundlage, -n foundation; basis
der Grundsatz, ̈e principle; grundsätzlich on principle
die Grundschule, -n elementary school
das Grundstück, -e property, estate
die Gruppe, -n group
*der Gruß, ̈e greeting

*grüßen to greet
gucken to look
gültig valid
der/das Gummi, -s rubber
günstig convenient, favorable
*gut (besser, best-) good, well, OK; gut gegen or zu good to
das Gut, ̈er farm; estate
die Güte goodness, kindness; du meine ~ goodness gracious
*das Gymnasium, Gymnasien high school; der Gymnasiast, -en, -en *(m)*/die Gymnasiastin, -nen *(f)* pupil at Gymnasium

*das Haar, -e hair; *der Haartrockner, - hairdryer
*haben to have; to possess
der Hafen, ̈ harbor, port
haften to adhere
der Häftling, -e convict
der Hahn, ̈e rooster; faucet
*halb half; halblaut in an undertone; halbfaul half rotten
die Hälfte, -n half
die Halle, -n hall, vestibule
*der Hals, ̈e neck
der Halt support; stop
halt stop
haltbar durable
*halten (ä; ie, a) to hold; to stop; ~ von to think of ~ für to regard as
*die Haltestelle, -n (bus) stop
die Haltung attitude; position
der Hammer, ̈ hammer
hämmern to hammer
*die Hand, ̈e hand
der Handel trade
handeln to act; to treat; sich ~ um to concern; es handelt von it's a matter of
handfest firm
handgeschrieben handwritten
die Handlung, -en plot; action
*der Handschuh, -e glove
*die Handtasche, -n purse, pocketbook
*das Handtuch, ̈er towel
das Handwerk, -e handicraft, trade

handwerklich pertaining to craft
*hängen (i, a) to hang
harmonisch in harmony
*hart (ä) hard, solid; difficult; stiff
der Haß hate
*hassen to hate
*häßlich ugly
hastig hastily
häufig often, frequent
das Haupt, ̈er head; principal
der Hauptbahnhof, ̈e main train station
die Hauptidee, -n main idea
die Hauptsache, -n main thing
hauptsächlich essentially, mainly
die Hauptschule, -n classes 1-9 for students intending to learn a trade; der Hauptschüler, - *(m)*/die Hauptschülerin, -nen *(f)* student in Hauptschule
das Hauptseminar, -e main seminar
*die Hauptstadt, ̈e capital
die Hauptstraße, -n main street
*das Haus, ̈er house; die Hausarbeit, -en house work; home work; der Hausmann, ̈er man who keeps house; die Hausfrau, -en woman who keeps house
der Haushalt, -e household
der Haushaltsplan, ̈e housekeeping schedule
häuslich domestic
die Haustür, -en front door
die Haut, ̈e skin
*heben (o, o) to lift, raise
die Hecke, -n hedge
das Heer, -e army
*das Heft, -e notebook
heftig vigorous; intense
heilen to heal
heilig holy
das Heim, -e home; institution; heim home (ward)
die Heimat, -en native country

or place; **die Heimatstadt, ⁻e**
home town; **der Heimweg, -e**
way home
heimlich secret
die Heirat, -en marriage
***heiraten** to marry
***heiß** hot
***heißen (ie, ei)** to be called; to
mean; **es heißt** it states
heiter cheerful
der Held, -en, -en hero
***helfen (i; a, o)** (+ *dat.*) to help
***hell** bright, light
***das Hemd, -en** shirt
***her** here
herab·stürzen [ist] to fall; to
hurry down
herauf up; toward
heraus out
**heraus·bringen (brachte
heraus, herausgebracht)** to
bring out; to publish
heraus·kriegen to figure out;
to get out
das Herbizid, -e herbicide
***der Herbst, -e** autumn
der Herd, -e (cooking) range
***herein** into
***herein·kommen (kam herein,
[ist] o)** to come in
***der Herr, -n, -en** Mr.;
gentleman
***herrlich** magnificent
herrschen to rule
her·stellen to produce,
manufacture; to establish
herum around; about
herunter down here
hervorragend excellent
**hervor·ziehen (zog hervor,
hervorgezogen)** to pull out
***das Herz, -ens, -en** heart;
***herzlich** heartily
***heute** today; **heutzutage**
nowadays
heutig present-day
***hier** here; **hierher** here
***die Hilfe, -n** help; **hilflos**
helpless
die Hilfsarbeit, -en unskilled
work
***der Himmel, -** heaven; sky

***hin** there; away; gone
hinauf up there
hinauf·schieben (o, o) to push
up
hinaus out; beyond
**hinaus·gehen (ging hinaus, [ist]
hinausgegangen)** to leave; to
go outside
hinaus·schmuggeln to
smuggle out
hindern to prevent
hinein in; inside; into
hin·fallen (ä; ie, [ist] a) to fall
hin·legen to put there
sich hin·setzen to sit down
***hinten** in the rear
***hinter** *(acc./dat.)* behind;
hintereinander in
succession; **hinterher**
afterward
hinterher·werfen (i; a, o) to
throw after
die Hinterseite, -n back
die Hin- und Rückfahrt, -en
round trip
hinunter down; below
der Hinweis, -e hint
**hin·ziehen (zog hin, [ist]
hingezogen)** to move there
hinzu·fügen to add
**hinzu·ziehen (zog hinzu,
hinzugezogen)** to consult
die Hinzuziehung consulting
das Hirn, -e brain
historisch historical
die Hitze heat
***das Hobby, -s** hobby
***hoch (höher, höchst-)** high
das Hochhaus, ⁻er high-rise
die Hochschule, -n university;
der Hochschullehrer, -
university professor
***höchst** highest; utmost;
höchstens at most
das Hochwasser, - high water
die Hochzeit, -en wedding
***der Hof, ⁻e** farm; court
***hoffen** to hope
***hoffentlich** I (we) hope;
hopefully
***die Hoffnung, -en** hope;
hoffnungslos hopeless

***höflich (gegen)** polite (to)
die Höflichkeit politeness
die Höhe, -n height
hohl hollow
der Hohn scorn
höhnisch mocking
***holen** to get
***das Holz** wood
hörbar audible
***hören** to hear; to listen to; ~
auf to take advice
der Hörer, - listener; telephone
receiver
der Hörsaal, *pl.* **Hörsäle**
auditorium
***die Hose, -n** trousers
***das Hotel, -s** hotel
***hübsch** pretty
der Hügel, - hill
***das Huhn, ⁻er** chicken
human humane
der Humor humor; **humorlos**
humorless; **humorvoll**
humorous
***der Hund, -e** dog; **auf den ~
kommen** to go to the dogs;
das Hundeleben, - dog's life;
hundemüde extremely tired
***hundert** hundred
***der Hunger** hunger
***hungrig** hungry
hupen to honk
***husten** to cough
***der Hut, ⁻e** hat
die Hütte, -n cabin, hut
hysterisch hysterical

das Ideal, -e ideal
idealistisch idealistic
***die Idee, -n** idea; **sich die ~
aus dem Kopf schlagen** to
give up on an idea
identifizieren to identify
die Identität identity
der Idiot, -en, -en idiot
idyllisch peaceful, idyllic
ihretwegen on her (their)
account
die Illusion, -en illusion
illustrieren to illustrate
die Illustrierte, -n -n
illustrated magazine

*immer always; ~ mehr more and more; ~ wieder again and again

immerhin after all, still, nevertheless

der Import, -e import

*in (acc./dat.) in, at, into, to

indem while; in that

das Individuum, Individuen individual

die Industrialisierung industrialization

*die Industrie, -n industry; der Industriekaufmann, ¨er company clerk; die Industrieproduktion industrial production

die Information, -en information

informieren to inform; informiert informed

*der Ingenieur, -e engineer

*der Inhalt, -e content

inhuman inhumane

innen in; inside; die Innentasche, -n inside pocket; die Innenstadt, center of city, inner city

inner interior; inner

*innerhalb (+ gen.) inside of

innerlich internal; die Innerlichkeit rich inner life

inoffiziell unofficial

das Insektizid, -e insecticide

die Insel, -n island

insgesamt altogether

das Institut , -e institute

die Institution, -en institution

*das Instrument, -e instrument

intelligent intelligent

intensiv intense

der Inter-City inter-city train (stops only at large cities)

*interessant interesting

das Interesse, -n interest

*sich interessieren (für) to be interested (in); interessiert (an + dat.) interested (in)

international international

die Interpretation, -en interpretation

interpretieren to interpret

das Interview, -s interview

interviewen to interview

intolerant intolerant

inwiefern in what respect

*inzwischen meanwhile

*irgend some; any; at all; irgendein some; any; irgendwelch any (kind)

*irgendwann sometime

*irgendwie somehow

*irgendwo somewhere

die Ironie irony

ironisch ironical

irre crazy; lost

sich irren to be mistaken

der Irrtum, ¨er mistake

isoliert isolated

die Isolierung isolation

*(das) Italien Italy; der Italiener,-(m)/die Italienerin, -nen (f) Italian; italienisch Italian

*ja yes

*die Jacke, -n jacket

das Jackett, -s (man's) suit jacket

die Jagd, -en hunt

jagen to hunt

der Jäger, - hunter

*das Jahr, -e year

die Jahreszeit, -en season

*das Jahrhundert, -e century

-jährig . . . years old

jährlich annual

das Jahrzehnt, -e decade

(das) Japan Japan; der Japaner, -(m)/die Japanerin, -nen (f) Japanese; japanisch Japanese

der Jazz jazz

*je each; for each case; je ... desto the . . . the

jedenfalls in any case, at all events

*jeder every

*jedermann everyone, everybody

*jedesmal every time

jedoch however, nevertheless

jemals ever

*jemand somebody

*jener that; the former

*jenseits (+ gen.) on the other side; beyond

*jetzt now

jeweils at any given time, from time to time

*der Job, -s job; auf Jobsuche gehen to look for a job

jobben to work

das Journal, -e journal

*der Journalist, -en, -en (m)/die Journalistin, -nen (f) journalist

*die Jugend youth

*der/die Jugendliche (noun decl. like adj) young person

die Jugendsprache youth slang

*jung (ü) young

*der Junge, -n, -n boy

der Jurist, -en, -en (m)/die Juristin, -nen (f) lawyer

die Jusos (die Jungsozialisten) young socialists; youth organization of the Social Democratic Party (SPD)

das Kabarett, -e cabaret

die Kabine, -n cabin

*der Kaffee coffee

der Kaiser, - emperor

der Kakao cocoa

der Kalender, - calendar

die Kalorie, -n calorie

*kalt (ä) cold; die Kälte cold

*die Kamera, -s camera

der Kamerad, -en, -en companion

*der Kamm, ¨e comb

*(sich) kämmen to comb one's hair

der Kampf, ¨e fight

*kämpfen to fight

die Kanne, -n pot

die Kantine, -n canteen

der Kanzler, - chancellor

das Kapital capital (money)

der Kapitän, -e captain

*kaputt broken; exhausted; kaputt-gehen to go to pieces

die Karaffe, -n carafe

*die Karte, -n card; menu; ticket; eine ~ lösen to buy a

ticket
*die Kartoffel, -n potato
*der Käse, - cheese
die Kaskade, -n cascade
*die Kasse, -n box office;
cashier
*die Kassette, -n cassette; *der
Kassettenrecorder, -
cassette recorder
der Kasten, ⸚ box
die Katastrophe, -n
catastrophe
die Kategorie, -n category
*die Katze, -n cat;
katzenfreundlich two-faced;
ein Katzensprung a stone's
throw; die Katzenmusik
caterwauling, racket
kauen to chew
der Kauf purchase
*kaufen to buy
der Käufer, - (m)/die Käuferin,
-nen (f) buyer; das
Kaufhaus, ⸚er department
store; der Kaufmann, ⸚er or
-leute merchant
*kaum hardly
der Kavalier, -e gentleman,
cavalier
kehren to sweep
*kein no, not a, none, not any
kein ... mehr no longer
keiner no one
keineswegs not at all
*der Keller, - cellar, basement
*der Kellner, - waiter; die
Kellnerin, -nen waitress
*kennen (a, a) to know; to be
acquainted with
*kennen·lernen to meet,
become acquainted with
der Kenner, - connoisseur
die Kenntnis, -se knowledge,
information
der Kerl, -e fellow
die Kernkraft nuclear power
die Kette, -n chain; necklace
der Kfz-Mechaniker
(Kraftfahrzeugmechaniker), -
auto mechanic
*das Kilogramm, -e kilogram
*der Kilometer, - kilometer

*das Kind, -er child
der Kindergarten, ⸚
kindergarten
die Kindergeschichte, -n
children's story
kinderlieb fond of children
*das Kino, -s cinema
der Kiosk, -e kiosk
*die Kirche, -n church
die Kirsche, -n cherry
das Kissen, - pillow
die Klage, -n complaint
klagen to complain
*klar clear; certainly
*die Klasse, -n class; erster ~
first class; klasse (coll.)
great
klassifizieren to classify
klauen to steal (coll.)
*die Klausur, -en (university)
examination
*das Klavier, -e piano
kleben to glue; to stick
*das Kleid, -er dress
kleiden to dress
*die Kleidung clothing
*klein little
die Kleinigkeit, -en trifle
klettern (ist) to climb
das Klima climate
die Klingel, -n bell
klingeln to ring
klingen (a, u) to sound
die Klinik, -en clinic
das Klischee, -s cliché
*klopfen to knock
*klug (ü) clever, intelligent;
klugerweise wisely
knapp brief
der Knecht, -e servant; farm
hand
die Kneipe, -n pub
das Knie, - knee
der Knochen, - bone
der Knopf, ⸚e button; das
Knopfloch, ⸚er buttonhole
der Koch, ⸚e cook
*kochen to cook
der Kode, -s code
*der Koffer, - trunk, suitcase;
das Kofferradio, -s portable
radio; *der Kofferraum, ⸚e

trunk (car)
der Kognak, -s Cognac
der Kohldampf hunger
(slang); ~ haben to be
hungry
die Kohle, -n coal; money
(slang)
kohlschwarz coal black
*der Kollege, -n, -n (m)/die
Kollegin, -nen (f) colleague
(das) Köln Cologne
komisch funny; strange;
komischerweise strangely
enough
das Komitee, -s committee
das Komma, -s comma
*kommen (kam, [ist] o) to come
der Kommentar, -e
commentary
kommentieren to comment
der Kommilitone, -n, -n (m)/die
Kommilitonin, -nen (f) fellow
student
die Kommunikation, -en
communication
das Kommunionskleid, -er
communion dress
der Kommunist, -en, -en
communist
das Komplement, -e
complement
die Komplikation, -en
complication
kompliziert complicated
die Komponente, -n
component
komponieren to compose
der Komponist, -en, -en
composer
die Komposition, -en musical
composition
das Kompositum, Komposita
compound (word)
der Konditor, -en (m) / die
Konditorin, -nen (f) pastry
chef; *die Konditorei, -en
pastry shop; café
die Konferenz, -en conference
der Konflikt, -e conflict
die Konjunktion, -en
conjunction
konkret concrete; real

die Konkurrenz   competition
konkurrieren   to compete
*können   can, to be able to
konservativ   conservative
die Konstruktion, -en
   construction
der Konsum   consumption; der
   Konsument, -en, -en
   consumer
konsumieren   to consume
der Kontakt, -e   contact
das Konto, -s   account
das Kontor, -e   office
der Kontrast, -e   contrast
die Kontrolle, -n   control
kontrollieren   to control
das Konzept, -e   concept
*das Konzert, -e   concert, recital
*der Kopf, ¨e   head; aus dem ~
   schlagen   to banish from
   one's thoughts; den ~ in den
   Sand stecken   to ignore
   danger; den ~ hängen lassen
   to be depressed; die
   Kopfschmerzen (pl.)
   headache
die Kopie, -n   copy
*der Korb, ¨e   basket
der Kordon, -s   cordon, barrier
der Kork, -e   cork
das Korn   grain
*der Körper, -   body; körperlich
   bodily, physical
der Korrespondent, -en, -en
   (m)/die Korrespondentin,
   -nen (f)   correspondent
der Korridor, -e   corridor
*korrigieren   to correct
kostbar   valuable; expensive
*kosten   to cost; to try a food;
   kostenlos   free, without
   charge
die Kosten (pl)   expenses; das
   geht auf ~ von   it is at the
   expense of
das Kotelett, -s   cutlet, chop
die Kraft, ¨e   force; kräftig
   strong
das Kraftwerk, -e   power
   station
der Kragen, -   collar
der Krahn, ¨e   crane

*krank (ä)   ill
der/die Kranke (noun decl. like
   adj.)   patient
*das Krankenhaus, ¨er   hospital
die Krankenkasse, -n   medical
   insurance; das
   Krankenkassenmitglied, -er
   member of medical insurance
   plan
der Krankenpfleger, -   nurse
   (m)
der Krankenschein, -e   medical
   report
*die Krankenschwester, -n
   nurse (f)
*der Krankenwagen, -
   ambulance
*die Krankheit, -en   illness
*die Krawatte, -n   tie
der Krebs, -e   cancer; crab
der Kredit, -e   credit
*die Kreide   chalk
der Kreis, -e   circle; district;
   county
kreisen   to circle
das Kreuz, -e   cross
kreuzen   to cross
die Kreuzung, -en   crosswalk,
   intersection
kriechen (o, [ist] o)   to crawl
*der Krieg, -e   war
kriegen   to get, obtain
der Krimi, -s   detective story or
   film
der Kriminalroman, -e
   detective novel
die Krise, -n   crisis
das Kriterium, Kriterien
   criterion
die Kritik, -en   criticism
kritisch   critical
*kritisieren   to criticize
die Krücke, -n   crutch
der Krug, ¨e   pitcher; mug
krumm   crooked, bent
*die Küche, -n   kitchen
*der Kuchen, -   cake
die Kugel, -n   ball; bullet
*der Kugelschreiber, -   ball-
   point pen
*die Kuh, ¨e   cow
*kühl   cool, chilly; die Kühle

   coolness
kühlen   to cool
*der Kühlschrank, ¨e
   refrigerator
kultiviert   cultivated
die Kultur, -en   culture;
   kulturell   cultural
sich kümmern um   to be
   concerned about, care
der Kunde, -n, -n (m) / die
   Kundin, -nen (f)   customer
kündigen   to give notice, lay off
*die Kunst, ¨e   art; das
   Kunstmuseum, -museen   art
   museum; das Kunstwerk, -e
   work of art
*der Künstler, - (m) / die
   Künstlerin, -nen (f)   artist
*der Kurs, -e   course
kursivgedruckt   italics
die Kurve, -n   curve
*kurz (ü)   short; kurz danach
   shortly afterwards
die Kurzgeschichte, -n   short
   story
kürzlich   recently
*die Kusine, -n   cousin
der Kuß, Küsse   kiss
*küssen   to kiss
die Küste, -n   coast
der Kutter, -   cutter

das Labyrinth, -e   labyrinth
lächeln   to smile
*lachen (über + acc.)   to laugh
   (about)
lächerlich   ridiculous
*der Laden, ¨   store
die Lage, -n   situation; position
das Lager, -   depot; camp
lahm   lame
*die Lampe, -n   lamp; das
   Lämpchen, -   small lamp
*das Land, ¨er   land, state,
   country; auf dem ~   in the
   country
landen [ist]   to land
die Landessprache, -n
   language of a country
die Landkarte, -n   map
*die Landschaft, -en   landscape
die Landstraße, -n   highway

der Landwirt, -e farmer; **die Landwirtschaft** farming
*lang (ä) long; **längere Zeit** for some time
*lange a long time
die Länge length
*langsam slow
längst long since
*langweilig boring
*der Lärm noise
*lassen (ä; ließ, a) to let; to leave
der Lastwagen, - truck
*laufen (äu; ie, [ist] au) to run
*die Laune, -n mood; **gute ~ haben** to be in a good mood; **das macht ~** that's fun
*laut noisy, loud
lauter clear; pure; nothing but
läuten to ring
der Lautsprecher, - loudspeaker
die Lawine, -n avalanche
*leben to live
*das Leben, - life; **der Lebensstil, -e** life style; **die Lebenszeit, -en** lifetime; **der Lebensunterhalt** livelihood; **die Lebensweise, -n** manner of living; life style
*lebendig lively; alive
*die Lebensmittel (pl.) food, provisions
die Leberwurst, ⸚e liverwurst
lebhaft lively
lecker delicious
das Leder, - leather
ledig single, unmarried
*leer empty
*legen to lay, put
lehnen to lean
das Lehrbuch, ⸚er textbook
die Lehre, -n apprenticeship; instruction
*lehren to teach
*der Lehrer, - (m) / **die Lehrerin, -nen** (f) teacher
*der Lehrling, -e apprentice
der Lehrplan, ⸚e schedule; syllabus
die Lehrstelle, -n apprenticeship position

der Leib body
*leicht easy; light
die Leichtathletik track and field sports; **das Leichtathletiktreffen, -** track meet
das Leid pain, suffering, torment
*leid tun to feel sorry
*leiden (litt, gelitten) to suffer; **ich kann ihn nicht ~** I cannot stand him
die Leidenschaft, -en passion
*leider unfortunately
leihen (ie, ie) to lend; to borrow
*leise soft, quiet
leisten to perform
*sich leisten to afford
leiten to lead
der Leiter, - leader
die Lektüre, -n literature, reading
*lernen to learn
*lesen (ie; a, e) to read; **die Leseratte, -n** bookworm; **der Lesestoff, -e** reading matter; **das Lesestück, -e** reading selection
*letzt last
leuchten to shine
*die Leute (pl.) people
liberal liberal
*das Licht, -er light
*lieb dear; **~ haben** to be fond of
*die Liebe love
*lieben to love
liebenswürdig charming
*lieber rather
das Liebeslied, -er love song
das Liebespaar, -e loving couple
lieblich lovely; sweet
der Liebling, -e darling; favorite; **die Lieblingsgeschichte, -n** favorite story; **die Lieblingslektüre, -n** favorite book; **das Lieblingswort, ⸚er** favorite word
liebst favorite

*liebsten: am ~ best liked, most of all
*das Lied, -er song
das Liederbuch, ⸚er song book
der Liedermacher, - (m) / **die Liedermacherin, -nen** (f) writer of popular and folk songs
*liegen (a, e) to lie, be located
die Lilie, -n lily
der Limerick, -s limerick
*die Limonade, -n soft drink
die Linde, -n linden tree
die Linie, -n line
*links left
die Lippe, -n lip
der Lippenstift, -e lipstick
die Liste, -n list
*der Liter, - liter
literarisch literary
die Literatur literature
loben to praise
das Loch, ⸚er hole
locker loose
*der Löffel, - spoon
die Logik logic
logisch logical
der Lohn, ⸚e reward; wages
sich lohnen to pay off, be worthwhile
das Lokal, -e restaurant; place
die Lokomotive, -n locomotive
das Los, -e fate; lottery tickets
*los released; loose; **was ist los?** what's wrong?
lösen to solve; to loosen, untie; **eine Karte ~** to buy a ticket
los·gehen (ging los, ist losgegangen) to start
los·lassen (läßt los, ließ los, losgelassen) to set free; to let go
die Lösung; -en solution
*die Luft air
die Lufthansa German airline
*die Luftpost airmail
die Lüge, -n lie
lügen (o, o) to lie
*die Lust pleasure; desire; **~ haben** to be in the mood, to feel like
*lustig jolly, amusing; **sich über**

etwas oder jemanden ~
machen   to make fun of
something or somebody
die Lyrik   lyric; poetry

*machen   to make; to do; ich
mache mir nichts aus Fisch
I don't care for fish; sich an
die Arbeit ~   to begin
working
die Macht, ¨e   power
mächtig   powerful; der/die
Mächtige (noun decl. like
adj.) the powerful one
machtlos   powerless
*das Mädchen, -   girl;
mädchenhaft   girlish
*der Magen, ¨   stomach
magisch   magic
mähen   to mow
mahlen (mahlte, gemahlen)   to
grind
die Mahlzeit, -en   meal
die Makrele, -n   mackerel
*mal   once; [drei]mal [three]
times; flavoring particle to
soften commands
*das Mal, -e   time(s)
*malen   to paint
der Maler, - (m)/die Malerin,
-nen   painter
die Malerei, -en   painting,
picture
*man   one (impersonal pron.)
*manch   many a; some
*manchmal   sometimes
der Mangel, ¨   lack
manipulieren   to manipulate
*der Mann, ¨er   man; husband;
männlich   male, masculine
die Mannschaft, -en   team
*der Mantel, ¨   coat
die Mappe, -n   briefcase
*das Märchen, -   fairy tale
die Margarine   margarine
die Marionette, -n   marionette,
puppet
*die Mark   mark (German
monetary unit)
die Marke, -n   label, brand
*der Markt, ¨e   market; die
Markthalle, -n   covered

market; der Marktstand, ¨e
market booth; die
Marktnische, -n   segment of
the market
*die Marmelade, -n   jam
marschieren (ist)   to march
*die Maschine, -n   machine
das Maschinengewehr, -e
machine gun
der Maschinenschlosser, -
machinist
das Maß, -e   measure
die Masse, -n   mass, quantity
mäßig   moderate
massiv   massive
die Maßnahme, -n   measure,
move
der Maßstab, ¨e   unit of
measurement
das Match, -e   match, game
das Material, -ien   material
*die Mathematik   mathematics
der Matrose, -n, -n   sailor
*die Mauer, -n   wall
der Maurer, -   bricklayer
die Maus, ¨e   mouse; mausetot
dead as a doornail
*der Mechaniker, - (m)/die
Mechanikerin, -nen (f)
mechanic
meckern   to complain
die Medaille, -n   medal
das Medikament, -e   medicine,
drug
das Medium, Medien   medium
*die Medizin   medicine; drug
der Mediziner, - (m)/die
Medizinerin, -nen (f) medical
doctor
*das Meer, -e   sea, ocean
das Mehl   flour
*mehr   more; immer ~   more
and more
*mehrere   several
das Mehrfamilienhaus, ¨er
apartment house
die Mehrheit, -en   majority
mehrmals   repeatedly
*meinen   to be of the opinion; to
intend, mean
*meinetwegen   as far as I am
concerned

*die Meinung, -en   opinion;
meiner ~ nach   in my
opinion; ich bin deiner ~   I
am of your opinion
die Meinungsverschiedenheit,
-en   difference of opinion
*meist   most
*meistens   mostly
der Meister, - (m)/die Meisterin,
-nen (f)   master;
foreman/forelady
meisterhaft   excellent, masterly
die Meisterschaft, -en   mastery;
championship
die Melancholie   melancholy
melden   to inform, notify
die Melodie, -n   melody
die Melone, -n   melon; head
(slang)
*die Menge, -n   great quantity;
crowd
*der Mensch, -en, -en   human
being; Mensch!   man!
menschenfeindlich
misanthropic
das Menschenfleisch   flesh
der Menschenfresser, - (m) / die
Menschenfresserin, -nen (f)
cannibal
menschenfreundlich   sociable;
philanthropic
der Menschenstrom   steam of
people
das Menschentum   humanity
menschlich   human
*merken   to notice; to realize
*merkwürdig   strange;
remarkable
messen (i; a, e)   to measure
*das Messer, -   knife
das Metall, -e   metal
*der Meter, -   meter
die Methode, -n   method
*der Metzger, - (m)/die
Metzgerin, -nen (f)   butcher
*die Metzgerei, -en   butcher
shop
der Meuchelmörder, - (m)/die
Meuchelmörderin, -nen (f)
assassin
mies   miserable
*die Miete, -n   rent

*mieten   to rent
der Mieter, - (m)/die Mieterin,
-nen (f)   tenant
der Mikrocomputer, -
microcomputer
der Mikroprozessor, -en
microprocessor
*die Milch   milk
militärisch   military
die Milliarde, -n   billion
*die Million, -en   million
mindestens   at least
das Minimum, Minima
minimum
der Minister, - (m) / die
Ministerin, -nen (f)   Cabinet
member
*die Minute, -n   minute
mischen   to mix
mißbrauchen   to abuse
der Mißerfolg, -e   failure
das Mißtrauen   mistrust
mißtrauisch (gegen)
suspicious (towards)
das Mißverständnis, -se
misunderstanding
*mißverstehen (mißverstand,
mißverstanden)   to
misunderstand
*mit (+ dat.)   with, at, by
die Mitarbeit   collaboration
mit·arbeiten   to collaborate
der Mitarbeiter, - (m) / die
Mitarbeiterin, -nen (f)
collaborator, coworker
mit·bringen (brachte mit,
mitgebracht)   to bring along
*miteinander   together
das Mitgefühl   sympathy
das Mitglied, -er   member
der Mit-Konsum   co-
consumption
das Mitleid   pity
mit·machen   to go along (with);
to join in
der Mitmensch, -en, -en   fellow
creature
mit·nehmen (nimmt mit; a,
mitgenommen)   to take along
mit·planen   to join in the
planning
die Mitschuld   complicity;

mitschuldig   accessory
der Mitschüler, - (m)/die
Mitschülerin, -nen (f)   fellow
student
mit·singen (a, u)   to sing along
*der Mittag, -e   noon; *das
Mittagessen, -   lunch, dinner;
*mittags   at noon; die
Mittagspause, -n   lunch hour
*die Mitte, -n   center
mit·teilen   to inform; to share
*das Mittel, -   means
der Mittelpunkt, -e   center
der Mittelstand   middle class
der Mittelwesten   midwest
mitten in   in the middle (of)
die Mitternacht   midnight
mittlere   (the) middle one
die Mittlere Reife   diploma
from Realschule
mittlerweile   in the meantime
der/die Mitversicherte (noun
decl. like adj.)   co-insured,
dependent
*die Möbel (pl.)   furniture
die Mobilität   mobility
möblieren   to furnish
die Mode, -n   fashion; das
Modejournal, -e   fashion
magazine
das Modell, -e   model
der Modellbauer, -   pattern
maker
modern   modern
*mögen   to like
*möglich   possible;
möglicherweise   possibly;
möglichst [bald]   as [soon] as
possible
die Möglichkeit, -en   possibility
*der Moment, -e   moment
*der Monat, -e   month;
monatlich   monthly
*der Mond, -e   moon
monoton   monotonous
das Moped, -s   small motorcycle
die Moral   morals; moral (of
story)
moralisierend   moralizing
der Mord, -e   murder
*morgen   tomorrow
*der Morgen, -   morning; der

Morgenmantel, ⸚   dressing
gown
*morgens   in the morning
die Morgenstunde, -n   early
morning hour
das Motiv, -e   motive; theme
*der Motor, -en   motor, engine
*das Motorrad, ⸚er   motorcycle
das Motto, -s   slogan, motto
*müde   tired
die Müdigkeit   tiredness
die Mühe, -n   effort; mühevoll
laborious; troublesome
die Mühle, -n   mill
der Müll   trash, refuse; der
Mülleimer, -   garbage can
der Müller, - (m)   miller; die
Müllerin, -nen (f)   miller,
miller's wife
der Müllwagen, -   garbage
truck
*der Mund, ⸚er   mouth;
mündlich   verbal
munter   cheerful
murmeln   to mutter
*das Museum, Museen
museum
*die Musik   music; musikalisch
musical
der Musikant, -en, -en
musician
der Musikautomat, -en, -en
juke box
der Musiker, - (m) / die
Musikerin, -nen (f)
musician, composer
das Musikgeschäft, -e   music
store
die Musikhochschule, -n
conservatory
der Musikprofessor, -en (m)/die
Musikprofessorin, -nen (f)
music professor
das Musikstück, -e
composition
die Musikstunde, -n   music
lesson
*müssen (muß; mußte, gemußt)
must, to have to
der Mut   courage, spirit; mutig
courageous
*die Mutter, ⸚   mother;

mütterlicherseits on the mother's side

die Mütze, -n hat, cap

die Mythologie, -n mythology

na well; come now; what did I tell you

*nach (+ dat.) after; according to

*der Nachbar, -n, -n neighbor

die Nachbarschaft, -en neighborhood

*nachdem afterwards; after

nach·denken (dachte nach, nachgedacht) to reflect; nachdenklich reflective, thoughtful

nacheinander one after the other

nach·erzählen to retell

die Nacherzählung, -en retelling of a story

nach·gehen (ging nach, [ist] nachgegangen) to pursue; die Uhr geht nach the watch is slow

*nachher later

nach·lassen (läßt nach; ließ nach, nachgelassen) to leave behind; to get weaker; to give up

*der Nachmittag, -e afternoon

*nachmittags in the afternoon

der Nachname, -ns, -n last name

die Nachricht, -en message; (plural) news; der Nachrichtendienst, -e radio news service; das Nachrichtenmagazin, -e news magazine

nach·rüsten to catch up in rearming

nach·schauen to go and see; to gaze after

*nächst next

*die Nacht, ⸚e night; nächtlich at night

der Nachteil, -e disadvantage

*der Nachtisch, -e dessert

nackt naked

die Nadel, -n needle

der Nagel, ⸚ nail

*nahe (näher, nächst-) near, close; ~ der Uni near the university

die Nähe nearness; in der ~ not far

*nähen to sew

nahe·stehen (stand nahe, nahegestanden) to be close; ich stehe ihm nahe I am close to him

naiv naive

*der Name, -ns, -n name; namens by name of, called

*nämlich of course, namely, you see

der Narr, -en, -en fool

*die Nase, -n nose

*naß wet

die Nation, -en nation

national national

die Nationalität, -en nationality

die NATO North Atlantic Treaty Organization

*die Natur nature; disposition; von ~ aus by nature

*natürlich natural; of course

der Naturschutz preservation of nature

die Naturwissenschaft, -en natural or physical science

der Nebel, - mist, fog; neblig foggy

*neben (+ acc./dat.) next to, beside; nebenan next door; nebenbei by the way

*der Neffe, -n, -n nephew

negativ negative

*nehmen (nimmt; a, genommen) to take

der Neid envy; neidisch (auf + acc.) envious (of)

*nein no

*nennen (a, a) to call

der Nerv, -en nerve; es geht mir auf die Nerven that gets on my nerves

nervös nervous

die Nervosität nervousness

nesteln to fasten, to tie

*nett nice, kind; pleasant

*neu new; neuest latest

die Neugier curiosity; *neugierig (auf + acc.) curious (about)

die Neuigkeit, -en news

neulich lately

*nicht not; nicht nur ... sondern auch not only . . . but also

*die Nichte, -n niece

der Nichtraucher, - non-smoker

*nichts nothing; ~ weiter nothing more

nicken to nod

*nie never

nieder down

nieder·fahren (ä; u, a) to run over

nieder·legen to pull down

niedrig low

niemals never, ever

*niemand nobody

*nirgends nowhere

nirgendwo no where

die Nische, -n niche, recess

*noch still, yet; in addition

die Nonne, -n nun

die Nonsenssprache, -n nonsense language, meaningless sounds

(das) Nordamerika North America

(das) Nordbayern North Bavaria

*der Norden north; nördlich northern

die Norm, -en norm

normal normal; normalerweise normally, usually

die Nostalgie nostalgia

die Note, -n grade

*nötig necessary

die Notiz, -en note; notice

*die Null, -en zero

*die Nummer, -n number

*nun now

*nur only

der Nutzen profit; advantage

nützen to be of use; nützlich profitable; advantageous; du warst mir nützlich you were helpful to me

*ob if, whether
*oben above; upstairs; nach ~ gehen to go upstairs
*der Ober, - waiter
die Oberfläche, -n surface
oberflächlich superficial
*oberhalb (+ gen.) above
der Oberidiot, -en, -en superidiot
obig above; foregoing, above-mentioned
*das Obst fruit; die Obsttorte, -n cake with fruit on top
*obwohl although
*oder or
*der Ofen, ¨ stove; oven
*offen open; frank
öffentlich public
die Öffentlichkeit public
offiziell official
der Offizier, -e officer (military)
*öffnen to open
die Öffnung, -en opening
*oft (ö) often
öfters several times
*ohne (+ acc.) without; ohne daß without; *ohne ... zu (+ inf.) without
*das Ohr, -en ear
die Ökologie ecology
ökologisch ecologic
das Öl, -e oil
die Olympiade, -n Olympic Games
*die Oma, -s grandma
der Omnibus, -se public bus
*der Onkel, - uncle
*der Opa, -s grandpa
die Oper, -n opera
die Operation, -en operation; surgery
operieren to operate
das Opfer, - victim
die Opposition opposition (party)
ordentlich orderly, neat, tidy
ordnen to order, to arrange
die Ordnung, -en order, regulation; arrangement;

ordnungsliebend tidy, orderly
die Organisation, -en organization
der Organismus, Organismen organism
die Orientierungsstufe, -n orientation level at school, consisting of classes 5 and 6
das Original, -e original
*der Ort, -e place, spot
*der Osten east; Orient; der Osteuropäer, - East European; östlich eastern
die Ostern (pl.) Easter
*(das) Österreich Austria; österreichisch Austrian
die Ostsee Baltic Sea
der Overall, -s overall
der Ozean, -e ocean

*das Paar, -e pair; couple
*paar: ein ~ a few
das Päckchen, - small parcel
*packen to pack (up); grab
die Packung, -en wrapper
*das Paket, -e package; bundle
der Pakt, -e pact
der Panzer, - armor plate; tank
*das Papier, -e paper; document
die Pappe, -n cardboard; das Pappschild, -er cardboard sign
der Parasit, -en, -en parasite
das Parfum, -s perfume
*der Park, -s park
*parken to park; das Parkhaus, ¨er parking garage
*der Parkplatz, ¨e parking space
das Parlament, -e parliament
die Parole, -n slogan
die Parodie, -n parody
die Partei, -en party (political)
die Partikel, -n particle
*der Partner, - (m) / die Partnerin, -nen (f) partner; spouse; die Partnerschaft, -en partnership
*die Party, -s party
der Paß, Pässe passport
passé outdated
*passen (+ dat.) to fit

*passieren [ist] (+ dat.) to happen, to take place
passiv passive
pathetisch pathetic
*der Patient, -en, -en (m) / die Patientin, -nen (f) patient
die Pause, -n pause; intermission
peinlich embarrassing
die Pension, -en pension; small hotel
perplex perplexed
*die Person, -en person; die Personalabteilung, -en personnel department
das Personal staff, personnel
personifizieren to personify
persönlich personal; das Persönliche personal quality; die Persönlichkeit, -en personality
die Perspektive, -n perspective; prospect
pervers perverse
der Pfarrer, - (m) / die Pfarrerin, -nen (f) pastor
der Pfeffer pepper
die Pfeife, -n pipe; whistle
*der Pfennig, -e one hundredth of a mark
*das Pferd, -e horse
pflanzen to plant
*die Pflanze, -n plant
das Pflaster, - bandage; pavement
pflegen to nurse, to take care of
die Pflicht, -en duty
pflücken to pick
*das Pfund, -e pound
das Phänomen, -e phenomenon
die Phantasie, -n imagination; fantasy; phantasielos without imagination, phantasievoll imaginative; phantastisch fantastic, marvelous
die Philosophie, -n philosophy
das Photo, -s photograph
die Photographie, -n photography; picture

der Pianist, -en, -en (m) / die Pianistin, -nen (f) pianist
*das Picknick, -s or -e picnic
piepsen to chirp; bei dir piept's wohl you must be crazy
die Pille, -n pill
der Pilot, -en, -en (m) / die Pilotin, -nen (f) pilot
der Pinsel, - brush
das Plakat, -e poster
*der Plan, ̈e plan; der Planer, - designer
planen to plan, to design
die Planung, -en planning
die Plastikfolie, -n plastic foil or wrap
die Plastiktasche, -n plastic bag
*die Platte, -n record; *der Plattenspieler, - record player
*der Platz, ̈e place; seat; nicht am ~ not suitable, not in order
plausibel plausible
*plötzlich suddenly
das Plusquamperfekt past perfect tense
(das) Polen Poland
*die Politik politics; *der Politiker, - (m) / die Politikerin, -nen (f) politician; politisch political
*die Polizei police; police station; das Polizeirevier, -e police station
*der Polizist, -en, -en (m) / die Polizistin, nen (f) police officer
populär popular
die Portion, -en portion, ration
positiv positive
*die Post post office; mail
der Posten, - guard
*das/der Poster, - poster
die Postkarte, -n postcard
die Postleitzahl, -en zip code
das Präfix, -e prefix
*praktisch practical
die Präsentierschachtel, -n merchandising box

der Präsident, -en, -en (m)/die Präsidentin, -nen (f) president
*der Preis, -e price; prize
preiswert inexpensive
die Presse, -n the press
pressen to press
das Prestige prestige
*prima great; first-rate
primär primary
primitiv primitive
das Prinzip, -ien principle
die Priorität, -en priority; nach Prioritäten in priority
privat private; das Privatleben private life, privacy; der Privatmann, ̈er private person; die Privatperson, -en private individual
die Privatsphäre, -n private world
das Privileg, -ien privilege
*pro per, for
die Probe, -n test
probieren to try out; to taste; to test
*das Problem, -e problem
das Produkt, -e product; outcome
die Produktion, -en production; die Produktionskette, -n production chain
produzieren to produce
*der Professor, -en (m) / die Professorin, -nen (f) professor
der Profit, -e profit
profitieren to profit
pro forma as a matter of form
*das Programm, -e program; schedule
das Projekt, -e project
prompt immediately
das Pronomen, Pronomina pronoun
prosaisch prosaic
der Prospekt, -e prospect; prospectus
der Protest, -e protest
protestieren to protest
provisorisch temporary

das Prozent, -e percent, percentage
der Prozeß, Prozesse process; trial
prüfen to test
*die Prüfung, -en examination
psychisch psychical, mental
psychologisch psychological
*das Publikum audience, public
*der Pullover, - sweater
pulsieren to pulsate
der Punkt, -e dot; point
*pünktlich on time; punctual
die Puppe, -n doll
*putzen to clean; to polish

der Quadratmeter, - square meter
die Qual, -en pain, misery
die Qualifikation, -en qualification
qualifiziert qualified
die Qualität, -en quality
die Quantität, -en quantity
der Quatsch nonsense
die Quelle, -n spring; source
quer oblique
die Quittung, -en receipt

der Rabe, -n raven
der Rabenvater, ̈ harsh father who neglects his children
*das Rad, ̈er wheel; bicycle; die Radtour, -en bicycle tour
*rad·fahren (ä; u, [ist] a) to ride a bike
der Radiergummi, -s eraser
*das Radio, -s radio
der Rahmen frame
die Rakete, -n rocket
der Rand, ̈er edge
der Rang, ̈e rank; die Rangliste, -n table or list with ranked order
der Rasen, - lawn
*der Rasierapparat, -e razor
*sich rasieren to shave
*der Rat advice, suggestion
der Rat, ̈e council; *das Rathaus, ̈er town hall
*raten (ä; ie, a) to advise; to guess; ratsam advisable;

ratlos perplexed
der Rauch smoke; **der Raucher, -** smoker
*****rauchen** to smoke; **rauchig** smoky
*****der Raum, ¨e** room; space; district
räumlich spatial
raus = heraus out, outside
raus·tragen (ä; u, a) to carry outside
reagieren to react
die Reaktion, -en reaction
die Realschule, -n school from 5th to 10th class that leads to the degree of "Mittlere Reife" and prepares pupils for careers in trade, industry, etc.
rechnen to calculate
*****recht** right; just; **einigen Menschen kann man es nie ~ machen** you just can't please some people; **~ haben** to be right; **~ behalten** to be right; **das ist mir ~** it suits me
*****das Recht, -e** right; law; justice
*****rechts** to or on the right side
*****der Rechtsanwalt, ¨e** (m)/ **die Rechtsanwältin, -nen** (f) lawyer; **der Rechtsanwaltsgehilfe, -n** law clerk
der Recorder recorder
die Rede, -n speech; **eine ~ halten** to give a speech; **indirekte ~** indirect discourse; **die Redewendung, -en** idiom
*****reden** to talk
der Redner, - speaker
reduzieren to reduce
*****das Referat, -e** report, essay; **einen ~ halten** to give a report
reflektieren to reflect
die Reform, -en reform
das Regal, -e shelf
die Regel, -n rule; **in der ~** normally
regelmäßig regular
*****der Regen** rain; **der Regenmantel, ¨** raincoat; *****der Regenschirm, -e**

umbrella; **der saure Regen** acid rain
regieren to govern
*****die Regierung, -en** government
regional regional
registrieren to take note of
*****regnen** to rain; **regnerisch** rainy
rehabilitieren to rehabilitate
reiben (ie, ie) to rub
*****reich** rich
reichen to pass, hand, give
*****reif** ripe
*****die Reihe, -n** row; **du bist an der Reihe** it's your turn; **die Reihenfolge, -n** sequence
der Reim, -e rhyme
*****rein** clear; pure
rein = herein in, inside
reinigen to clean
*****der Reis** rice
*****die Reise, -n** journey, tour; **das Reisebuch, ¨er** guidebook **der Reiseführer, -** travel guide; guidebook; *****das Reisebüro, -s** travel agency
*****reisen ([ist])** to travel
reißen (i, i) to tear
*****reiten (ritt, [ist] geritten)** to ride (a horse)
die Reklame, -n advertisement
der Rekord, -e record
relativ relative(ly)
relevant relevant
die Religion, -en religion
*****rennen (a, [ist] a)** to run; to race
die Renovierung, -en renovation
die Rente, -n pension; **der Rentner, -** (m)/**die Rentnerin, -nen** (f) pensioner
die Reparatur, -en repair; **die Reparaturwerkstatt, ¨en** repair shop
*****reparieren** to repair
das Repertoire, -s repertory
die Republik, -en republic
repräsentieren to represent
*****reservieren** to reserve
resigniert resigned
der Respekt respect; **die**

Respektsperson, -en authority figure; **respektvoll** respectful; **respektabel** respectable
respektieren to respect
das Ressentiment, -s resentment
der Rest, -e rest; remains
*****das Restaurant, -s** restaurant
das Resultat, -e result
*****retten** to save
die Revolte, -n revolt
die Revolution, -en revolution
das Rezept, -e recipe, prescription
die Rezession, -en recession
rezitieren to recite
richten to direct at; adjust, correct
der Richter, - judge
*****richtig** right
*****die Richtung, -en** direction
*****riechen (o, o)** to smell
riesig gigantic, immense
der Riese, -n, -n giant
der Ring, -e ring
das Risiko, Risiken risk
*****der Rock, ¨e** skirt; coat
*****der Rock** rock music; **die Rockmusik** rock music
die Rockband, -s rock band
*****roh** raw; brutal
das Rohr, -e pipe
*****die Rolle, -n** role; **das Rollenspiel, -e** role play
rollen to roll
der Roman, -e novel
der Röntgenstrahl, -en x-ray
die Rose, -n rose
*****rot (ö)** red; **~ werden** to blush; **rothaarig** red-haired
die Routinearbeit routine job
die Routineberufe (pl) routine jobs
routiniert well-trained, experienced
die Rübe, -n turnip; head (slang)
der Rücken, - back
die Rückfahrkarte, -n return ticket
die Rückfahrt, en

return journey
der Rucksack, ⁻e backpack
die Rückseite, -n back side
die Rücksicht, -en discretion,
  consideration
der Ruf, -e call; reputation
*rufen (ie, u) to call
die Ruhe quiet, peace
ruhen to rest; ruhelos
  restless
*ruhig quiet, silent
der Ruhm glory, fame
*rund round
die Runde, -n circle; match;
  party
rund·fliegen (o, [ist] o) to circle
  an area
der Rundfunk radio,
  broadcasting
runter = herunter down
der Russe, -n, -n (m)/die
  Russin, -nen (f) Russian

*die Sache, -n matter, thing
der Sack, ⁻e sack, bag
*der Saft, ⁻e juice
*sagen to say, tell
*die Sahne cream
*der Salat, -e salad, lettuce
die Salbe, -m ointment, salve
das Salz, -e salt; salzig salty
*sammeln to collect
die Sammlung, -en collection
sämtlich all, entire
der Sand sand
sanft gentle; easy; smooth
der Sänger, - (m) / die
  Sängerin, -nen (f) singer,
  folksinger
*satt satisfied with food or
  drink
*der Satz, ⁻e sentence; das
  Satzpaar, -e group of two
  sentences; couplet; der
  Satzteil, -e part of a sentence
*sauber clean
säubern to clean up
saudumm extremely stupid
*sauer sour; angry
der Sauerstoff oxygen
saugen to suck
*das Schach chess

die Schachtel, -n box
*schade (um) what a pity
  (about)
*schaden (+ dat.) to harm, to
  hurt
der Schaden, ⁻ damage; injury;
  schädigen to harm;
  schädlich harmful
der Schadstoff, -e pollutant
das Schaf, -e sheep; der
  Schafskopf, ⁻e fool
*schaffen to provide; to get it
  done
schälen to peel
*die Schallplatte, -n record
schalten to switch
der Schalter, - switch; counter
*scharf (ä) hot; sharp
der Schatten, - shade; shadow
der Schatz, ⁻e sweetheart
schätzen to value; to guess
schauen to look
die Schaufel, -n shovel
das Schaufenster, - store
  window
das Schauspiel, -e drama, play
der Schauspieler, - actor / die
  Schauspielerin, -nen
  actress
der Scheck, -s check
scheiden (ie, [ist] ie) to
  separate
der Schein, -e gleam, shine;
  appearance; certificate; der
  Scheinwerfer, - floodlight;
  headlight
*scheinen (ie, ie) to shine; to
  appear
*schenken to give as a present
die Schere, -n scissors
die Scheune, -n barn
die Schicht, -en class, level
*schick chic
*schicken to send
das Schicksal, -e fate
*schieben (o, o) to push
schief oblique; bent; distorted
*schießen (o, geschossen) to
  shoot
*das Schiff, -e ship
das Schild, -er sign; shield
schimpfen to scold

*der Schirm,-e umbrella
schizophren schizoid
die Schlacht, -en battle
schlachten to slaughter
der Schlaf sleep; die
  Schlafratte, -n sound
  sleeper, sleepy-head; der
  Schlafsack, ⁻e sleeping bag;
  *das Schlafzimmer, -
  bedroom
*schlafen (ä; ie, a) to sleep
schlaflos sleepless
schläfrig sleepy
der Schlag, ⁻e blow, stroke
*schlagen (ä; u, a) to hit; to beat
schlagend striking; impressive
die Schlägerei, -en brawl
die Schlagzeile, -n headline
die Schlange, -n snake;
  waiting line, queue
*schlank slender
*schlecht bad; spoiled
*schließen (o, geschlossen) to
  shut
*schließlich finally; after all
*schlimm severe; bad
*das Schloß, Schlösser lock;
  castle
der Schlosser, - locksmith;
  pipe fitter
der Schluck, -e sip
schlucken to swallow
der Schluß, Schlüsse end,
  conclusion; Schlüsse ziehen
  to draw conclusions
*der Schlüssel, - key
das Schlüsselloch, ⁻er keyhole
*schmal narrow; slim, slender
*schmecken to taste; das
  schmeckt mir it tastes good
der Schmerz, -en pain
schmerzen to hurt
schmierig greasy, oily
schminken to put on make-up
der Schmutz dirt
*schmutzig dirty
*der Schnee snow; schneeweiß
  white as snow
*schneiden (schnitt,
  geschnitten) to cut
der Schneider, - tailor / die
  Schneiderin, -nen

seamstress
*schneien to snow
*schnell fast, quick
die Schnellstraße, -n
expressway
der Schnellzug, -̈e fast train
that stops only in larger cities
*das Schnitzel, - cutlet
der Schnupfen head cold
*die Schokolade, -n chocolate
*schon already
*schön beautiful; nice; OK
die Schönheit, -en beauty
der Schornstein, -e chimney
*der Schrank, -̈e closet
die Schraube, -n screw; eine ~
locker haben to be slightly
crazy
der Schraubenzieher, -
screwdriver
der Schreck, -e scare; fear;
schrecklich frightful,
horrible; very (coll.)
der Schrei, -e scream
*schreiben (ie, ie) to write
das Schreiben, - official letter
die Schreibmaschine, -n
typewriter
das Schreibpapier stationery
*der Schreibtisch, -e desk
das Schreibzeug writing
utensils
schreien (ie, ie) to scream,
shout
der Schreiner, - cabinetmaker
schreiten (schritt, ist
geschritten) to step; to
proceed
die Schrift, -en writing;
handwriting; schriftlich
written
schrill shrill
der Schritt, -e step; ~
annehmen to fall into step
der Schrubber, - scrubber
schüchtern shy
*der Schuh, -e shoe; wo der ~
drückt where the difficulty is
die Schularbeit, -en
homework, home assignment
die Schuld, -en obligation;
debt; fault, blame; schuld sein

(an + dat.) to be guilty (of)
*schulden to owe
*schuldig guilty; indebted;
schuldlos (an + dat.)
blameless (of); er ist mir Geld
~ he owes me money
*die Schule, -n school; der
Schultyp, -en type of school;
die Schularbeit, -en school
work
*der Schüler - (m)/die Schülerin,
-nen (f) pupil
die Schulter, -n shoulder
der Schuß, Schüsse gunshot
die Schüssel, -n bowl
der Schuster, - shoemaker
schütteln to shake
der Schutz protection
schützen to protect
*schwach weak
die Schwäche, -n weakness
die Schwachheit, -en weakness
der Schwamm, -̈e sponge
schwanger pregnant
*schwarz black; ~ auf weiß
black and white (written);
schwarzgerändert black-
rimmed
der Schwarzwald Black Forest
der Schwede, -n, -n/die
Schwedin, -nen Swede
der Schwefel sulphur
das Schwefeldioxid sulphur
dioxide
schweigen (ie, ie) to be silent;
schweigsam taciturn
*das Schwein, -e pig; ~ haben
to be lucky
*die Schweiz Switzerland; in
die ~ to Switzerland
*der Schweizer, - (m)/die
Schweizerin, -nen (f) Swiss
*schwer heavy; difficult
schwer·fallen (ä; fiel, [ist]
gefallen) to find difficult
*die Schwester, -n sister
schwierig difficult, hard
die Schwierigkeit, -en
difficulty
*das Schwimmbad, -̈er
swimming pool
das Schwimmbecken, -

swimming pool
*schwimmen (a, [ist] o) to swim
die Schwimmstunde, -n
swimming lesson
schwitzen to sweat
*der See, -n lake
*die See ocean
der Seemann, -leute sailor
das Segel, - sail
*segeln [ist] to sail
*sehen (ie; a, e) to see
sehenswert worth seeing
die Sehenswürdigkeit, -en
object of interest; sight
*sehr very, greatly, much
die Seide, -n silk
*die Seife, -n soap; seifig
soapy
*sein to be
seinetwegen on his account
*seit (+ dat.) since
*seit (conj.) since; *seitdem
(conj.) since; (adv.) since
then
*die Seite, -n page; side; die
Seitenstraße, -n side street
*der Sekretär, -e (m)/die
Sekretärin, -nen (f) secretary
der Sekt champagne
der Sektor, -en sector
*die Sekunde, -n second
*selber oneself
*selbst oneself; selbständig
self-supporting, independent;
selbstgerecht self-righteous;
selbstverständlich obvious;
of course; die Selbst-
bedienung self-service; das
Selbstgespräch, -e
monologue; der Selbstmord,
-e suicide, ~ begehen to
commit suicide
*selten rare
*das Semester, - semester; der
Semesterbeginn beginning
of the semester; erstes ~
first-semester student
*das Seminar, -e seminar; die
Seminararbeit, -en seminar
paper; der Seminarraum, -̈e
seminar room
*senden (sandte, gesandt) to

send; (gesendet) to
broadcast
die Sendung, -en broadcast,
program (radio, TV)
senkrecht vertical
der Service service
servieren to serve
*der Sessel, - armchair
*setzen to set; to place; sich
setzen to sit down
seufzen to sigh
*sicher secure; sure
die Sicherheit security; die
Sicherheitsvorschrift, -en
safety rule
sichern to secure
sichtbar visible
der Sieg, -e victory
siezen to address somebody
formally (with Sie)
das Signal, -e sign, signal
die Silbe, -n syllable
silbern silver
das Silber silver
*singen (a, u) to sing
*sinken (a, [ist] u) to sink
der Sinn, -e sense; sinnlos
foolish; meaningless; sinnvoll
meaningful, significant
sittlich moral, ethical
die Situation, -en situation
der Sitz, -e seat
*sitzen (saß, gesessen) to sit;
er hat gesessen he was in
jail
skeptisch skeptical,
suspicious
*der Ski, -er ski
*ski·laufen (äu; ie, [ist] au) to
ski
skrupellos unscrupulous
*so so; *so ... wie as . . . as
*sobald as soon as
*die Socke, -n sock
so daß so that
soeben just, just now
*das Sofa, -s couch, sofa
*sofort immediately
der Sog, -e wake of a ship;
undertow
*sogar even
sogenannt so-called

*sogleich at once
*der Sohn, -̈e son
solange as long as
*solch such
*der Soldat, -en, -en soldier
die Solidarität solidarity
*sollen to be obliged
*der Sommer, - summer
sonderbar strange, odd
*sondern but, on the contrary
*die Sonne, -n sun; die
Sonnenbrille, -n sunglasses
sonnig sunny
*sonst else, otherwise
*die Sorge, -n sorrow; care
sorgen to take care of; sich
sorgen um to worry about;
ich sorge für ihn I take care
of him
*sorgfältig careful
*soviel as far as, as much
soweit so far as
sowie as soon as, as well as
*sowieso anyhow
die Sowjets Soviets
die Sowjetunion Soviet Union
*sowohl ... als auch not only . . .
but also
sozial social
der Sozialarbeiter, - (m)/die
Sozialarbeiterin, -nen (f)
social worker
der Sozialdemokrat, -en, -en
member of Social Democratic
Party
die Sozialhilfe, -n social aid
sozialistisch socialist
der Sozialpädagoge, -n, -n
(m)/die Sozialpädagogin, -nen
social worker (with university
degree)
sozusagen so to speak
die Spannung, -en tension
*sparen to save; sparsam
saving, economical
*der Spaß, -̈e fun; joke; der
Spaßvogel, -̈ jokester
*spät late
spätestens at the latest
spazieren·fahren (ä; u, [ist] a)
to go for a drive
*spazieren·gehen (ging, [ist]

gegangen) to go for a walk
*der Spaziergang, -̈e walk, stroll
*die Speise, -n food; meal; die
Speisekarte, -n menu
das Spektrum spectrum
der Spezialist, -en, -en (m)/die
Spezialistin, -nen (f)
specialist
die Sphäre, -n sphere
*der Spiegel, - mirror
*das Spiel, -e play, game; der
Spielraum, -̈e margin;
latitude; die Spielkarte, -n
playing card; das Spielzeug, -e
toy; die Spielregel, -n rules
of the game
*spielen to play
spinnen (a, o) to spin; du
spinnst you're crazy
spitz sharp; pointed; sarcastic
die Spitze, -n point
spontan spontaneous
*der Sport sport; ~ treiben to
engage in sports; das
Sportgeschäft, -e sporting
goods store; die Sportgruppe,
-n sport group; der
Sportplatz, -̈e playing field;
*der Sportverein, -e sports
club; der Sportler, - (m.)/die
Sportlerin, -nen (f.) athlete
*sportlich athletic
der Spott ridicule; scorn
*die Sprache, -n language;
speech; sprachlich
linguistic; grammatical;
related to speech; sprachlos
speechless, flabbergasted
*sprechen (i; a, o) to speak, talk
der Sprecher, - (m)/die
Sprecherin, -nen (f) speaker
die Sprechstunde, -n office
hour; die Sprechstundenhilfe,
-n medical assistant,
receptionist
das Sprichwort, -̈er proverb
*springen (a, [ist] u) to jump
der Spruch, -̈e motto
sprühen to spray
*spülen to rinse; to wash dishes
*die Spülmaschine, -n
automatic dishwasher

spüren   to feel, to sense

*der Staat, -en   state; country; staatlich   governmental

das Städele   small town (dialect)

das Stadion, Stadien   stadium

*die Stadt, ̈e   town, city; die Stadthalle, -n   building for meetings and events; die Stadtmitte, -n   center of the city; der Stadtplan, ̈e   city map; das Stadttheater, -   theater of a city; das Stadtviertel, -   quarter, district; die Stadtrundfahrt, -en   city sightseeing tour; das Städtchen, -   little city

städtisch   urban, municipal

der Stahl   steel

das Stakkato, -s   staccato

der Stall, ̈e   stable

der Stamm, ̈e   tree trunk

stammen   to originate

der Stand, ̈e   booth; class

der Standpunkt, -e   point of view

*stark (ä)   strong

die Stärke   strength; force

die Station, -en   station

die Statistik, -en   statistic

*statt (+ gen.)   instead of; statt dessen   instead; *statt ... zu   instead of

statt·finden (a, u)   to take place

der Staub   dust; ~ saugen   to vacuum; der Staubsauger, -   vacuum cleaner

stechen (i; a, o)   to pierce; to sting

*stecken   to stick; to put

*stehen (stand, gestanden)   to stand; to be situated; stehend   standing

stehen·bleiben (ie, [ist] ie)   to stop

die Stehlampe, -n   floor lamp

*stehlen (ie; a, o)   to steal

steigen (ie; [ist] ie)   to climb; to mount; steigend   increasing

*der Stein, -e   stone

*die Stelle, -n   place; position, job

*stellen   to put

die Stellung, -en   position

*sterben (i; a, [ist] o)   to die

der Sterbetag, -e   day of death

das Stereo, -n   abbreviation for *die Stereoanlage, -n   stereo set

stereotyp   stereotypic

*der Stern, -e   star

stets   always

die Steuer, -n   tax

*der Steward, -s (m)/die Stewardeß, Stewardessen (f)   flight attendant

das Stichwort, -e   cue, catch-word

der Stickstoff   nitrogen

der Stiefel, -   boot

der Stil, -e   style

*still   calm, silent

still·stehen (stand; gestanden)   to stand still

*die Stimme, -n   voice

*stimmen   to be correct, be in order; das ~   that's right

die Stimmung, -en   mood

stinken (a, u)   to stink

das Stipendium, die Stipendien   scholarship

die Stirn(e), -en   forehead; front

der Stock, ̈e   stick, walking stick

*der Stock, Stockwerke   floor

stocken   to hesitate; to stop; stockend   by stops and starts

*der Stoff, -e   material; topic

stolz (auf + acc.)   proud (of)

stoppen   to stop

das Stoppschild, -er   stop sign

stören   to disturb, interrupt

*stoßen (ö; ie, o)   to push; to hit

*die Strafe, -n   punishment, fine

der Strahl, -en   beam, flash, ray

strahlen   to radiate, beam

*die Straße, -n   street, road

*die Straßenbahn, -en   streetcar; das Straßencafé, -s   sidewalk café; der Straßenhändler, -   street vendor; der Straßenrand, ̈er   roadside

streben   to strive

streichen (i, i)   to paint; to stroke

das Streichholz, ̈er   match

streifen   to graze

der Streifenwagen, -   police car

der Streik, -s   strike

*streiken   to strike

der Streit, -e   quarrel

(sich) streiten (stritt, gestritten)   to quarrel

streng   strict; harsh; streng gegen   strictly against

der Streß   stress

das Stroh   straw

*der Strumpf, ̈e   stocking

*das Stück, -e   piece; (theater) play

die Stube, -n   room, living room

*der Student, -en, -en (m)/die Studentin, -nen (f)   student; *das Studentenheim, -e   dormitory; die Studentenschaft, -en   student body

*studieren   to study; to attend a university

das Studium, die Studien   study; university education

die Stufe, -n   step; level

*der Stuhl, ̈e   chair

stumm   mute

*die Stunde, -n   hour; lesson; stundenlang   for hours

der Stundenlohn, ̈e   hourly wage

der Stundenplan, ̈e   class schedule

-stündig   over a period of . . . hours

stur   pig-headed

der Sturm, ̈e   storm

der Sturz, ̈e   fall; crash

stürzen [ist]   to plunge, fall

das Substantiv, -e   noun

die Subvention, -en   subsidy

die Suche   search

*suchen   to look for

(das) Südamerika   South America

*der Süden   south; südlich   southern

die Summe, -n   sum, total

sündigen   to sin

super   super
*der Supermarkt, ¨e   supermarket
*die Suppe, -n   soup
*süß   sweet; cute
das Sylvester, -   New Year's Eve
das Symbol, -e   symbol; symbolisch   symbolic
der Sympathisant, -en, -en   sympathizer, person who supports a view
sympathisch   congenial; sie ist mir ~   I like her
das Symptom, -e   symptom
das System, -e   system
systematisch   systematic
die Szene, -n   scene

der Tabak   tobacco
die Tabelle, -n   chart, table
*die Tablette,-n   tablet, pill
*die Tafel, -n   blackboard; chart
*der Tag, -e   day; die Tageszeit, -en   time of day
tagelang   for days
*täglich   daily
das Tal, ¨er   valley
der Tank, -s   tank
*tanken   to refuel, fill up
*die Tankstelle, -n   gas station; der Tankwart, -e   gas station attendant
die Tanne, -n   fir tree; der Tannenbaum, ¨e   Christmas tree
*die Tante, -n   aunt
*der Tanz, ¨e   dance
*tanzen   to dance
*die Tasche, -n   pocket; bag; das Taschenbuch, ¨er   pocket book, paperback; die Taschenlampe, -n   flashlight; das Taschentuch, ¨er   handkerchief
*die Tasse, -n   cup; nicht alle Tassen im Schrank haben   to be crazy
*die Tat, -en   deed, act; in der ~   in fact
der Täter, -   perpetrator
*tätig   active, busy
die Tatsache, -n   fact

tatsächlich   indeed, really
taufen   to baptize
täuschen   to deceive
*tausend   thousand
*das Taxi, -s   cab; *der Taxifahrer, - (m) / die Taxifahrerin, -nen (f)   cab driver; der Taxistand   cab stand
die Technik   technology; technique; technisch   technical
technisiert   pertaining to technology
*der Tee, -s   tea
*der Teenager, -   teenager
*der Teil, -e   part, section; zum ~   partly, sometimes
*teilen   to divide
teil·nehmen (an + dat.) (nimmt teil; a, teilgenommen)   to take part (in)
der Teilnehmer, - (m)/die Teilnehmerin, -nen (f)   participant
teils   in part
die Teilung, -en   division, separation
teilweise   partly
die Teilzeitarbeit, -en   part-time job
*das Telefon, -e   telephone; das Telefonbuch, ¨er   telephone book; das Telefongespräch, -e   telephone call
*telefonieren mit   to call; telefonisch   by telephone
die Telefonzelle, -n   phone booth
*der Teller, -   plate
*die Temperatur, -en   temperature
das Tempo   speed
*das Tennis   tennis; das Tennismatch, -s   tennis set; der Tennisplatz, ¨e   tennis court; der Tennisschuh, -e   tennis shoe
*der Teppich, -e   carpet
der Termin, -e   date, deadline
der Test, -s   test
testen   to test

*teuer   expensive; das ist mir ~   that is dear to me
der Text, -e   text
*das Theater, -   theater; ins ~   to the theater
die Theke, -n   bar, counter
das Thema, Themen   theme; subject
die Theorie, -n   theory
das Thermometer, -   thermometer
die Thermosflasche, -n   thermos bottle
der Thron, -e   throne
ticken   to tick
*das Ticket, -s   ticket
*tief   deep
die Tiefe, -n   depth
*das Tier, -e   animal; ein großes ~   an important person (a big fish); der Tierarzt, ¨e (m)/die Tierärztin, -nen (f)   veterinarian; tierisch   animal-like; tierlieb   fond of animals
tippen   to tip; to type
*der Tisch, -e   table; den ~ decken   to set the table; die Tischdecke, -n   tablecloth
der Tischler, -   cabinet maker
das Tischtennis   table tennis
der Titel, -   title
*die Tochter, ¨   daughter
*der Tod, -e   death
*die Toilette, -n   toilet
tolerant   tolerant
tolerieren   to tolerate
*toll   marvelous, great, fantastic; mad
der Ton, ¨e   sound
*das Tonband, ¨er   tape; *das Tonbandgerät, -e   tape recorder
der Topf, ¨e   pot; jar
topographisch   topographical
*das Tor, -e   gate
*die Torte, -n   cake (in layers)
*tot   dead
total   total
der/die Tote (noun decl. like adj.)   dead person
*töten   to kill

das Totenbett, -en   deathbed

*die Tour, -en   tour, trip

*der Tourist, -en, -en *(m)* / die Touristin, -nen *(f)*   tourist

die Tradition, -en   tradition; traditionell   traditional

*tragen (ä; u, a)   to carry, to bear; to wear; tragbar   portable, wearable

die Tragik   tragedy

tragisch   tragic

die Tragödie, -n   tragedy

trainieren   to train, exercise

das Training   training

der Traktor, -en   tractor

trampen   to hitchhike

die Träne, -n   tear

die Transaktion, -en   transaction

die Transportmöglichkeit, -en   various means of transportation

*trauen (+ *dat.*)   to trust

der Traum, ⸚e   dream; traumhaft   as nice as in a dream; der Traumberuf, -e   dream job

träumen   to dream; träumerisch   dreamy

*traurig (über + *acc.*)   sad (about)

*(sich) treffen (i; traf, o)   to meet (with somebody)

das Treffen, -   meeting

*treiben (ie, ie)   to push, set into motion; to occupy oneself with something

*trennen   to separate

*die Treppe, -n   stairs

*treten (tritt; a, e)   to kick; ~ [ist]   to step

*treu   faithful, loyal

trinkbar   drinkable

*trinken (a, u)   to drink

der Tritt, -e   step; kick

triumphierend   triumphant

*trocken   dry

der Tropfen, -   drop

tropfen   to drip

der Trost   consolation

*trotz (+ *gen.*)   in spite of

*trotzdem   nevertheless

*das Tuch, ⸚er   cloth

*tüchtig   capable; qualified

*tun (tat, getan)   to do

*die Tür, -en   door

die Türkei   Turkey

der Turm, ⸚e   tower

turnen   to do gymnastics

*die Tüte, -n   bag

der Typ, -en   type; typisch   typical

*die U-Bahn, -en   subway

*üben   to practice

*über (+ *acc./dat.*)   over, above, on top; more; by way of

*überall   everywhere

überbrücken   to bridge over

übereinander   on top of each other

überein·stimmen   to agree with

überfüllt   overloaded

übergeben (i; a, e)   to hand over

übergehen (überging, übergangen)   to pass over

überglücklich   overjoyed

*überhaupt   generally; really; at all

*(sich) überlegen   to reflect on überlegend   pondering

*übermorgen   the day after tomorrow

übernachten   to stay overnight

das Übernatürliche   supernatural

übernehmen (übernimmt; a, übernommen)   to take over

*überraschen   to surprise; überrascht (durch)   surprised (by)

die Überraschung, -en   surprise

überreden   to persuade

die Überschrift, -en   title

der Überschuh, -e   overshoe

übersehen (ie; a, e)   to overlook

übersetzen   to translate; übersetzbar   translatable

übertreffen (i; übertraf, o)   to surpass

überzeugen   to convince; überzeugt (von)   convinced (by); überzeugend   convincing

die Überzeugung, -en   conviction

üblich   usual, common

*übrig   remaining

*übrigens   by the way; moreover

*die Übung, -en   practice, exercise

*das Ufer, -   shore, bank

*die Uhr, -en   clock, watch; die ~ geht nach   the watch is slow; die Uhrensammlung, -en   watch or clock collection

*um (+ *acc.*)   about; around; approximately; near; um ... willen (+ *gen*)   for the sake of

*um ... zu   in order to

umarmen   to embrace, hug

die Umarmung, -en   embrace, hug

um·blicken   to look around

um·drehen   to turn around

um·fallen (ä; fiel um, [ist] a)   to fall over

die Umfrage, -n   inquiry; poll

umgangssprachlich   colloquial

umgeben (i; a, e)   to surround

um·schreiben (ie, ie)   to rewrite, to express in other words

umsonst   free of charge; in vain

der Umstand, ⸚e   circumstance; trouble, fuss

um·steigen (ie, [ist] ie)   to change *(train, bus)*

die Umwelt, -en   environment

das Umweltbewußtsein   environmental awareness

umweltfreundlich   environmentally sound

der Umweltschutz   environmental protection

die Umweltverschmutzung   pollution

sich um·wenden (wandte um, umgewandt)   to turn around

*um·ziehen (zog um, [ist] umgezogen)   to move

unabhängig   independent

die Unabhängigkeit   independence

unausstehlich   insufferable

unbedingt   absolute;

unconditional
unbestimmt vague,
  undetermined
unbeweglich inflexible
***und** and; ~ **so weiter** and so
  on
undemokratisch undemocratic
undenkbar unthinkable
unecht not genuine, fake
unehrlich dishonest
unerträglich intolerable
unerwünscht unwanted
unfair unfair
***der Unfall, ⁻e** accident
die Unfreiheit, -en lack of
  freedom
unfreundlich unfriendly
***ungeduldig** impatient
***ungefähr** about, approximate
ungefährlich not dangerous
ungerecht unjust
***ungesund** unhealthy
ungewöhnlich unusual
unglaublich incredible
***das Unglück, -e** misfortune
unglücklich unhappy;
  unglücklicherweise
  unfortunately
ungültig invalid
***unhöflich** impolite
***die Uni, -s** (*abbrev. for*
  Universität)
die Uniform, -en uniform
***die Universität, -en** university;
  auf die ~ gehen to attend a
  university
unkultiviert uncultivated
unlogisch illogical
unmißverständlich
  unmistakable
unmittelbar direct, immediate
***unmöglich** impossible
unnahbar unapproachable
die Unordnung disorder; mess
unpassend unsuitable, not
  fitting
das Unpersönliche impersonal
das Unrecht injustice; fault
unruhig restless
die Unschuld innocence
unsicher unsure; insecure
der Unsinn nonsense

***unten** down; downstairs
***unter** (+ *acc./dat.*) under,
  below, underneath; ~ **uns**
  between us
die Unterabteilung, -en
  subsection
***unterbrechen (i; a, o)** to
  interrupt
unterdrücken to suppress,
  repress
der Untergrund underground;
  die Untergrundliteratur
  underground literature; **die**
  Untergrundbahn, -en
  subway
***unterhalb** (+ *gen.*) under,
  beneath
***unterhalten (ä; ie, a)** to
  entertain; **sich ~** to have a
  conversation
die Unterhaltung, -en
  entertainment; conversation
unternehmen (unternimmt; a,
  unternommen) to undertake
die Unternehmung, -en
  undertaking
die Unterqualifizierung
  underqualification
der Unterricht instruction
unterrichten to teach
unterscheiden (ie, ie) to
  distinguish
der Unterschied, -e difference
unterschreiben (ie, ie) to sign
die Unterschrift, -en signature
die Unterseite, -n underside
unterstützen to support
untersuchen to examine
die Untersuchung, -en
  examination
unterwegs on the way
untrennbar inseparable
unwahrscheinlich improbable
unwichtig unimportant
die Unwissenheit ignorance
unzufrieden dissatisfied
der Urgroßvater, ⁻ great-
  grandfather
***der Urlaub, -e** vacation
die Ursache, -n reason, cause
der Ursprung, ⁻e origin
das Urteil, -e judgment; **ein ~**

fällen to pass judgment
urteilen to judge
***die USA** (*pl.*) United States of
  America
***usw.** (*abbrev. for* **und so weiter**)
  et cetera

***der Vater, ⁻** father
die Vegetation, -en vegetation
sich verabreden to make a
  date or appointment;
  verabredet sein to have an
  appointment or date
die Verabredung, -en
  appointment, date
sich verabschieden to say
  good-by
verallgemeinern to generalize
die Verallgemeinerung, -en
  generalization
sich verändern to change,
  transform
die Veränderung, -en
  transformation
die Veranstaltung, -en event;
  performance
verantwortlich (für)
  responsible (for)
verantwortungsvoll
  responsible
verarbeiten to process
verbessern to improve; to
  correct
die Verbesserung, -en
  improvement
***verbieten (o, o)** to prohibit
verbinden (a, u) to join,
  connect
die Verbindung, -en fraternity;
  relation
das Verbot, -e prohibition
der Verbrauch consumption,
  use; **der Verbraucher, -**
  consumer
verbrauchen to consume
das Verbrechen, - crime; **der**
  Verbrecher, - (*m.*) / **die**
  Verbrecherin, -nen (*f.*)
  criminal
verbrennen (verbrannte,
  verbrannt) to consume, to
  burn

*verbringen (verbrachte, verbracht) to spend time
verdammt damned
verderben (i; a, o) to spoil
*verdienen to earn; to deserve
der Verdienst profit; merit
verdunkeln to obscure
*der Verein, -e club
die Verfassung, -en constitution
verfolgen to follow, pursue
die Vergangenheit, -en past
vergebens in vain
*vergessen (vergißt; vergaß, vergessen) to forget; vergeßlich forgetful
der Vergleich, -e comparison
vergleichen (i, i) to compare
das Vergnügen, - pleasure, fun; sich vergnügen to have a good time; viel ~! have a good time!
vergnügt cheerful; delighted
vergrößern to enlarge; to increase
verhaften to arrest
das Verhalten conduct, behavior; das Verhaltensmuster behavior pattern
sich verhalten (ä; ie, a) to conduct oneself
das Verhältnis, -se relations; situation
verhandeln to negotiate
die Verhandlung, -en negotiation
verheiratet married
verhindern to prevent
der Verkauf, ⸚e sale; *der Verkäufer, - (m)/die Verkäuferin, -nen (f) salesperson
*verkaufen to sell
*der Verkehr traffic; das Verkehrsamt, ⸚er tourist office; die Verkehrsampel, -n traffic light; das Verkehrsmittel, - vehicle, means of transportation; das Verkehrszeichen, - traffic sign

verknallt in love
verkürzen to shorten
*verlangen to demand; to desire
verlangsamen to slow down
*verlassen (verläßt; verließ, verlassen) to leave; to abandon
verlegen embarrassed
*verletzen to injure
die Verletzung, -en injury
sich verlieben to fall in love
verliebt (in + acc.) in love (with)
*verlieren (o, o) to lose
sich verloben to become engaged
verlobt mit engaged with
der/die Verlobte (noun decl. like adj) person engaged to be married
die Verlobung, -en engagement
verlogen insincere
der Verlust, -e loss
vermeiden (ie, ie) to avoid
vermieten to rent out
vermuten to suppose, presume
vernichten to destroy
vernünftig reasonable, sensible
veröffentlichen to publish
verpacken to wrap up
die Verpackung, -en wrapping
verpassen to miss (opportunity, train)
sich verpflichten to promise
verraten (ä; ie, a) to betray; to show
verreisen to go on a trip
*verrückt crazy
der Vers, -e verse
versammeln to collect; sich ~ to meet
die Versammlung, -en gathering; meeting
*verschieden different
verschlagen: es verschlägt ihm die Stimme it takes away his voice
verschließen (o, o) to lock up
verschlossen closed up, reserved, taciturn
die Verschmutzung pollution
die Verschwendung waste

verschwinden (a; [ist] u) to vanish, disappear
versichern to insure; to assure
die Versicherung, -en insurance
die Version, -en version
sich verspäten to be late
die Verspätung, -en delay
*versprechen (i; a, o) to promise
verstädtern to become urbanized; to get used to life in a city
verständlich understandable
das Verständnis, -se understanding; sympathy
(sich) verstecken to hide
*verstehen (verstand, verstanden) to understand; es versteht sich that is obvious; sich verstehen to get along
verstorben deceased
der Versuch, -e attempt; experiment
*versuchen to try
die Versuchung, -en temptation
verteilen to distribute
der Vertrag, ⸚e contract
*vertrauen (+ dat.) to trust
das Vertrauen trust
vertreten (vertritt; a, e) to represent
der Vertreter representative
versursachen to bring about, cause
vervollständigen to complete
die Verwaltung, -en administration
(sich) verwandeln to change, transform
die Verwandlung, -en change; metamorphosis
verwandt (mit) related (to)
der/die Verwandte (noun decl. like adj.) relative
die Verwandtschaft, -en relation
verwechseln to confuse
verweigern to refuse
die Verwünschung, -en curse
verzeihen (ie, ie) (+ dat. of

person)　to pardon, forgive

*die Verzeihung　pardon

verzweifeln　to despair

die Verzweiflung　despair, desperation

*der Vetter, -n　cousin *(m)*

vibrieren　to vibrate

der Videorecorder, -　video recorder

*viel　a lot, much

*vielleicht　perhaps

*das Viertel, -　fourth; quarter; die Viertelstunde　a quarter of an hour

violett　violet

visuell　visual

das Visum, Visa　visa

*der Vogel, ⁝　bird

die Vokabel, -n　word, especially from foreign language

das Vokabular, -e　vocabulary

*das Volk, ⁝er　people; nation; *das Volkslied, -er　folk song; der Volkssänger, - folksinger; der Volkswirt, -e economist

die Volkspolizei　East German Police; ~kreisamt　district office of police

*voll (von)　full (of); complete

*der Volleyball　volleyball

völlig　total, entire

vollkommen　complete

*von *(+ dat.)*　of, from, by; ~ jetzt ab　from now on

der Vopo, -s *(abbrev. for der Volkspolizist, -en -en)*　East German policeman

*vor *(+ acc./dat.)*　before, previous; in front of; ~ allem above all; ~ Jahren　years ago; ~ kurzem　recently

die Voraussetzung, -en precondition

*vorbei　over; gone

vorbei·gehen (ging vorbei, [ist] vorbeigegangen)　to go past

vorbei·schieben (o, o)　to push past

*vor·bereiten　to prepare; vorbereitet (auf + *acc.*)

prepared for

die Vorbereitung, -en preparation

*vorgestern　the day before yesterday

*vor·haben　to intend

das Vorhaben　plan, intention

*der Vorhang, ⁝e　curtain, drape

*vorher　before; beforehand

vorhin　a short time ago

*vorig　former, preceding, previous

vor·kommen (kam vor, [ist] vorgekommen)　to happen

vor·legen　to present; to show

vor·lesen (ie; a, e)　to read aloud; to lecture

*die Vorlesung, -en　lecture; der Vorlesungssaal, -säle　lecture hall

die Vorliebe, -n　preference

*der Vormittag, -e　morning

vorn　in front

der Vorname, -ns, -n　first name

der Vorort, -e　suburb

der Vorschlag, ⁝e　proposal

*vorschlagen (ä; u, a)　to propose, suggest

die Vorschrift, -en　regulation

die Vorsicht　precaution

vorsichtig　cautious, careful

die Vorstadt, ⁝e　suburb

*vor·stellen　to introduce; sich *(dat.)* vor·stellen　to imagine

*die Vorstellung, -en performance; introduction; idea

das Vorstellungsvermögen imagination

der Vorteil, -e　advantage

der Vortrag, ⁝e　lecture

vorüber　gone, over

das Vorurteil, -e　prejudice

*vorwärts　forwards

vor·werfen (i; a, o)　to reproach

der Vorwurf, ⁝e　reproach

vor·zeigen　to display; to produce

vor·ziehen (zog vor, vorgezogen) to prefer

vorzüglich　excellent, first-rate

die Waage, -n　scale

waagrecht　horizontal

*wach　awake; alert

*wachsen (ä; u, [ist] a)　to grow

das Wachstum　growth

der Wachtmeister, -　guard, policeman

die Waffe, -n　weapon

das Waffenarsenal, -e　arsenal

wagen　to dare

*der Wagen, -　carriage; car

die Wahl, -en　choice

*wählen　to choose; to elect

*wahr　true; real; correct

*während (+ *gen.*)　during, while

*die Wahrheit, -en　truth

*wahrscheinlich　probably, likely; plausible

*der Wald, ⁝er　forest, woods

das Waldland　woodland

das Waldsterben　dying forests

*die Wand, ⁝e　wall

der Wanderer, - *(m.)* / die Wanderin, -nen *(f.)*　hiker

*wandern [ist]　to hike, go on foot

*die Wanderung, -en　hike

*wann　when

*die Ware, -n　article; goods *(pl.)*

das Warenhaus, ⁝er department store

*warm (ä)　warm; warmherzig warmhearted

die Wärme　warmth

warnen　to warn

(das) Warschau　Warsaw

*warten　to wait; ~ auf (+ *acc.*) to wait for

*warum　why

*was　what

*was für　what sort, what kind

*die Wäsche　linen, clothes, laundry

*waschen (ä; u, a,)　to wash; waschbar　washable

die Wäscherei, -en　laundry; das Wäschereiauto, -s laundry truck

*die Waschmaschine, -n

washing machine; **der Waschraum, ⁻e** lavatory

*__das Wasser, -__ water; **~ auf seine Mühle** grist to his mill; **der Wasserhahn, ⁻e** faucet; **die Wassermühle, -n** water mill; **die Wasserratte, -n** person fond of swimming

*__das WC__ toilet

der Wechsel, - change, alteration

wechseln to change; to exchange; to replace

*__wecken__ to wake

der Wecker, - alarm clock

*__weder__ neither; *__weder ... noch__ neither . . . nor

*__der Weg, -e__ way; road; path; direction; **sich auf den ~ machen** to set out

*__weg__ gone, away; lost

*__wegen__ (+ _gen._) because of, owing to

*__weg·fahren (ä; u, [ist] a)__ to drive away, go away

*__weg·gehen (ging weg, ist weggegangen)__ to go away

*__weg·laufen (äu; ie, [ist] au)__ to run away

*__weg·nehmen (nimmt weg; a, weggenommen)__ to take away

*__weg·werfen (i; a, o)__ to discard, throw away

das Wegwerffeuerzeug, -e disposable cigarette lighter

weh woe; oh **~** alas

*__weh tun__ (+ _dat._) to hurt

der Wehrdienst military service

(sich) wehren to resist

weiblich feminine

*__weich__ soft

sich weigern to refuse

*__das Weihnachten, -__ Christmas; **der Weihnachtsmann, ⁻er** Father Christmas, Santa Claus; **der Weihnachtsbaum, ⁻e** Christmas tree

*__weil__ because, since

die Weile a short while

*__der Wein, -e__ wine

*__weinen__ to cry

die Weise, -n manner, way, method; **auf diese ~** in this way

*__weiß__ white

*__weit__ wide; far, distant; **~ und breit** far and wide

*__weiter__ further; additional

weiter·arbeiten to continue to work

weiter·bilden to continue to train

die Weiterführung, -en continuation

weiter·gehen (ging weiter, ist weitergegangen) to go on walking

weiterhin from then on

weiter·kommen (a, [ist] o) to advance; come on

weiter·treiben (trieb weiter, weitergetrieben) to force forward; to drive on

weitgeöffnet wide-open

der Weizen wheat

*__welcher__ which

die Welle, -n wave

*__die Welt, -en__ world; **weltberühmt** world famous; **der Weltkrieg, -e** world war; **das Weltfestspiel, -e** world festival

*__wenden (wandte, gewandt)__ to turn

*__wenig__ little, slightly, not much

*__ein wenig__ a little bit

*__wenigstens__ at least

*__wenn__ when, whenever; if

*__werden (i; u, [ist] o)__ to become

*__werfen (i; a, o)__ to throw

*__das Werk, -e__ work; deed; factory; *__die Werkstatt, ⁻en__ workshop; **das Werkzeug, -e** tool; **der Werkzeugmacher, -** tool and die maker

*__wert__ valued; worth; **wertvoll** valuable; precious

der Wert, -e value

das Werturteil, -e value judgment

*__weshalb__ why

*__wessen__ whose

*__der Westen__ west; West;

westeuropäisch West European; **westlich** western

*__das Wetter, -__ weather; **der Wetterbericht, -e** weather report

der Wettkampf, ⁻e contest

*__wichtig__ important

widersprechen (i; a, o) to contradict

*__wie__ how

*__wieder__ again

wieder·geben (i; a, e) to reproduce, render

*__wiederholen__ to repeat

wieder·sehen (ie; a, e) to see again

*__das Wiedersehen, -__ reunion; **auf ~** good-by

wiegen (o, o) to weigh

die Wiese, -n meadow

wieso why, how come

*__wieviel__ how much; **wie viele** how many

*__wild__ wild

der Wille, -ns, -n will, determination

*__willkommen__ welcome

*__der Wind, -e__ wind

*__winken__ to wave

*__der Winter,-__ winter

wirken to bring about; to do

*__wirklich__ really; true

*__die Wirklichkeit, -en__ reality

wirksam effective

die Wirkung, -en effect

der Wirt, -e innkeeper, host; **das Wirtshaus, ⁻er** restaurant

die Wirtschaft, -en restaurant; economy

wischen to wipe

*__wissen (weiß; wußte, gewußt)__ to know

die Wissenschaft, -en science, knowledge; **der Wissenschaftler, -** _(m)_ / **die Wissenschaftlerin, -nen** _(f)_ scientist, scholar; **wissenschaftlich** scientific

*__der Witz, -e__ joke

witzig funny; witty

*__wo__ where; in which

*die Woche, -n   week; in einer ~
in one week, next week; vor
einer ~   one week ago, last
week; *das Wochenende, -n
weekend; das Wochen-
endhaus, ⁻er   cottage; der
Wochentag, -e   weekday
wofür   what for
*woher   where from
*wohin   where to, where
*wohl   well; probably
*wohnen   to live, reside;
wohnlich   pleasant to live in
der Wohnort, -e   place of
residence; die Wohnstraße, -n
residential street; das
Wohnviertel, -   residential
district; das Wohnheim, -e
dormitory
*die Wohnung, -en   residence,
apartment
der Wolf, ⁻e   wolf
*die Wolke, -n   cloud
*wollen   to want, wish; to
intend
womit   by what means
*das Wort, ⁻er   word; die
Wortbildung, -en   word
formation; wörtlich   literal;
wortlos   without saying a
word; der Wortschatz
vocabulary
das Wort, -e   connected words
(in pl.)
*das Wörterbuch, ⁻er   dictionary
wozu   to what purpose, why
das Wunder, -   miracle, wonder;
*wunderbar   wonderful;
*wunderschön   very
beautiful, very nice
*(sich) wundern   to be
surprised; to wonder
*der Wunsch, ⁻e   wish
*wünschen   to wish
wurscht: das ist mir ~   it
doesn't matter to me (colloq.)
*die Wurst, ⁻e   sausage; das
Wurstbrot, -e   cold meat
sandwich; das Würstchen, -
small sausage
der Wüstling, -e   lecher
die Wut   rage, fury

wütend (auf + acc.)   furious
(with, at)

*z.B. (abbrev. for zum Beispiel)
for example
*die Zahl, -en   number
zahlbar   payable
*zahlen   to pay
*zählen   to count
zahlreich   numerous
der Zahltag, -e   payday
*der Zahn, ⁻e   tooth; *der
Zahnarzt, ⁻e (m) / die
Zahnärztin, -nen (f)   dentist;
*die Zahnbürste, -n
toothbrush; *die Zahnpaste, -
n   toothpaste
zart   tender
zärtlich   affectionate, tender,
loving
der Zaun, ⁻e   fence
das Zeichen, -   sign, symbol
die Zeichnung, -en   drawing,
sketch
*zeigen   to show, to point
*die Zeile, -n   line
*die Zeit, -en   time; era; zeitig
early; at the right time; vor
kurzer Zeit   a short while ago
*die Zeitschrift, -en   journal;
magazine; der
Zeitschriftenartikel, -
magazine article
*die Zeitung, -en   newspaper;
der Zeitungsartikel, -
newspaper article; der
Zeitungsjunge, -n,
-n   paper boy; der
Zeitungsverkäufer, -   news
vendor
die Zelle, -n   cell
*das Zelt, -e   tent
*zelten   to camp, tent
zentral   central
das Zentrum, Zentren   center
(of a city)
zerfallen (ä; zerfiel, [ist] a)   to
fall apart, disintegrate
*zerstören   to destroy
der Zettel, -   note, slip of paper
das Zeug   stuff; clothes;
utensils; du redest dummes ~

you're talking nonsense
das Zeugnis, -se   testimony;
grades, report card
*ziehen (zog, gezogen)   to pull;
move
das Ziel, -e   goal, aim
*ziemlich   rather; quite
*die Zigarette, -n   cigarette
die Zigarre, -n   cigar
*das Zimmer, -   room
das Zitat, -e   quotation
zitieren   to cite; to quote
zittern   to tremble, shiver
zivil   civilian
der Zivildienst   civilian service
in place of military service
die Zivilisation, -en   civilization
*zu   to; too; shut
zucken   to twitch
*der Zucker   sugar
zu·decken   to cover
zueinander   to each other
*zuerst   first; at first
der Zufall, ⁻e   chance
zu·fallen (ä; fiel zu, [ist] a)   to
close
zufällig   accidental, incidental
*zufrieden (mit)   content,
satisfied (with)
*der Zug, ⁻e   train
der Zugang, ⁻e   entrance
zu·geben (i; a, e)   to admit
zu·gehen (ging zu, [ist]
zugegangen)   to go toward
zugleich   at the same time
zu·hören   to listen
zu·kommen (a, [ist] o)   to
approach
die Zukunft   future; zukünftig
future; zukunftssicher   long
term (job)
die Zulassung, -en   admittance
zuletzt   at last, finally; the last
time
*zu·machen   to close
zunächst   first of all
zu·ordnen   to associate with; to
arrange
*zurück   back; backwards;
behind
zurück·bleiben (ie, [ist] ie)   to
remain; to fall behind

zurück·halten (ä, ie, a)   to hold back

zurück·kommen (a, [ist] o)   to come back

sich zurück·lehnen   to lean back

zurück·reichen   to hand back

zurück·treten (tritt; trat, [ist] getreten)   to step back

zurück·zahlen   to pay back

*zusammen   together

zusammen·drängen   to crowd together, press together

zusammen·falten   to fold

zusammen·fassen   to summarize

die Zusammenfassung, -en   summary

der Zusammenhang, -̈e   context

zusammen·hängen   to be connected with

zusammen·stellen   to put together

der Zustand, -̈e   condition, situation

zu·stimmen   to agree to

zu·treten (tritt zu; a, [ist] e)   to step up to

zuverlässig   reliable

*zuviel   too much

zu·wenden (wandte zu, zugewandt)   to turn toward

*zwar   to be sure, course, indeed

*der Zweck, -e   purpose

*der Zweifel, -   doubt

zweifelhaft   doubtful

zweifeln   to doubt; ~an (+ dat.)   to doubt in

zweitens   in the second place

der Zwerg, -e   dwarf

der Zwieback, -e   biscuit, rusk

*zwingen (a, u)   to compel

der Zwirnsfaden, -̈   piece of yarn

*zwischen (+ acc./dat.)   between

die Zwischenstation, -en   way station

zynisch   cynical

English-German Vocabulary

The English-German end vocabulary contains the words needed in the grammar exercises that require students to express English sentences in German. The definitions provided are limited to the context of a particular exercise. Strong and irregular weak verbs are indicated with a raised degree mark (°). Their principal parts can be found in the Appendix. Separable-prefix verbs are indicated with a raised dot: **an·fahren°**.

about über
accident der Unfall, ¨e
acquaintance der/die Bekannte *(noun decl. like adj.)*
across über; ~ **the street from us** uns gegenüber
act as if tun, als ob
actually eigentlich
after nach *(prep.)*; nachdem *(conj.)*
afternoon der Nachmittag, -e; **this ~** heute nachmittag; **afternoons** nachmittags
agree: I ~ with [you] ich bin [deiner] Meinung
airplane das Flugzeug, -e
all all, alle; ~ **day** den ganzen Tag; ~ **the same to me** mir gleich
alone allein
along entlang; ~ **the river** den Fluß entlang; **bring ~** mit·bringen°
already schon
also auch
although obwohl
always immer
amazed: to be amazed (at) sich wundern (über)
ambulance der Krankenwagen, -
American der Amerikaner, - *(m.)* / die Amerikanerin, -nen *(f.)*; amerikanisch *(adj.)*

and und
annoy ärgern
answer antworten; ~ **a question** auf eine Frage antworten
anymore nicht mehr
anything etwas
apartment die Wohnung, -en
apple der Apfel, ¨
around um; ~ **here** hier
arrive kommen°; an·kommen°
as: ~ **if** als ob
ask fragen
at [seven] um [sieben]; ~ **the movies** im Kino; ~ **home** zu Hause; ~ **the railroad station** am Bahnhof; ~ **the post office** bei der Post
Austria Österreich

back zurück; **come back** zurück·kommen°
bad schlecht; **too ~** schade
beat schlagen°
because weil, da; denn
become werden°; **to ~ of** werden aus...
bed das Bett, -en
beer das Bier, -e
before ehe, bevor
behave sich benehmen°
behind hinter
believe glauben

belong gehören (+ *dat.*)
beside neben
best best-
better besser
bicycle das Fahrrad, ¨er
biking: to go ~ rad·fahren°
bird der Vogel, ¨
birthday der Geburtstag, -e; **for [his] ~** zum Geburtstag
bloom blühen
book das Buch, ¨er
boring langweilig
bottle die Flasche, -n
box office die Kasse; **at the ~** an der Kasse
bring bringen°; ~ **along** mit·bringen°
brown braun
bus der Bus, -se
but aber; sondern
buy kaufen
by: ~ **the way** übrigens; ~ **Sunday** bis Sonntag

café das Café, -s; **to a ~** ins Café
cake der Kuchen, -
call up *(telephone)* an·rufen°
can können; ~ **not be helped** läßt sich nicht ändern
car das Auto, -s
change (sich) ändern
cheese der Käse, -

city die Stadt ⸚e; **in(to) the ~** in die Stadt

city hall das Rathaus, ⸚er

class die Klasse, -n; **to travel [first] ~** [erster] Klasse fahren°

clothes die Kleidung; die Sachen (pl.); die Kleider (pl.)

coffee der Kaffee

cold kalt; die Erkältung; **to catch a ~** sich erkälten

comb der Kamm, ⸚e

come kommen°; **~ with me** komm doch mit; **~ back** zurück·kommen°

command befehlen°

compare vergleichen°

completely ganz

concert das Konzert, -e

cook kochen

cost kosten

could könnte

country das Land, ⸚er; **to the ~** aufs Land

course: of ~ selbstverständlich, natürlich

cream die Sahne

curious(ly) neugierig

cut schneiden°

day der Tag, -e

describe beschreiben°

different andere, anders; **to be of a ~ opinion** anderer Meinung sein

difficult schwer

dinner das Abendessen, -

dishes das Geschirr, -(e)

do machen, tun°

doctor der Arzt, ⸚e/die Ärztin, -nen

dog der Hund, -e

dozen das Dutzend, -e

dream träumen

drink trinken°

drive fahren°

drugstore die Drogerie, -n; **to the ~** in die (zur) Drogerie

easy leicht

eat essen°

either: isn't [bad] ~ auch nicht [schlecht]

electrician der Elektriker, -

elegant elegant

English (person) der Engländer, - (m.) / die Engländerin, -nen (f.)

enough genug

evening der Abend, -e; **this ~** heute abend; **in the ~** am Abend, abends

every jeder

everything alles

excellent ausgezeichnet

exception die Ausnahme, -n

expensive teuer

experience die Erfahrung, -en; erleben

express aus·drücken

famous berühmt, bekannt

father der Vater, ⸚

feel sich fühlen; **~ sorry for** leid tun; **I ~ better** es geht mir (ich fühle mich) besser

few wenige; **a ~** einige

film der Film, -e

find finden°

first erst; **to travel ~ class** erster Klasse fahren°

fish der Fisch, -e

five fünf

flower die Blume, -n

fly fliegen°

follow folgen (+ dat.)

food das Essen, -

for für; **~ [his] birthday** zum Geburtstag; **~ a long time** lange; **~ a week** seit einer Woche

foreigner der Ausländer, -; die Ausländerin, -nen

forget vergessen°

France (das) Frankreich

freeze frieren°

frequently häufig, oft

Friday der Freitag; **on ~** am Freitag

friend der Freund, -e/die Freundin, -nen; der/die Bekannte (noun decl. like adj.) **boy~** Freund; **girl~** Freundin

friendly freundlich

from von

fry braten°

funny lustig, komisch

furniture das Möbel, -

garden der Garten, ⸚

German der/die Deutsche (noun decl. like adj.); **he is ~** er ist Deutscher; **~ (language)** (das) Deutsch

Germany Deutschland

get bekommen°; **~ from Hamburg to Berlin** von Hamburg nach Berlin kommen; **~ tired** müde werden; **~ off** frei bekommen°; **~ in** ein·steigen°; **~ up** auf·stehen°

gift das Geschenk, -e

girl das Mädchen, -; **girl friend** die Freundin, -nen

give geben°; (as present) schenken

glass das Glas, ⸚er; **wine~** das Weinglas

go (on foot) gehen°; (by vehicle) fahren°

good gut

grandparents die Großeltern (pl.)

great toll

guest der Gast, ⸚e

had: ~ to mußte

hair das Haar, -e

happy froh; glücklich

hard schwer; hart

hasn't: ~ it? nicht? nicht wahr?

have haben; **~ to** müssen; **would~to** müßte; **~ [the electrician] come** [den Elektriker] kommen lassen

hear hören

help helfen°; **can't be helped** läßt sich nicht ändern

here hier; **around ~** hier

hey! Du (informal)

hi Tag!

high hoch

hike wandern

history die Geschichte, -n

hold halten°

home: at ~ zu Hause; **~** (*direction*) nach Hause

hope hoffen; **I ~** hoffentlich

hour die Stunde, -n; **in an ~** in einer Stunde

house das Haus, ⸚er

how wie; **~ nice** wie schön

hurry (up) sich beeilen

hurt weh tun° (+ *dat.*); schmerzen (+ *dat.*)

husband der Mann, ⸚er

idea die Idee, -n

if wenn; (*whether*) ob; **~ only** wenn nur

ill krank

immediately sofort

inform informieren

information die Information, -en

inn das Gasthaus, ⸚er; der Gasthof, ⸚e

instead anstatt

interest interessieren

invite ein·laden°

Italy (das) Italien

jacket die Jacke, -n

key der Schlüssel, -

knife das Messer, -

know (*to know a fact*) wissen°; (*to be acquainted with*) kennen°

lake der See, -n

last letzt; vorig-; **~ night** gestern abend

later später

laugh lachen

learn lernen

leave lassen°; weg·gehen°; **~ the café** das Café verlassen°

leg das Bein, -e

let lassen°; **let's** laß(t) uns doch

letter der Brief, -e

lie liegen°

life das Leben, -

like mögen; **would [you] ~** möchten [Sie]; **would ~ to help** gern helfen°; (*prep.*) **speak ~ him** so sprechen wie er; **~ something** gefallen° (+ *dat.*); **~ someone** gern haben

listen, Trudi hör mal, Trudi!

live wohnen; leben

long lang(e); **a ~ time** lange

longer: no ~ nicht mehr

look schauen; **~ (at)** an·schauen; an·sehen°; **~ for** suchen; **~ as if** aus·sehen°, als ob ...

lose verlieren°

lot: a ~ viel; **a ~ of** eine Menge

mad: to be mad sich ärgern

man der Mann, ⸚er

many viele

mark die Mark

married couple das Ehepaar, -e

may dürfen°

mean meinen

meat das Fleisch

meet kennen·lernen; begegnen (+ *dat.*); treffen°, sich treffen° mit

minute die Minute, -n

Monday der Montag

money das Geld, -er

month der Monat, -e

more mehr; **any ~** nicht mehr

morning der Morgen, -

most meist; **~ of the time** meistens

mother die Mutter, ⸚

mountain der Berg, -e

move (*change residence*) um·ziehen°

movies das Kino, -s; die Filme; **to the ~** ins Kino; **at the ~** im Kino

much viel

museum das Museum, Museen (*pl.*); **to the ~** ins Museum

musician der Musiker,-/die Musikerin, -nen

must müssen

natural(ly) natürlich

necktie die Krawatte, -n

need brauchen

neighbor der Nachbar, -n, -n/die Nachbarin, -nen

next nächst; **next to** neben

nice nett; schön; **how ~** wie schön

no nein; kein; **~ thanks** nein, danke

not nicht

nothing nichts

nothing more nichts mehr

notice merken, bemerken

now jetzt

obey gehorchen (+ *dat.*)

of course natürlich, selbstverständlich

off frei; **get ~** frei bekommen

official der Beamte (*noun decl. like adj.*), die Beamtin, -nen

often oft

oh o; oh; ach

okay gut; **is it ~** ist es [Ihnen] recht?

old alt

on an; auf; **~ Sunday** am Sonntag; **~ the street** auf der Straße

once einmal

only nur; **if ~ it** wenn es nur

open öffnen

opera die Oper, -n; **to the ~** in die Oper

opinion die Meinung, -en; **in [my] ~** [meiner] Meinung nach; **to be of a different ~** anderer Meinung sein

or oder

order bestellen

ought sollen; **he ~ to** er müßte

outside draußen

over über

own (*verb*) besitzen°; (*adj.*) eigen

pack packen; ein·packen

parents die Eltern (*pl.*)

park der Park, -s; **to go for a walk through the ~** im Park spazieren·gehen°

party   die Party, -s; das Fest, -e;
  to have (give) a ~   ein Fest
  machen (geben)
pay   bezahlen
people   die Leute (*pl.*)
pharmacist   der Apotheker, -
photographer   der Fotograf, -en,
  -en
piano   das Klavier, -e
pick up   ab·holen
picture   das Bild, -er
plan   der Plan, ˝e
play   spielen
please   bitte
policeman   der Polizist, -en, -en
post office   die Post; **to the** ~
  auf die Post; **at the** ~   bei der
  Post
practice   üben
prefer   vor·ziehen°; lieber: ~ (**to**
  travel)   lieber (fahren)
prepare   vor·bereiten
probably   wohl, wahrscheinlich
professor   der Professor, -en/die
  Professorin, -nen
purchase   kaufen
put   stellen; stecken; setzen;
  legen; ~ **on (clothing)**
  an·ziehen°

question   die Frage, -n

railroad station   der Bahnhof, ˝e
rain   regnen; der Regen
raincoat   der Regenmantel, ˝
react   reagieren
read   lesen°
ready   fertig
realize   merken, bemerken
really   wirklich
relative   der/die Verwandte
  (*noun decl. like adj.*)
remember   sich erinnern an (+
  acc.)
remodel   um·bilden
repair   reparieren
report   das Referat, -e; **give a** ~
  einen Referat halten°
reserve   reservieren
restaurant   das Restaurant, -s;
  to a ~   ins Restaurant

rice   der Reis
right   recht; **to be** ~   recht
  haben
river   der Fluß, Flüsse
roast   braten°
run   laufen°; (*water*) fließen°

salad   der Salat, -e
same   gleich; **it's all the** ~ **to**
  [**me**]   es ist [mir] gleich
sandwich   das Brot, -e
Saturday   der Samstag, -e; **on** ~
  am Samstag
say   sagen
sea   das Meer, -e; die See, -n
seat   der Platz, ˝e
second   zweit-
see   sehen°; (*to visit*) besuchen
sell   verkaufen
seminar   das Seminar, -e; **to the**
  ~   ins Seminar; ~ **paper**   die
  Seminar arbeit, -en
send   schicken; ~ **for**   kommen
  lassen°
several   einige
should   sollen; ~ **go**   sollte
  gehen; ~ **have known**   hätte
  wissen sollen
shut   zu·machen; schließen°
shy   schüchtern
sick   krank
simply   einfach
since   seit
sing   singen°
singer   der Sänger, -/die
  Sängerin, -nen
sister   die Schwester, -n
sit   sitzen°
sleep   schlafen°
slowly   langsam
smile   lächeln
so   so
some   manche
something   etwas
sometimes   manchmal
son   der Sohn, ˝e
soon   bald
sorry: I'm ~   es tut mir leid; **I**
  feel ~ **for (her)**   (sie) tut mir
  leid
speak (to or with)   sprechen°
  (mit); reden (mit)

spend (time)   verbringen°
spite: in ~ **of**   trotz
stamp   die Briefmarke, -n
stand   stehen°
station (train)   der Bahnhof, ˝e
stay   bleiben°
still   noch
store   der Laden, ˝, das Geschäft,
  -e
story   die Geschichte, -n
street   die Straße, -n; **across the**
  ~ **from us**   uns gegenüber; **on**
  the ~   auf der Straße
stupid   dumm; doof
such   solch-; ~ **a**   solch ein, so
  ein
sudden: all of a ~   plötzlich
suddenly   plötzlich
suitcase   der Koffer, -
summer   der Sommer, -
sun   die Sonne, -n
Sunday   der Sonntag, -e; **on** ~
  [am] Sonntag
supermarket   der Supermarkt,
  ˝e
sure   sicher
surely   sicher, bestimmt, wohl
sweet   süß
swim   schwimmen°
Switzerland   die Schweiz; **to** ~
  in die Schweiz; **in** ~   in der
  Schweiz

table   der Tisch, -e
take   nehmen°; bringen°; ~
  along   mit·bringen°;
  mit·nehmen°
talk (to)   reden (mit)
teacher   der Lehrer, -/die
  Lehrerin, -nen
tell   erzählen
tennis   das Tennis
than   als
thanks   danke
that   das; (*conj.*) daß
theater   das Theater, -; **to the** ~
  (*to buy tickets*) zum Theater; **to**
  the ~ (*to see performance*) ins
  Theater
then   dann
there   dort; da; ~ **is/are**   es gibt
these   diese

think denken°; **think about** nach·denken° (über); überlegen

this dies-

through durch; **to go for a walk ~ the park** im Park spazieren·gehen°

ticket die Karte, -n; das Ticket -s

time die Zeit; **for a long ~** lange

tired müde

to auf; in; nach (*with cities and masc. and neut. countries*); zu; **~ the movies** ins Kino; **~ the city** in die Stadt; **~ the post office** auf die Post; **~ the drugstore** in die (zur) Drogerie; **~ Switzerland** in die Schweiz; **~ the opera** in die Oper

today heute

together zusammen

tomorrow morgen; **~ evening** morgen abend

tonight heute abend

too zu; **~ bad** schade

towards gegen; **~ evening** gegen Abend

train der Zug, ̈e

train station der Bahnhof, ̈e; **from the ~** vom Bahnhof

travel fahren°; reisen

TV das Fernsehen; **watch ~** fern·sehen°

TV set der Fernseher, -

umbrella der Regenschirm, -e

uncle der Onkel, -

understand verstehen°; **understood: it's ~** es versteht sich

unfortunately leider

until bis

upset: to get ~ sich ärgern

use gebrauchen

very sehr

village das Dorf, ̈er

visit besuchen; der Besuch, -e; **for a ~** zu Besuch

wait warten; **~ for** warten auf

waiter der Ober, -; der Kellner, - (*m.*)/die Kellnerin, -nen (*f.*)

walk: to go for a ~ spazieren·gehen°

want wollen

warm warm

was war

watch TV fern·sehen°

water das Wasser; **~ bottle** die Wasserflasche, -n

way der Weg, -e; **by the ~** übrigens

wear an·ziehen°

weather das Wetter

week die Woche, -n

weekend das Wochenende, -n

weird seltsam; komisch

well, ... na

what was

when als, wenn, wann

where wo; **~ to** wohin; **~ from** woher

whether ob

which welch-

why warum; **~ not** warum nicht

window das Fenster, -

wine der Wein; **~ glass** das Weinglas

wish wünschen; **I ~** ich wünschte, ich wollte

with mit

without ohne

woman die Frau, -en

wonderful wunderbar; wunderschön

word das Wort, ̈er

work arbeiten; die Arbeit; **to do the ~** die Arbeit machen

would würde; **~ like to help** würde gern helfen; **~ have to** müßte; **it ~ be nice** es wäre schön

write schreiben°

yellow gelb

yes ja

yesterday gestern

yet schon; noch

Index